FOREWORD
CARMELO EZPELETA

The year 2014 provided race fans with arguably one of the best MotoGP™ seasons in recent memory, as Marc Marquez put on what can only be described as a sensational performance, whilst his rivals fought tooth and nail to stop him.

Valentino Rossi showed that age does not stop you from getting faster, Jorge Lorenzo fought back tremendously after one of his worst starts to a season, and Dani Pedrosa proved that Marquez was beatable after being the first to do so this year. Yet more so than ever it was the rest of the field that made this season so special.

Ducati's revival saw the team grace the podium numerous times with riders Andrea Dovizioso and Cal Crutchlow, whilst Andrea Iannone went fairing-to-fairing with Marquez on various occasions. The new 'Open' class, which was the latest evolution of the previously named CRT class, showcased a raft of new talents that have made a name for themselves – most notably Aleix Espargaro on the Forward Yamaha.

And following this gem of a season I am pleased once again to introduce the latest edition of the *MotoGP Season Review* from Evro Publishing, which will look back at a season that has given so much to the motorcycle-racing fan. Glance back at a season that saw World Champion Marc Marquez's early dominance challenged in style by old and new rivals alike, with the desire to win tested at every single occasion in all kinds of conditions.

Britain's Cal Crutchlow bounced back from a very tough start of the year with Ducati to score a podium in tricky conditions at Aragón, whilst Rookie Scott Redding showed huge amounts of potential on the 'Open' class Honda, regularly beating far more experienced rivals on the same machinery. And I am also pleased for Bradley Smith, who celebrated his contract extension with the Tech3 team with his first-ever MotoGP™ podium at Phillip Island. And with Redding and Crutchlow both switching to satellite Honda machinery next year, the scene is set for some top British performances.

But it was not just the MotoGP™ class that brought us fireworks week in week out. Moto2™ and Moto3™ are continuing to prove exceptional feeder classes on the world stage, where racecraft and outright speed are a must. And the riders have not disappointed. Moto2™ saw Tito Rabat win the title in style, whilst the class also saw the emergence of Maverick

Viñales as an enormous talent in his Rookie year, earning him a MotoGP™ ride for 2105, as he fought it out with Rabat, Mika Kallio, Dominique Aegerter and many more.

Moto3™ was more spectacular than ever as a mêlée of at least ten riders were capable of winning almost every race. Jack Miller, Alex Marquez, Romano Fenati, Alex Rins, Danny Kent, John McPhee – just a few of the names that made the class so spectacular. And it was great to see the title come down to the final few corners in the last race in Valencia, where Miller won, yet Marquez took the title – making it the first time in history that two brothers have ever done so.

So enjoy reliving the 2014 season, and I look forward to welcoming you all next year.

CARMELO EZPELETA
DORNA SPORTS CEO
NOVEMBER 2014

Published in November 2014

A catalogue record for this book is available from the British Library

ISBN 978-0-9928209-8-5

Published by Evro Publishing, Westrow House, Holwell, Sherborne, Dorset DT9 5LF

Printed and bound in the UK by Gomer Press, Llandysul Enterprise Park, Llandysul, Ceredigion SA44 4JL

This product is officially licensed by Dorna SL, owners of the MotoGP trademark (© Dorna 2014)

Editorial Director Mark Hughes
Design Richard Parsons
Special Sales & Advertising Manager
David Dew (david@motocom.co.uk)
Photography Front cover, race action and portraits by Andrew Northcott/AJRN Sports Photography; side-on studio technical images of bikes (pp13–29) by Dorna; other technical images (pp13–29) by Neil Spalding

Author's acknowledgements
My gratitude goes to long-time contributors Andrew Northcott, Neil Spalding, Mat Oxley and Peter Clifford for helping get the Official MotoGP Season Review back on the road.

Thanks also to my BT Sport colleagues Keith Huewen, Gavin Emmett and Neil Hodgson, and the producers, cameramen and sound recordists who got us on air.

In the MotoGP press office Matt Birt, Nick Harris, Nereo Balazin, Venancio Luis Nieto, Dean Adams and many others kept me on my toes. Thanks also to Martin Raines.

www.evropublishing.com

EVRO
PUBLISHING

CONTENTS
MotoGP™ 2014

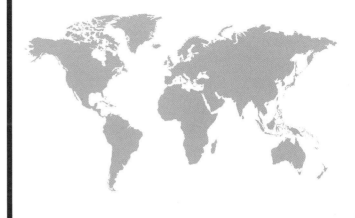

A YEAR OF REVELATIONS

Everyone knew Marc Marquez would be strong again in 2014. But few expected that Valentino Rossi would be reborn

And the young man shall teach the old men, and lead them also. Marc Marquez's second season in the class of kings was just as impressive as his hard-to-beat rookie championship. It was impressive in many ways, especially in the way it started with ten victories. No-one in the modern era has started a season in such a fashion, and this from a fresh-faced 21-year-old who sometimes looks more male model than motorcycle racer.

But most interesting of all was the effect Marquez had on his rivals during 2014. In 2013 they seemed mostly shell-shocked. They were astonished by his speed, but most of them surely believed he could not sustain it long enough to win the crown, that he would crash and ruin his title chances.

This year they knew that probably would not happen. Jorge Lorenzo, the man from whom Marquez took the championship last year, struggled to cope with that reality. His shocking start to 2014 – first-lap crash in Qatar, ridiculous jump start in Texas – suggested that he was still destabilised by Marquez's arrival and still flailing around for an answer.

Valentino Rossi, on the other hand, seemed to accept the new order and determined to learn from it. Perhaps that was easier for him because he has already been knocked down and has learned how to pick himself back up.

Rossi's renaissance was every bit as remarkable as Marquez's relentless ride towards joining him in legendary status. At the end of his lacklustre Yamaha comeback season everyone nodded sagely and muttered that old cliché: you can't teach an old dog new tricks. But Rossi is an old dog – okay, a middle-aged dog, to be precise – and he did learn new tricks, thus proving everyone wrong, even five-time 500 king Mick Doohan, who had gone with the consensus and stated that sportsmen can only last ten years at the top. Last

ABOVE LEFT Somehow, Jorge Lorenzo always seemed excluded from the other boys' games… He had a terrible start to the year but turned it round.

ABOVE RIGHT Dani Pedrosa's side of the Repsol Honda garage struggled against Marc Marquez's.

season was Rossi's 14th at the top of the class of kings and he was still running with the fastest men in the world.

It is impossible to know what goes on in Rossi's head. He has his place in history and he is Babylonian wealthy, and yet he is still prepared to lay life and limb on the line every other weekend for seven months of each year. When Doohan talks of the ten-year rule, he's mostly referring to golfers, tennis players and so on. Players of games, not sports, as Hemingway had it. Such players play at the top for a decade, then drift into retirement, having had enough of the white heat of competition and the peripatetic lifestyle – and having more than enough in the bank. Few of them ever need to worry about injuries and worse.

Rossi knows the risks – Marco Simoncelli, October 2011 and all – and yet he happily treads into the danger zone in search of more glory. There can only be one reason for this: love. Love of riding motorcycles, love of racing motorcycles, love of the racing life and, of course, love of winning.

He still holds the same breathless joy for racing motorcycles as he did in August 1996, when he rode rings around veteran champion Jorge Martinez at Brno to score his first GP win. At Phillip Island in October, the occasion of his 250th premier-class start and his 108th GP win, he bubbled over with enthusiasm, not just about winning the race but also the sheer joy of riding the ragged edge at GP racing's finest track. It's not often that a rider gets the chance to fully enjoy a race – there's always too much going on and too much than can go wrong – but on the Island he was able to do just that.

'Sincerely, I was excited!' he said after that race. 'The last few laps were fantastic: coming through the final corner, 120 miles an hour, right on the edge, elbow on the tarmac, knowing I had a seven-second advantage. Was great!'

Loving what you do is all very well. But it is not enough to be the best at it. During 2014 Rossi refashioned himself, having spent plenty of time during the winter watching and learning from Marquez. He knew he had to change the way he rides a motorcycle to get the most out of the latest bikes and tyres. Most riders find it impossible to radically change their technique at any time in their careers, but Rossi managed to do this as a 35-year-old.

He transformed the way he sits and moves on the motorcycle, leaning his upper body far to the inside of the bike to aid turning and then moving forwards on corner exits to reduce the need for the acceleration-killing anti-wheelie software to kick in.

'If you want to stay on top of racing you must look at what the fastest riders are doing,' he said during the season.

'I now use more of the top of my body to move outside of the bike to improve turning. Marc has a very different style, so I look at Dani and especially Jorge, because we have the same bike. I watch and I try to modify my position on the bike and the movement of the bike. I now move forward more to avoid wheelies.'

There were other reasons for his revival, of course. For his second year back at Yamaha he had a bike that was more tuned to his needs and Yamaha had a new gearbox that allowed clutch-less downshifts, which reduced Honda's advantage during braking.

'It makes the bike more stable so I can brake a lot deeper,' Rossi added. 'I can really use the engine braking to stop so I can divide grip more between the front and rear. Last year it was all on the front.'

He also had new crew chief Silvano Galbusera, whose arrival in Rossi's garage was not the last act of a desperate man, as most of us believed when we heard the news at Valencia in November 2013. Unlike Jeremy Burgess, Galbusera is an electronics whizz, which is important this far into the 21st century. Hardly surprising, but Rossi chose well. And Rossi can communicate with him in his mother tongue, which must help when discussing the finer details.

Marquez appeared as delighted at Rossi's resurgence as the man himself. After all, the old man is still the young man's hero – Marquez modelled himself on the nine-time champ and is still a fan. He admits that even now he visits the local shops every few weeks to purchase the latest Rossi replica scale model.

The pair get on because they share a similar attitude to life and to racing: always having fun off the bike, always up for a fight on it. But how long can it last? In the past, Rossi has always fallen out with his toughest rivals. As old friend Marco Melandri once opined, Rossi is happy to be your friend until you start beating him. But perhaps there is a difference with this friendship that will allow it to endure. Marquez is not threatening Rossi's throne – he had already lost it first to Jorge Lorenzo and then to Casey Stoner.

During 2014 Marquez's riding continued to draw oohs and aahs from spectators. He only knows one way to ride a motorcycle and that is at the very brink of disaster. It is a wonderful thing to watch: a rider crashing but not crashing.

Marquez has millions of fans but possibly none who can identify with him as Freddie Spencer can. Fast Freddie has much in common with the new king of MotoGP: he was still barely a grown man when he made it all the way to the top of motorcycling's highest peak and he has an otherworldly talent that has rivals and fans shaking their heads in wonder, unable to fathom what they have just witnessed.

Marquez may be MotoGP's current king of slide, but everyone on the grid can hang out the rear of a motorcycle until the cows come home. But the front? Spencer reckons that is Mighty Marc's real secret.

'Marc's success is more than just ability, it's his focus, it's how he methodically prepares and thinks about every corner,' says the American. 'It's about how he rotates the bike into the corner and how quick he does that. It's like he's over-turning and going beyond the grip level of the front tyre, so he's using speed and tyre movement to get the bike to pivot around the front tyre. That's exactly what I worked on as a kid in my back yard every single day: being able to know that the tyre's going to scrub and then using the brake and lean angle to pivot the bike around the front tyre.'

And yes, that is exactly what Marquez does.

'Most of the time I like to feel some movement in the front tyre, to feel that the tyre is sliding, because that's how I feel the limit,' Marc says. 'Sometimes you slide the front a lot and it looks like you will turn better, but then you cannot stop the bike, so you have to release the brake and then you go a bit wide. When you slide at that point and you have to use the front brake some more you have to be so careful because maybe you will lift the rear and then will come the [corner-entry] highside crash!'

During the season Marquez did not crash like he did in his rookie year but he crashed in many more races. Just once in 2013, but three times (in a row!) in 2014.

His Misano crash was the high point of Rossi's comeback, the moment Valentino was so fast that not even Marquez could keep up. The youngster was in over his head trying

to stay with the old dog. He kept running wide and crashing without crashing, and then he did crash.

Two weeks later at Aragón he did it again, staying out on slicks on a soaking racetrack and riding headlong against inevitability. Hot slicks can beguile a rider on a wet track – when they are hot they grip well, even in the rain. But then they start to cool down and the moment they slip below that critical temperature they suddenly offer zero grip.

But the real reason for both of those crashes was Marquez's head. The comfort of his gargantuan points lead allowed his mind to wander. During the first half of the season, whenever someone asked him whether he could win every race, he sensibly replied that he knew he would not be able to do so, that one day circumstances would conspire against him. That day came at Brno. What he also said was that when he could not win he must make sure he finished on the podium.

By Misano he lost sight of that plan. He wanted to win there so he could wrap up the title at Aragón, in front of his home fans. And after his Misano crash had postponed his coronation, he wanted to win at Aragón, again for his fans. That is a major loss of focus, something that his mentor Emilio Alzamora has no doubt already rectified for 2015 and beyond. After all, it is not only points you waste with a crash, you can also break bones. Then again, one of the great things about Marquez is that he lives for the moment, a characteristic that has something to do with the head injury he sustained at Sepang in 2011 that gave him double vision for five months.

'That was the most difficult moment of my career,' said Marc. 'I had five very long months with that injury and we visited six or seven different doctors to understand the problem. Some said I would be okay, others said maybe not.

BELOW Valentino Rossi justified his decision to make Silvano Galbusera his race engineer with a stunning return to race-winning form.

ABOVE New Brit on the block: Scott Redding achieved his ambition of being top customer Honda rider and will get a factory bike for 2015.

UPPER RIGHT The new head of Ducati Corse, Gigi Dall'Igna, started the lengthy process of turning the Desmosedici back into a race winner.

LOWER RIGHT MotoGP said 'goodbye' to Colin Edwards; he rode his last race, at Indianapolis, in camouflage leathers.

They couldn't guarantee I'd ride again but I always kept a positive mentality. One day I tried to ride my motocross bike with double vision but it was impossible. After the operation the eye got better and better, so a big thanks to the doctor who helped me to ride again and enjoy my hobby, which is riding motorbikes. The lesson from those five months was that you need to enjoy every moment, because you never know the future.'

While Lorenzo flailed around for an answer to Marquez, Dani Pedrosa happily cruised along in his shadow, trying no doubt to beat the young upstart but content to pick up the occasional win. In that sense he is the perfect team-mate, which is no doubt why HRC signed him for 2015 and 2016 – which will make it 11 years at Repsol Honda. That is longer than Giacomo Agostini spent at MV Agusta and surely an all-time record.

There is always much talk of Pedrosa's diminutive size, how it helps him, how it hinders him. Moto3's 2014 runner-up, Jack Miller, who may replace him in the Repsol squad in 2017, has no doubt about the effect Pedrosa's frame has had on his results. 'If Dani was bigger, he'd be a multiple MotoGP champion by now,' said the Aussie.

Lorenzo did eventually get his head together and the results started to come. After 14 rounds he finally won a race and then two weeks later he won another, this time beating his rivals on sheer speed, not circumstances. In terms of wins this was his worst season since his rookie year in MotoGP but once he had dug himself out of his hole he refused to engage in negativity.

'I never regret anything because you can't change your past, you can only learn a lesson,' he said. 'This year has been unfortunate because I was unfit at the start of the

season [following three significant operations during the winter], didn't plan the pre-season well and the bike wasn't competitive and the tyres were different, so everything made the start of the season very complicated. Then I made two mistakes at the first two races, so it was a complete disaster. Also I changed my trainer during the winter. At first things were worse, now they are better – it's two steps back and one forward. If Yamaha keep working like they have over the last months then we will have a good chance in 2015.'

Lorenzo was rookie of the year in 2008 and of course there was another new rookie this year. The end-of-season points standings tell us that the winner of the 2014 rookie of the year award was Pol Espargaro, MotoGP's latest Moto2 graduate. But what about considering Gigi Dall'Igna, who had his first go at designing a MotoGP bike? We will not count his Aprilia ART CRT machine because that was not a real MotoGP bike.

After half a decade of wandering in the wilderness, unable to find the exit door, Ducati finally seemed to find its way in 2014. And that was all down to one man: Dall'Igna. And it was not all about hardware and software.

A decade ago, when Ducati arrived in MotoGP, all guns blazing, Claudio Domenicali attributed the success of the Desmosedici to the race department's greatest advantage over the Japanese brands: better communication between those working at the track and those working at the factory. When Dall'Igna arrived at Ducati Corse in November 2013 he declared that the biggest problem he had to confront was the lack of communication between track and factory. So how on earth did they lose their way?

Dall'Igna shrugged his shoulder at that question. 'We are human beings, sometimes we lose the way.'

Like all good engineers, Dall'Igna is a bit of a philosopher. To solve problems no-one else can solve you have to have a global view of the world and be capable of looking in from the outside. In fact, fixing Ducati Corse's problem was incredibly simple. 'I've given the important people at the racetrack a role also in Bologna,' he added, 'so when they are home they can work on the problems from the racetrack.'

In recent years Ducati's MotoGP riders have always complained of three main problems: rear-suspension pumping, ferocious power delivery and understeer. After less than a year in Bologna Dall'Igna had fixed the first two and aims to fix the third with next year's GP15. He blames the understeer problem on geometry, and the ideal geometry could not be achieved with the existing bike because of engine size. The GP14.2, introduced at Aragón, featured more compact rear cylinders to allow the engine to be shifted up and back. But only the completely new and smaller GP15 engine will allow Dall'Igna to put the engine exactly where he wants it.

Andrea Dovizioso's Motegi result gives a good indication of how far Ducati has come since Dall'Igna walked into the Bologna race department last autumn. At Motegi 2013 Dovizioso finished 43 seconds down on the winner; this year he was just 14 seconds down. And at other races he was often much closer than that.

Dovizioso was impressive at Ducati. This was the former 125 World Champion's seventh season in the premier class and his most impressive yet. He is something of an Italian Eddie Lawson, though obviously without the four 500 world titles. The pair share a characteristic rare in racers – patience. Like Lawson, Dovizioso understands that there is no point in riding a bike beyond its limits. What is important is understanding those limits, then relaying that information to the engineers and then waiting patiently for the hardware and software. Lawson did just that at Yamaha, Honda and Cagiva. Dovizioso does the same at Ducati.

Like all top factory engineers up and down pit lane, Dall'Igna did not spend all of 2014 talking with his riders in the team garage or watching digital read-outs and flashing lights in the dyno room. Along with Honda's Shuhei Nakamoto and Yamaha's Kouichi Tsuji, he spent a lot of the year locked in meeting rooms at racetracks around the world, thrashing out the future of MotoGP with Corrado Cecchinelli.

Cecchinelli was Ducati's first MotoGP chief technician but jumped the fence some years ago. As MotoGP's Director of Technology he is now a Dorna man, which means he is an engineer who must look at his sport from the promoter's point of view rather than an engineer's. The factories and Dorna want entirely different things from the sport.

Dorna wants to reduce speeds – no great surprise when Pramac Ducati data told us that Andrea Iannone reached 224mph at Mugello – and would like to achieve that with an rpm limit. But the factories do not want an rpm limit. Honda prefers air-intake restrictors. Ducati does not want any restriction in performance because it has just designed an entirely new engine for 2015 and any limiters might require a redesign. Evidence for that assertion already exists with KTM's Moto3 engine: in response to a reduction in the Moto3 rev limit from 14,000rpm to 13,500rpm for 2015, the Austrian factory is building a new, narrower-bore engine to make the most of that change.

'I don't think we shouldn't be talking about the future,' says Dall'Igna. 'But the most important thing is to have the same rules for several years. What we should be talking about now is the rules from 2021, when maybe we should reduce the top speed by 20kph or 30kph, not the 4–5kph that may happen in 2016.'

Dorna also wants to restrict electronics, because this will also reduce costs, with a beneficial knock-on of making the bikes move around a bit more. Fewer electronics should force the riders to get more physical, which should improve the show. And that means more TV viewers, more income and more sponsorship. The factories insist that is all nonsense, of course, but then they are engineers, not showbusiness types.

The weird thing about the electronics issue is that the factories are the only people who want hi-tech rider controls. Dorna do not want them, the fans do not want them and the riders do not want them. The riders would prefer more basic safety controls that will save them from highsides while allowing them to ride their way, without so much interference from the little box.

The 2015 season will be MotoGP's last of open electronics competition. From 2016 all riders will use control software and the system will work like this. Cecchinelli will tell Magneti Marelli what is required and Magneti engineers will write the code. The manufacturers will be allowed to add software, but first Cecchinelli must approve it. Even then the factory software will not be dumped directly into the control ECU; instead the code will be written by Dorna's electronics people and then added to the system.

In theory, this should give everyone a more equal chance. The factory set to suffer the most is Honda, which currently enjoys the most advanced electronics on the grid. This may explain why HRC has been most vociferous in arguing against the introduction of a control ECU. We have one season to go before MotoGP undergoes its biggest technical transformation since the advent of the four-strokes. Riders and teams will have one eye on the present and one eye on the future.

BELOW Marc Marquez celebrates his second MotoGP crown at Motegi – the first time a Honda rider has secured the title at the company's track.

RIDERS' RIDER
OF THE YEAR 2014

What happens when you ask every rider who competed in more than one MotoGP race to name their best riders of the year? You have the Riders' Rider of the Year poll.

Since the first *Official MotoGP Season Review* of 2004, this poll has been conducted every year bar one and each time every eligible voter has contributed. The rules are simple: name your top six riders of the season in order and do not vote for yourself.

The scrutineers then do a few sums, awarding six points for a first place down to one point for a sixth place. The result is an alternative World Championship table. But as we are dealing with motorcycle racers, they do not always follow the rules, do they Valentino? Not everyone wants to name six of his opponents; a few of them want to make a point.

This is a secret ballot, so I am not going to tell you who voted for whom, but I can tell you this. When a previously unbeatable, or almost unbeatable, rider shows a weakness, his votes tumble. It happened to Rossi last year. It happened to Jorge Lorenzo and Dani Pedrosa this year.

PREVIOUS WINNERS

2004	VALENTINO ROSSI
2005	VALENTINO ROSSI
2006	LORIS CAPIROSSI
2007	CASEY STONER
2008	VALENTINO ROSSI
2009	VALENTINO ROSSI
2010	JORGE LORENZO
2012	JORGE LORENZO
2013	MARC MARQUEZ

The top three in our 2014 poll are the same as in the World Championship, but Rossi is a lot closer to Marquez than in real life, and Jorge is a lot further back. Andrea Dovizioso's super-professional season means that his peers voted him fourth, one place higher than in the World Championship table, at the expense of Pedrosa.

Aleix Espargaro was preferred by the voters to Dani, who he beat by the narrowest of margins, and to his younger brother – another reversal of what happened on track. Aleix's margin over Pol was substantial: double the number of voters put Aleix in their selection compared with Pol, who in turn was only a couple of votes ahead of Andrea Iannone.

Of the 27 voters, all but six put Marc Marquez as their number one and all but ten put Valentino Rossi second. The majority of the riders then shuffled the names of Pedrosa, Lorenzo, Dovizoso and one of the Espargaros into different orders.

After those six, the numbers of votes awarded to the rest of our top ten were quite small, but Scott Redding was included by six of his fellow riders and Bradley Smith by three. Only three other riders were mentioned: Stefan Bradl and Yonny Hernandez got one vote and Colin Edwards two – with one voter saying that it was a vote for 'his career'.

2014 TOP TEN

1st	MARC MARQUEZ	140
2nd	VALENTINO ROSSI	124
3rd	JORGE LORENZO	82
4th	ANDREA DOVIZIOSO	63
5th	ALEIX ESPARGARO	47
6th	DANI PEDROSA	46
7th	POL ESPARGARO	16
8th	ANDREA IANNONE	14
9th	BRADLEY SMITH	10
10th	SCOTT REDDING	7

HONDA
The Power of Dreams

PREMIER CLASS
CHAMPIONS
SINCE 1983

HONDA – PREMIER CLASS WORLD CHAMPIONS SINCE 1983
SPENCER - GARDNER - LAWSON - DOOHAN - CRIVILLE - ROSSI - HAYDEN - STONER - MARQUEZ

WWW.HONDAPRORACING.COM

SMALL CHANGES, BIG CONSEQUENCES

Gigi Dall'Igna joined Ducati Corse at the start of the year. He had just weeks to change MotoGP's rules and develop the bike

Yamaha scored a real victory over Honda when it decided that it could best 'help' the MotoGP class by making available leased factory engines to run on 24 litres of fuel to teams that had previously used CRT machines. Whereas Honda had committed resources to building its steel-valve-spring 'customer bike', the RC1000V, Yamaha simply rummaged through its engine parts bin and built some power units for lease. Because the deal was agreed at such a late stage, Yamaha was also persuaded to add a chassis, swingarm and linkage to the mix to help the recipients. This represented a major boost in effectiveness compared with the old CRT class. It was a bold step that was welcomed in most parts of the paddock.

And then Bridgestone dropped the bombshell: all 2014 races would be on the 'heat-resistant' versions of its tyres. These are slightly stiffer in construction and have a slightly harder edge, thus reducing the edge grip on which the Yamaha – and especially Jorge Lorenzo's Yamaha – thrives. Bridgestone's announcement was a direct result of the company being required to supply a range of softer compounds for the new Open Class (the old CRT class). Rather than the converted street engines of old, this subsidiary class was now populated with full-blown factory engines operating with limited electronics and more fuel, a lot more fuel – a completely different proposition in power terms. Bridgestone wanted to make sure its tyres were up to the job.

We did not really know it then, but Bridgestone's decision took away Yamaha's hopes of maintaining grip at high lean angles and also of beating Marquez, certainly for the first few races of the season. Bridgestone quickly understood the issues its decision had created: for those circuits where the medium tyre could take a softer edge construction, and to try and retrieve some of the Yamahas' lost grip, it was agreed that

TOP Ducati's first 2014 swingarm was not long enough; note the position of the stand bobbin.

ABOVE By the first race at Qatar a slightly longer version had been introduced; again observe the position of the stand support.

BOTTOM For Sachsenring Dovizioso and Iannone received new swingarms and rear linkages to help them in long, slow corners.

revised tyres would be made available, but they did not turn up until Jerez. Because Bridgestone's 2014 strategy was to use the tyres previously only specified for particularly tough circuits, at those circuits – Mugello being the first – riders would use the same tyre they had used the year before. This meant that Lorenzo's first really competitive run in 2014 was on a bike and tyre combination very similar to that of 2013.

Yamaha also uprated its seamless-shift gearbox for 2014. Rather than being seamless only from second to sixth, now it had the same N–1–2–3–4–5–6 pattern as the Hondas but only worked as a seamless gearbox while shifting up. The downshifts were conventional until Catalunya, when they became clutchless, not seamless – that would have required a new crankcase design and Yamaha, being a factory entry, had its engine design frozen for the year.

This year's Yamaha chassis was a logical extension of the strategy the company had been using for the previous two years. It had been following Lorenzo's preferences for ever stiffer and more precise handling, using the flex in the softer carcass of the 'quick-to-heat-up' Bridgestones to provide suspension. Jorge's style is to maintain corner speed by using big arcs and this works as long as he does not get stuck behind an ultra-fast, stop-turn-and-go Honda. The Yamaha has ended up longer than the Honda and this has the happy side effect of allowing faster starts before the wheelie control cuts in. Rossi struggled last year with the Yamaha, looking everywhere for something that would give him more front-wheel 'feel', so this year's chassis was certainly not to his taste

Something happened, however, after the third race, in Argentina. Someone decided that an experiment with flex was necessary, and Yamaha arrived at Jerez just a week later with two modified chassis. Sections of the main frame above the swingarm pivots had been cut out and plates welded in. Rossi went out of his way to love his new frame but Lorenzo tried his just once. And as it was Rossi who initially had favourable results, we expected a wholesale rethink on the direction Yamaha had been taking – but little new was seen subsequently.

It appears that halfway through the Le Mans meeting Lorenzo went back to a late 2013 chassis, which was slightly softer and as a result a little better with the new medium-compound rear tyre, the one with the edge design slightly modified to try to reinstate the grip levels of 2013. It was clear by this stage of the season that Lorenzo's confidence had been damaged, but in machinery terms he was rapidly getting back to a set-up similar to the one he enjoyed at the end of 2013.

The second major change for 2014 was the adoption of a new fuel limit of 20 litres, one litre down on previous years. Engine-related restrictions usually favour Honda, which has the best engine-development facilities in racing, so we expected Yamaha to struggle with this – and that duly happened. The first day of the first test at Sepang was a disaster for Yamaha, but after some overnight work the bike's throttle response was much improved.

Restricting fuel is supposed to limit performance and to give the factories justification for spending research and development budget for racing. But it does not seem to slow down the bike too much, as top speeds in 2014 were still as high as a bike can go without either spinning the rear tyre or turning over backwards.

The significant technical barrier that comes with tighter fuel restriction is the effect on initial throttle opening. Managing the addition of very small throttle openings is important and smooth throttle pick-up and drive off corners are vital to good lap times. Having spare fuel available at these moments makes a major difference to a bike's throttle reaction and the

FAR LEFT The Desmosedici started the year with a new fairing intended for quick side-to-side transitions. It was shorter than previous Ducati fairings.

LEFT From Sachsenring the design was more orientated to top speed, with more shoulder cover and bigger radiator ducts to make up for the cooling lost as the front wheel came progressively back.

rider's comfort zone. For Yamaha, it took several software upgrades to reinstate that smooth initial throttle response, which is so critical at high angles of lean. Along with the tyre modifications and the different chassis, this completed the work that returned Yamaha's bike to full competitiveness.

SPECIAL NEEDS?

Over at Ducati there was some intense scrutiny of the rulebook. Nothing in the regulations said that Ducati had to enter as a 'Factory MotoGP' team: if it took the Dorna ECU and its inertial platform, Ducati could put all of its bikes in MotoGP's Open Class category and benefit from 24 litres of fuel per race, 12 engines per year and softer-compound tyres.

Ducati announced that it would take the gamble and do just that. Dorna was pleased, for its master plan has all bikes running to the Open Class regulations in 2016. At the same time the spec software received a major upgrade, with many new functions and much more adjustment. The origins of the new software, available to all teams in the Open Class, were a mystery, but those who had access assured us that some of the many pages still had 'Ducati' written on them.

Gigi Dall'Igna, recruited from arch-rival Aprilia to be Ducati's head of racing, understands how to play with a rulebook. He had been insistent from the start that to develop the Ducati into a machine capable of taking on the Honda and Yamaha he would need to be able to change the design of his engines mid-year. Twelve engines without a design freeze were more than enough for this purpose, and the extra fuel allowed was a bonus. Honda and Yamaha were not happy, and neither were the owners of all the other Open Class MotoGP bikes once they had looked at the electronics upgrade and the complications it presented.

Some renegotiation was necessary. Just before the start of the season the new electronics were dumped – deemed way too complicated by the customer teams that are the mainstay of the Open Class – and a special clause was added to the factory regulations. This allowed any factory that had

'not achieved a race win in dry conditions during the 2013 season, or a new Motorcycle Manufacturer entering the Championship for the first time since the 2013 season' to be exempt from the factory engine homologation restrictions (five engines and frozen design) and the factory fuel limit (20 litres) until the start of 2016.

In addition, 'should any rider or combination of riders entered by the same Manufacturer, participating under these conditions, accumulate three race wins in dry conditions during the 2014 and/or 2015 seasons, then for all riders of that Manufacturer the tyre allocation will revert to the Factory Option specification. This revised tyre specification will apply to all races immediately after the stated results are achieved and remain in place until the end of the 2015 season.' This left only Honda and Yamaha subject to the full 'Factory MotoGP' regulations.

BELOW Cal Crutchlow discovered early in testing that the Ducati Desmosedici was never going to feel like the Yamaha he was used to.

TOP The initial chassis, seen in Qatar. Note the amount of material between the bearing holder and the 'fuel tank' cover. Later in the year this type of chassis was supplied to Hector Barbera at Avintia.

ABOVE By Silverstone the headstock had moved back; this is the third version of the chassis, and note that the adjustment is still 'full back'.

Ducati's progress has also been noticeably different this year. Dall'Igna has brought clear vision of the path he wants followed, the questions he needs answered and the manner in which the bike is to be developed.

The first iteration of the 2014 Desmosedici was designed in mid-2013 when Ducati Corse was being run by Bernhard Gobmeier. The bike was a major step forward from the 2013 design and brought some big changes. The engine was moved forward by around 70mm and the mass was centralised. This involved a new fuel tank design (in both 20- and 24-litre capacities), repackaging the ECU and electronics, and new fairing and bodywork. The chassis had new levels of adjustability, including Yamaha-style front engine mounts of adjustable length.

Dall'Igna's job is to develop this bike as far as he can while finding out what major changes might be needed to produce a bike that can compete with Honda and Yamaha. From the team's point of view he has brought direction and a plan. There was a clear decision to focus first on the bike's basic geometry.

At Qatar the bike looked extraordinary. The swingarm was set as long as it could be and the front end looked like it was set really short, although it seems more likely that

the top adjuster was fully back and the lower one further forward. The centre section of the bike would have been 'rolled forward' by this set-up.

Overall, however, as much weight as possible was being moved forward, and this was on a bike that was already over 70mm shorter at the front than the previous year. In addition Ducati tried all of its machines with a lot of fork showing above the top clamp and the back of the bike set high, so the centre was rolled forward, possibly lowering the crankshaft centre (and the mass of the motor) and raising the swingarm pivot. Unlike previous years there was a clear method: Dovizioso and Iannone tried different settings to the extent that both assessed all the options at some stage or other. Crutchlow was not part of this procedure as he was being given time simply to understand the bike, and it was clear he was not finding that easy.

Revised, longer swingarms quickly became available and by Le Mans there was also a new main frame that allowed the front end to be adjusted backwards by another 10mm. Almost immediately Dovizioso moved it to its fully back position. As soon as 340mm discs were allowed, on they went, and stayed. The air scoops that had been added to try to cool the 320mm discs also stayed; Ducati wanted as much speed as possible for as long as possible, and anything that helped hard and late braking was used.

For the tight, twisty Sachsenring there was a new fairing and another new swingarm, beefier at the front but noticeably thinner out near the axle, probably for more flex at this point. Finally, there was the Desmosedici 14.2, a completely new bike that was narrower in the middle, repackaged for better aerodynamics and to provide an easier platform for the rider to move around on.

Very early in the process it became obvious that new engine architecture would be needed. This will still be a 90-degree V4, but it will be smaller and probably heavier. Until now the Ducati engine has been noticeably light in weight according to many of the mechanics who have worked on it. Over the past two years the crankshaft has been made heavier, to the point where no more material can be accommodated inside the crankcases.

In addition to its duty of converting power delivered in straight lines into rotational motion, the crankshaft on a racing motorcycle is used to damp down the rate of its own acceleration. Power has to be delivered accurately and smoothly, especially at small throttle openings and high angles of lean. During 2014 Ducati conducted further crankshaft-inertia experiments using its external flywheel, and on more than one occasion a new flywheel was fitted part way through a session. Around the circumference of one particular flywheel there were high-density metal inserts, which must have made a very noticeable difference not only to throttle response but also to the bike's response during changes of direction.

The new engine will undoubtedly have a higher-inertia crankshaft, with as much of the weight as possible inside the crankcases on the centre line of the bike. It will also have a relocated gearbox so that Ducati achieve desired outcomes in both centre of mass and swingarm angle and position. The new engine will also be smaller so that Ducati stands a chance of repositioning it in the chassis going into the era of Michelin control tyres in 2016.

Ducati tried several other experiments during the year. One in particular caused a lot of comment but has never been satisfactorily explained by the team. This was the addition of a mass damper either side of the exhaust on the rear seat hump. A mass damper acts to control movement, and the Ducati has always had a reputation for being a little 'rough'. It is possible that Ducati was just seeking to smooth out that vibration for comfort reasons, to help maintain the rider's stamina reserves, but there are other vibrations that can be very destructive on a motorcycle. Chatter would be one of the main ones, and carbon swinging arms have something of a reputation for chattering when grip levels are high.

PRESERVING THE STATUS QUO

Factories do not have to go racing. The fact that they do, and they choose to risk their reputations by doing so, should be celebrated. It is a show, one we all enjoy, and it is an adventure for everyone involved, from the racers to the fans. It is also a sport and a commercial opportunity for some.

All of these aspects get thrown together when a rulebook is written. For the show, the aim is to get as many different bikes and riders as possible together on track and to allow them to compete. For the sport, those who have the best riders and machines should win – but not by too much for the sake of the show. The rulebook should also make it as easy as possible for new factories and sponsors to join and to compete. Heaven knows, this is a far more complex sport than it looks already. These are the pressures that are shaping the MotoGP rulebook.

It can be self-destructive to impose rules that restrict newcomers so that they cannot engineer solutions to the sort of problems they will inevitably face. The freezing of engine specifications at the start of the year and the very limited number of engines allowed are great ideas to reduce costs for the established and successful factories, but to a potential newcomer they represent a significant risk.

From a technical perspective, Ducati brought itself a load of problems in the 800cc era when it did not, or would not, realise just how much its success was down to the skills of one phenomenal rider. To try to get out of the resulting mess, Ducati has changed personnel and engineering philosophies – and spent a load of money. The rulebook was not helping. How can you develop your way out of trouble if significant chunks of the bike are frozen at the start of each year? And if you were a new entrant, why would you want to lay your reputation on the line just to make others look good?

There are three sections of the factory MotoGP rulebook that favour the current top dogs: the limited number of engines, the frozen engine design and the fuel limit. From an everyday perspective we do not really need a body of research on 1,000cc engines operating at over 17,000rpm and below 10-bar fuel pressure with indirect injection and limited fuel. Where is the practical application? It is the same thing with the frozen designs and restricted engine numbers – great for a display of technical excellence but little else.

I salute those who can get their bike going so well with these restrictions. They are superb engineers and should be respected as such. But the sport needs more factories and a good show.

The 2016 rules, with a common set of software and a control ECU and inertial platform, will level the playing field a little. But these new rules do not contain much that restricts performance. It can be argued that the current fuel limit at least slows down the bikes a bit, and that is increasingly necessary given the speeds we are seeing. The current factories do not like it, but a common rev limit would be a simple way to limit power development, and as a happy side effect it would even out the playing field.

The final decision on who was subject to which rules for 2014 was quite pragmatic, and the right thing to do, but it has to be said that the manner in which we got there was not particularly edifying.

BELOW Ducati's test bike seen at Mugello. Note the external flywheel and the adjustable-length front engine mounts. The flywheels can be changed mid-session, as can the position of the bolts holding the front of the engine.

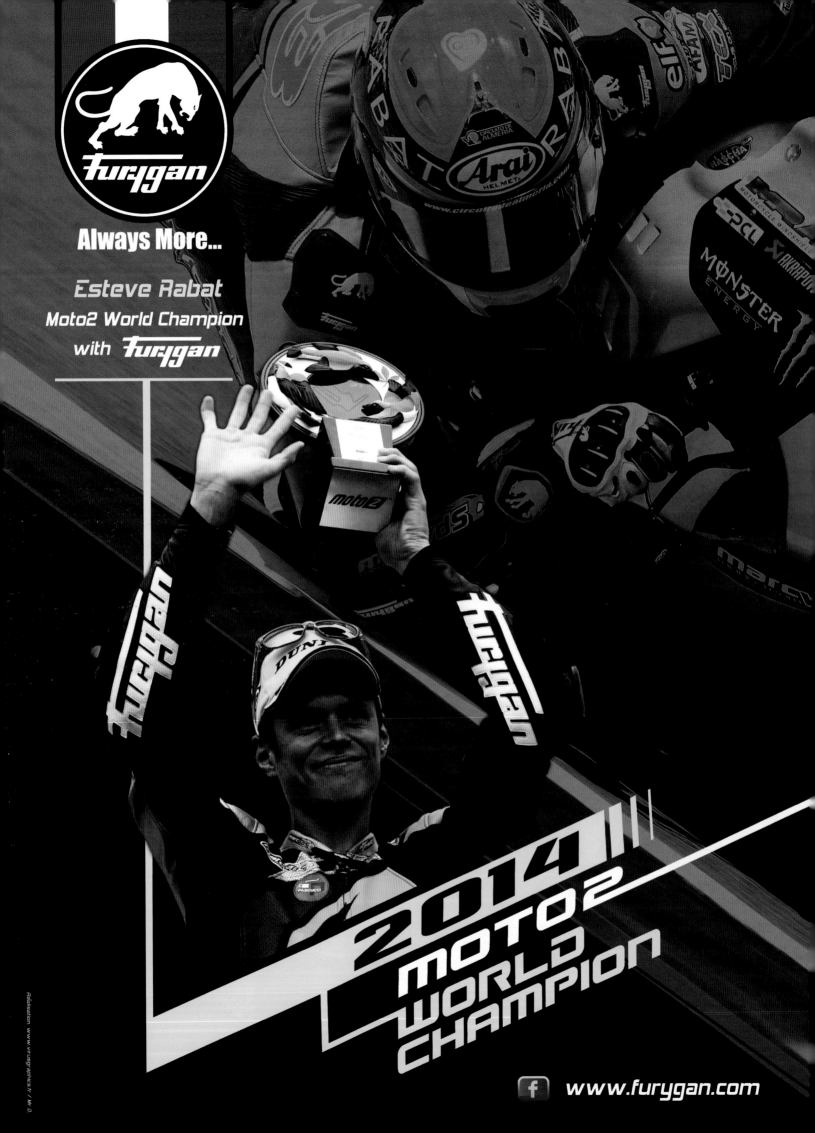

THE BIKES

HONDA
RC213V 2014

The Honda started the year as the best bike, and pretty much ended it like that too. It has the most advanced electronics and a design concept that fits well with Marc Marquez's riding style. With the requirement for a control Marelli ECU this year, Honda was the only manufacturer to have to make major changes to its software; all the other teams already used Marelli hardware and therefore had much less reprogramming to do.

The Honda RC213V is a 1,000cc, 90-degree V4 with pneumatic valve springs and a seamless-shift gearbox that works both on upshifts and downshifts. The gearbox is the key to a series of design decisions that lie behind some of Marquez's amazing rides. The bike looks twitchy on the brakes, but that allows a good rider to feel where the limits are before they arrive – the front twitches before it locks up. The gearbox design also means that the chassis does not pitch every time the rider changes gear, this extra stability allowing the bike to be taken closer to its limits more of the time.

The Honda noticeably does not need the big 340mm discs that the rest of the field consider normal; indeed, the Hondas quite often use carbon covers on the front discs to keep their temperature up. This is possible as the engine is used as a computer-controlled rear brake and has been designed to soak up massive over-rev stresses on corner entry. That would normally be a recipe for disaster, but to prevent destructive valve bounce the pneumatic valve system is capable of increasing the spring pressure temporarily to make sure the valves stay on the cam while also increasing the engine braking. The bike then relies on its sensors and the electronics manage the throttles to provide exactly the right amount of computer-controlled rear-wheel braking.

Honda had good luck too. In 2013 the company had struggled with Bridgestone's temperature-resistant 'option' tyres and arrived at Sepang for the first test of 2014 determined to fix that. It was only then that Honda discovered that these tyres would be standard fare in 2014. The company duly spent the pre-season testing period trying out three different levels of chassis flex before settling on the one that would work best for them. That advance planning, and a chassis design philosophy that does not rely on edge grip, served them well in 2014.

1 2 Dani Pedrosa and Marc Marquez use differently shaped top cowls and different brake lever lengths and throttle systems. There are conventional cables on Pedrosa's twistgrip and wires on Marquez's bike.

3 The Hondas did not suffer from the 'braking crisis' and even needed disc covers to keep their 320mm discs warm.

4 The only obvious change on the Repsol bikes during the year was a new exhaust system with longer primary pipes; this should have boosted mid-range power.

YAMAHA
YZR M1 2014

Yamaha had a bad start to the year. Its chosen set-up, and Bridgestones with slightly less edge grip, conspired to wreck Jorge Lorenzo's early-season confidence. Technically the major problems were pretty much fixed by Le Mans, and by Mugello Jorge could run at the front again, but it would take until the last third of the year before the wins started coming.

The Yamaha M1 maintains the same basic design concept that has lasted for the past decade. It is an in-line four-cylinder with a cross-plane and reverse-rotating crankshaft. The chassis is a twin-aluminium-beam 'web' design with the space between the front engine mounts and the underside of the beam now fully filled in. The beams are complex CNC-machined structures with an 'open-web' design and no inner skin. Yamaha uses its technical ability to change the wall thickness of the material to get the right flex and stiffness ratios, and the absence of significant amounts of welding means that the structure suffers less from heat-induced warping during production.

Yamaha continued development of its seamless gearbox, with the 2014 version having a revised design that was seamless in all gears, replacing the rushed second-to-sixth gearbox that had been débuted at Misano in 2013. It was still 'upwards only', however, as the engine freeze – which was intended to limit costs – prevented Yamaha from fitting the revised mechanism that would be required to work seamlessly downwards as well. Yamaha worked hard on its slipper clutch and throttle auto-blip mechanism to get downshifts as smooth as possible and limit the advantage that Honda held into corners.

The Yamaha is a careful development of the bike Valentino Rossi first rode in 2005, and until this year it had been looked after by the same group of engineers all the way through. Over that same period Yamaha has faced very hard times. The in-line four concept that Yamaha has stuck with for years is not the most fuel-efficient: it has irregular intake and exhaust pulses that lower the efficiency of the airbox and exhaust system, and an extra set of gears to reverse the direction of the engine's rotation. Logically this engine should not be as good as the Honda unit, yet after Yamaha's slow start its bikes were capable of matching the Hondas on the straights.

Younger men are coming to the fore and taking the project forward. It will be interesting to see if they are given the budget to make significant changes.

1 At the start of the year Jorge Lorenzo tried increasing front-end rigidity with this solid top triple clamp.

2 The small lever on the clip lifts the gate to allow neutral to be selected on the seamless-shift N–1–2–3–4–5–6 gearbox.

3 New exhaust systems were débuted at Assen and helped to smooth the power at low revs.

4 Yamaha modified two chassis for more flex; Lorenzo did not like the feel but Rossi used them all year.

DUCATI
DESMOSEDICI GP14

Ducati had had a reasonable year in 2013, which was clearly an experimental season for its aluminium beam frames with a big focus on understanding how to change the flex and the direction in which to go for the geometry. After Audi's takeover of Ducati, the major change was the appointment of Bernhard Gobmeier, the ex-BMW Superbike racing boss, to run the Ducati Corse project.

It was Gobmeier's design that was débuted at the first test in Malaysia. By the time the bike arrived, however, Gobmeier had gone, back to Germany to help oversee all of the VW group's racing activities. His replacement as head of Ducati Corse was ex-Aprilia chief Gigi Dall'Igna, and it did not take long for him to make his mark.

Dall'Igna essentially renegotiated the rulebook, getting Ducati out of the need to freeze its engine design as well as increasing the number of engines available for the season to 12 and the race fuel allowance to 24 litres. He then set about developing Gobmeier's design, his first goal being to find the right geometry for the bike. Three swingarms and chassis later he had it almost as good as he could hope for. He had a bike that the two Andreas – Dovizioso and Iannone – could put on the front of the grid. That did not always turn into strong race results as the bike still had an appetite for tyres and did not really want to hold a line in corners, but it was great on circuits where its riders could point and squirt it out of corners.

At Aragón Ducati débuted a 'GP14-2' version of the bike that carried forward the development: it was shorter at the front, longer and more flexible at the rear, narrower in the middle, and had new bodywork. A lot of work had gone into fine-tuning throttle response with flywheels and electronic mapping, and overall power levels increased from an engine that could rev to 18,000rpm – a lot for a power unit with a 48mm stroke.

Cal Crutchlow did not benefit from these changes as the 'works' riders from mid-season onwards were the two Andreas. Nevertheless, Crutchlow was able to put in some excellent performances on a chassis very similar to the one on which he started the year – which tends to indicate that engine development has had more of an impact on performance than the process of chassis development.

1 Cal Crutchlow's bike with the ultra-high-inertia flywheel fitted. Note also the number of cooling ducts around the front brake discs.

2 The test bike at Mugello with its mass dampers fitted.

3 The 'GP14-2' version had the headstock bearing moved back even further (compare this photo with those on page 16).

4 The 'GP14-2' version is also noticeably narrower in the middle, probably requiring a narrower rear cylinder head.

THE CIRCUIT OF WALES

The Circuit of Wales is a £315m world-class motorsport and destination informed and inspired by nature and regeneration.

A business hub for high-technology excellence in the automotive and technology centres, the Circuit of Wales will provide:

- A state-of-the-art, purpose-built motorcycle Grand Prix circuit and facilities, attracting national and international motorsports

- A centre for low-carbon research and development, providing a base for leading educational institutions

- The home of advance manufacturing, precision engineering and automotive performance companies

- An elite indoor performance academy aimed at developing industry talent

- Leading educational, safety and training automotive infrastructure facilities

- A range of complementary Leisure & Retail offerings in the picturesque Rassau Valley

For further information contact
www.circuitofwales.com

HONDA
RCV1000R

Honda built and sold the RCV1000R, a bike that is a treasure house of information on how to race in MotoGP but for one glaring exception – it is just too slow. To keep the price down and to sit with the original concept of an Open Class bike, Honda built a cheaper version of its all-conquering V4 with steel valve springs, a very conventional double-dog gearbox and lower-spec components all round.

The chassis is full-spec RCV, just a year out of date, and the bike handled well. Everyone immediately junked the as-delivered 42mm Moto2-spec Ohlins forks and went for full-through-rod 48mm forks. The Honda used the full Dorna ECU and inertial platform, which gave HRC a lot of information on using the control software.

When the severity of the horsepower shortfall became obvious, the rev limit was raised, just enough to make the 22-litre fuel tank too small. Many of the usual small adjustments were not permitted, with the bike having one linkage and one swingarm position. Occasionally, just before a rider's home race, a works linkage might arrive in his garage.

1 The chassis is virtually identical to the works chassis of one year ago.

2 Scott Redding had the use of the latest Showa suspension and Nissin brakes.

3 Honda went back to an entirely conventional 'double dogger' gearbox to keep costs down.

YAMAHA
M1 OPEN SPEC

Yamaha provided an engine plan, and the temporary loan of a chassis and swingarm. Forward got FTR to make all the extra bits, including the bodywork, and off the team went. Forward was supposed to make its own chassis too, but the riders clearly liked the idea of using one-year-old, out-of-date works Yamaha stuff.

After leaving his post as FTR's chief designer, Mark Butler built a chassis for Forward using the Yamaha chassis as a jig. It clearly worked well, and the fact that it was a lot 'softer' made it particularly effective in slower corners. The riders, however, could not see any benefit in moving away from Yamaha's proven machinery.

Colin Edwards was replaced by Alex de Angelis mid-season and that was supposed to result in more testing of the in-house chassis – but that did not seem to happen.

1 FTR initially built all the additional parts required to make the Yamaha chassis serviceable.

2 The airbox and the packaging of the airbox and pneumatic valve systems is identical to the works bikes.

APRILIA
ART GP14

There were two Aprilia-based teams on the grid in 2014: Paul Bird Motorsport (PBM) with its own chassis and the more factory-based Ioda team.

Paul Bird's operation continued to use its British-built GPMS chassis, which was totally conventional-looking and never quite able to make the best of the grip on offer.

Ioda went with the Aprilia-built ART chassis. This was clearly experimental, with a new swinging arm and main frame compared with the 2013 bike. Both the frame and the swinging arm were noticeably weak-looking, as if Aprilia wanted the bike to twist torsionally – something that normally is all but eliminated. The chassis appeared to remain unchanged all year and the only visible developments were to fairings and air intakes.

1 On its own bike Aprilia used a chassis with a very flexible main beam.

2 Aprilia used two different air-intake systems during the year.

AVINTIA
KAWASAKI ZX-10R

Kawasaki donated a lot of ex-World Superbike parts, including chassis and suspension. Akira in France then built pneumatic-valve-spring cylinder heads for the engines, to World Superbike spec. It all sounded like a serious effort.

Over the first few rounds the original black paint went missing from the frames and Inmotec in Pamplona welded a lot of material around the steering head while also lengthening and strengthening the swingarm. In later races new swingarms and a chassis reinforced around the swingarm pivot were tried. The bike never really showed well, demonstrating how difficult it is to build a competitive machine. The converted Kawasaki in-line-four superbike has none of the cross-plane and reverse-rotating crankshaft technology of the last of the Kawasaki MotoGP bikes, and it showed. The engine revved to at least 16,000rpm and while power was enhanced usability was not. From a purely competitive angle, the previous year's FTR chassis would have been better developed and quite possibly quicker on track.

1 The first change was a new swingarm to replace the extended superbike race item.

2 The top-up tank for the Akira pneumatic-valve cylinder head was situated under the seat hump.

SUZUKI
GSX-RR

Suzuki tested its new MotoGP design for nearly two years before it came to the track. An across-the-frame four-cylinder, it follows a completely different philosophy from the company's previous V4.

Just like the similar Yamaha, the Suzuki has a cross-plane and reverse-rotating crank. The chassis is a very slight-looking aluminium beam frame. During 2014 Suzuki tested several identical-looking chassis, all with different rigidities, and concentrated on getting a functional software suite to work in the new 'control' ECU.

Long-time test rider Randy de Puniet was given one race on the Suzuki, at Valencia, as a prelude to a full two-rider team for 2015. Suzuki will benefit from the newly introduced 'new-entrant' regulations, which will allow 24 litres of fuel per race and 12 engines a year with no design freeze.

1 Suzuki transferred to the Marelli control ECU at the start of the year and has been redeveloping its software ever since.

2 Several different exhaust systems were tried during testing, this classic megaphone being the last of them.

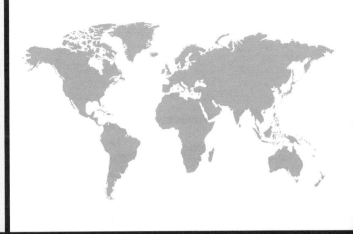

THE SEASON IN FOCUS

From the factory men to the wild cards, every MotoGP rider's season analysed

CHAMPIONSHIP

	Rider	Nation	Team	Points
1	Marquez	SPA	Repsol Honda Team	362
2	Rossi	ITA	Movistar Yamaha MotoGP	295
3	Lorenzo	SPA	Movistar Yamaha MotoGP	263
4	Pedrosa	SPA	Repsol Honda Team	246
5	Dovizioso	ITA	Ducati Team	187
6	P Espargaro	SPA	Monster Yamaha Tech3	136
7	A Espargaro	SPA	NGM Forward Racing	126
8	Smith	GBR	Monster Yamaha Tech3	121
9	Bradl	GER	LCR Honda MotoGP	117
10	Iannone	ITA	Pramac Racing	102
11	Bautista	SPA	GO&FUN Honda Gresini	89
12	Redding	GBR	GO&FUN Honda Gresini	81
13	Crutchlow	GBR	Ducati Team	74
14	Aoyama	JPN	Drive M7 Aspar	68
15	Hernandez	COL	Energy T.I. Pramac Racing	53
16	Hayden	USA	Drive M7 Aspar	47
17	Abraham	CZE	Cardion AB Motoracing	33
18	Barbera	SPA	Avintia Racing	26
19	Pirro	ITA	Ducati Team	18
20	Petrucci	ITA	Octo IodaRacing Team	17
21	De Angelis	RSM	NGM Forward Racing	14
22	Edwards	USA	NGM Forward Racing	11
23	Parkes	AUS	Paul Bird Motorsport	9
24	Laverty	GBR	Paul Bird Motorsport	9
25	Di Meglio	FRA	Avintia Racing	9
26	Nakasuga	JPN	YAMALUBE Racing Team	4
27	Camier	GBR	Drive M7 Aspar	1

1 MARC MARQUEZ
REPSOL HONDA TEAM

NATIONALITY Spanish
DATE OF BIRTH 17 February 1993
2014 SEASON 13 wins, 14 rostrums,
13 pole positions, 12 fastest laps
TOTAL POINTS 362

Marc carried on where he left off last year, effectively retaining his championship with a run of form in the first half of the season that destroyed the opposition. Pole position in the first eight races and winning the first ten races gave him a lead of 89 points after Indianapolis.

His subdued fourth place at Brno was a serious anti-climax and led to a couple of mistakes as he tried to set up the chance to retain the title on home soil at Aragón. To Honda's barely disguised pleasure, that had to wait until Motegi, where Marc became the first Honda rider to secure the title at Honda's own circuit, which he did with an uncharacteristically cautious third place. He also became the youngest rider ever to retain motorcycle racing's top championship, taking that distinction from Mike Hailwood.

The champion went through this year with the same *joie de vivre* that characterised his rookie year in MotoGP. He had the bike sliding at the rear as he ran his front wheel up inside curves, he regularly pushed the front beyond the limit, and he was ruthless when he needed to be – as with Lorenzo at Silverstone. He also had to cope with several new varieties of flag-to-flag race and won them.

Is there a weakness in his game? Well, he is not the best starter but that does not seem to matter. More than once, in France and Malaysia for instance, he recovered from being punted down the field in first-lap incidents only to come back and win.

Marc Marquez is the best man on the best bike.

2 VALENTINO ROSSI
MOVISTAR YAMAHA MOTOGP

NATIONALITY Italian
DATE OF BIRTH 16 February 1979
2014 SEASON 2 wins, 13 rostrums,
1 pole position, 1 fastest lap
TOTAL POINTS 295

It took four races for Valentino to work out where he stood. Once he knew that he could be a regular podium contender, the old Valentino reappeared both on and off the track. He repeatedly reminded the media that he was 'happy with the way my team is working', in other words pointing out that he was right to change crew chiefs. His riding style altered dramatically: he used much more upper-body lean than before, and appeared to be as fit as he was a decade ago.

Valentino's wins also harked back to earlier championships. Make no mistake, these were not gifts or products of strange circumstances (as you could say about Assen 2013). With new race engineer Silvano Galbusera, the team was able to recreate the old Jerry Burgess magic of throwing a fix at the bike on Saturday night and transforming bad qualifying into a great race. Just two examples were the rostrum at Mugello from tenth on the grid and the win in Australia from eighth in qualifying.

The win in his back yard at Misano was an act of savage redemption, the great champion in merciless form in front of his friends, family and fans. At Phillip Island he celebrated like a teenager winning his first race. Nine years after his last win on the toughest track of all, he knew he had not lost it.

You would not normally expect Vale to get excited about second place, but he made it crystal clear that this time it mattered not because being runner-up meant anything to him but being top Yamaha rider most certainly did.

On this form he will be a championship contender in 2015.

3 JORGE LORENZO
MOVISTAR YAMAHA MOTOGP

Given his start to the season, third place in the championship can be considered a great result. After the first two races, which featured a first-lap crash and the mother of all jump starts, he was 16th in the championship. At Assen he suffered fearsome flashbacks to his 2013 wet-weather crash and could only finish 13th – and was still only fifth in the table. His fitness at the start of the season was affected by three operations in the close season, but it was the blows to his confidence that seemed most hurtful.

And yet Jorge summoned up a stunning second half to the year. From Indianapolis onwards he was never off the rostrum until Valencia, and he put together back-to-back wins at the very different Aragón and Motegi circuits, setting fastest lap at both. Other

factors added to the view of Jorge as a complicated character: there were a couple of rather strange tyre choices and after the three back-to-back October races he again raised questions about his fitness – which seemed to be taking self-criticism to new heights.

Many of his problems went back to Bridgestone's medium-compound rear slick for 2014. The original design, which Jorge hated, had stiffer edges and compromised Jorge's need for high speeds at high lean angles. When a revised design came through (a return to previous specification), he was happier.

As recently as mid-season, it was possible to believe that Jorge Lorenzo was a spent force. That would have been a mistake. When you have been a double MotoGP champion you do not give up easily.

NATIONALITY Spanish
DATE OF BIRTH 4 May 1987
2014 SEASON 2 wins, 11 rostrums, 1 pole position, 2 fastest laps
TOTAL POINTS 263

4 DANI PEDROSA
REPSOL HONDA TEAM

Right up to the Misano race in September, Dani Pedrosa looked like a certainty for second place in the championship. For once he started the season injury-free and in the first four races of the year he scored podium finishes to keep his team-mate in sight. Then things gradually started to slide away from him, although he did have the satisfaction of ending Marc Marquez's run of both pole positions and race wins.

After that win in the Czech Republic, Dani started, in complete contrast to his history, to give the rest a headstart during the remaining races. His pace towards the end of races was usually as good as that of the leaders, but by then the top three were too far away. There was also some bad luck, such as being rammed by Iannone in Australia,

but there were also the self-inflicted mistakes such as the crashes in Aragón and Malaysia.

There were also problems within the team. After it was decided that two of his mechanics would not be back for 2015, Dani's long-time race engineer Mike Leitner decided that he did not want to continue. Before things turned nasty at the end of the year, HRC signed up Dani for another two years alongside Marc Marquez; no doubt Honda sees the value of stability in the personnel department with the major rules changes coming up.

Despite the disappointing fourth-place finish, it is difficult – if not impossible – to think of someone who could do a better job than Dani and there is no doubting the effort he put in to try to match his team-mate this season.

NATIONALITY Spanish
DATE OF BIRTH 29 September 1985
2014 SEASON 1 win, 10 rostrums, 1 pole position, 3 fastest laps
TOTAL POINTS 246

5 ANDREA DOVIZIOSO
DUCATI TEAM

NATIONALITY Italian
DATE OF BIRTH 23 March 1989
2014 SEASON 2 rostrums, 1 pole position
TOTAL POINTS 187

Along with new racing department head Gigi Dall'Igna, Andrea gave Ducati reason for hope. He extracted the maximum from his machine whatever the circumstances and allied it to astute riding and impeccable racecraft. As the Ducati gradually improved, so Dovi became a regular front-row qualifier and a fixture at the front of the field. No-one could have predicted two top-three finishes in the first five races, or the run of three consecutive front-row starts after the summer break, but the clever ride to second in tricky conditions at Assen was completely in character. There was also a pole position, only the second of his MotoGP career, in Japan.

Even allowing for problems on tracks like the Sachsenring, where the bike spent a long time on its side, a record of only one crash – while tracking the leaders in Aragón – and a lowest finish of ninth speaks of a season of consistent excellence. He regularly got away with the leaders at the start of races but the effort of getting the bike to turn tended to wear out both the rider and the tyre. The rule concession allowing Ducati to run a softer tyre than the factory bikes did not always help, especially when it came to choosing race rubber.

There were times when Dovi struggled to hide his frustration with the limits of his bike, but there is no doubting his commitment to the Bologna cause or disguising his faith in Dall'Igna. It will be fascinating to see how the team fares with its redesigned bike next season.

6 POL ESPARGARO
MONSTER YAMAHA TECH3

NATIONALITY Spanish
DATE OF BIRTH 10 June 1991
2014 SEASON Rookie of the Year
TOTAL POINTS 136

The younger Espargaro brother was the only rookie on a Factory Option bike, having arrived as Moto2 champion and with a factory Yamaha contract in his pocket. That CV comes with a heavy load of expectation. Did Pol live up to it? The answer has to be 'yes', but with a couple of caveats.

Mid-season it looked as if he had sixth place overall – and first non-works rider – nailed down provided he could keep ahead of his brother, but Pol ended the season fighting his team-mate for that championship position. Sixth is much as the paddock expected at the start of the year but it should be pointed out that the satellite Hondas did not put up too much of a fight.

As you would expect from a fast rookie, there were a few crashes. Many of them were down to Pol's willingness to attack corners with the bike well out of shape in the way a Moto2 bike has to be ridden. However, all his race finishes were well within the top ten and there were flashes of real promise, including one front-row start and a fourth place. As befits a Moto2 graduate, Pol was also more than willing to go handlebar-to-handlebar with the opposition.

There is no doubt that Pol had an impressive rookie season – indeed it was usually difficult to remember he was a rookie. The trick now is to keep up the momentum and make sure that Yamaha has no option but to put him on a works bike in the near future.

NATIONALITY Spanish
DATE OF BIRTH 30 July 1989
2014 SEASON Open Class Champion,
1 rostrum, 1 pole position
TOTAL POINTS 126

For the third year in a row, Aleix dominated what used to be called CRT but this year metamorphosed into the Open Class. Leaving aside the arguments about whether his bike, essentially last year's satellite Yamaha, should ever have been allowed to enter as an Open Class machine, there was no doubt that Aleix was the best rider in the category.

He easily beat the customer Hondas, Avintia Kawasakis and PBM and Ioda Aprilias, but it should be noted that he also outshone his team-mate – first Colin Edwards and then Alex de Angelis. Things got a little more competitive, though, when Barbera was given a Ducati late in the year.

Aleix was clever in his use of the softer tyre allowed for Open Class bikes, especially in qualifying – as pole

position at Assen demonstrated. It took Pedrosa most of that race to get the last podium position off him as well.

Aleix did get on the rostrum at the somewhat chaotic Aragón race, but that was mainly thanks to taking the brave decision (Jorge Lorenzo's words) to pit first to change bikes. Some bad luck in Australia and a collision with Bautista in Malaysia (Aleix's fault) put what had looked like a safe sixth place in the championship in danger and he had to fight his little brother and Bradley Smith.

The voting in the official Riders' Rider of the Year poll (see pages 10–11) showed that Aleix is held in high regard by his peers. No-one was surprised – quite the reverse – when Suzuki recruited him to lead its team when the factory returns to MotoGP in 2015.

NATIONALITY British
DATE OF BIRTH 28 November 1990
2014 SEASON 1 rostrum
TOTAL POINTS 121

8 BRADLEY SMITH
MONSTER YAMAHA TECH3

After a very impressive rookie season in 2013, this was a make-or-break year for Bradley's ambitions to become a factory rider and he knew it. At the start of the year he said he had to leave the factory 'no option' by being top satellite rider by a distance.

After starting the season with front-row qualifying, things turned sour when a new chassis arrived and Bradley started crashing. By the time his race engineer, Guy Coulon, persuaded him to put the new chassis back in the truck, Bradley was a confused man. Things then spiralled down to the nadir of Sachsenring, where he crashed five times over the weekend.

After the summer break, he got things together again. He started to move up the championship from a low of 11th place and caught the Espargaro

brothers, with whom he had a splendid fight over sixth in the championship in the closing rounds. The position is irrelevant, but beating his team-mate Pol Espargaro and finishing top satellite rider was very relevant.

The highlight of his year was his first rostrum in MotoGP to add to the 23 he achieved in the smaller classes. That came in Australia where he was able to race the softer front tyre, unlike many of his opponents.

Bradley's team, Monster Yamaha Tech3, had enough faith in him to sign him for a third year after the Indianapolis GP when he was ninth overall. In 2015 he will once again line up alongside Pol, and their internecine battle will again provide one of the more interesting sub-plots of the season.

9 STEFAN BRADL
LCR HONDA MOTOGP

NATIONALITY German
DATE OF BIRTH 29 November 1989
TOTAL POINTS 117

The German's third year in MotoGP did not add to the single rostrum and pole position he scored in 2013. Thanks to some not very subtle hints from inside Honda, it was already obvious that the factory felt it needed to look elsewhere. With Scott Redding's form and the public courtship of Jack Miller added to the early signing of Cal Crutchlow, Stefan was left in no doubt that he would have to look for a new seat at the end of the year.

Frankly, Stefan did not threaten to finish on the podium at any point in the year and only twice started from the front row. But for his team's error on the start line at the Sachsenring, his home race, he could have bettered his best finish of fourth place. His team took the gamble of trying to change his bike's settings from wet to dry rather than change bikes after the warm-up lap and start from pitlane. Had they have managed it, Stefan would have had the best part of 30 seconds' start on the field. Unfortunately, the work on the front forks did not get finished and he suffered the embarrassment of fading through the field and finishing out of the points. As a metaphor for Stefan's season, the German race works well.

It is worth remembering that Stefan was still only 24 years old at the end of the season, so it is no surprise that he has been able to secure a decent ride for 2015. He will lead Forward Racing's team, which will again run only slightly out-of-date satellite Yamahas.

10 ANDREA IANNONE
PRAMAC RACING

NATIONALITY Italian
DATE OF BIRTH 9 August 1989
TOTAL POINTS 102

The young Italian may have been entered by Pramac, Ducati's satellite team, but halfway through the season he effectively became the second factory rider. He even referred to himself as such when he forgot to keep up the pretence. Cal Crutchlow's troubles adapting to the Desmosedici and his subsequent early signing by LCR Honda for 2015 meant that he was not going to get the goodies – so Andrea did.

Andrea's tendency to do a bit too much crashing was largely reined in and he played an important part in the Bologna factory's encouraging showing. He used the softer option tyre very well to qualify high up the grid and then regularly interfered with the (other) factory men early in races, even leading the race on the front row for six consecutive races after the summer break, Iannone was there three times.

There was a maturity and consistency to Andrea's riding that many observers, frankly, were surprised to see, although no-one could ever describe him as restrained; both Pedrosa and Crutchlow found reasons to criticise his riding publicly during the year. Ironically, the end of his season was seriously affected by an elbow injury sustained when none other than Marc Marquez rammed him in a wet Malaysian practice session.

Andrea's promotion to Ducati's factory team for 2015 was one of those open secrets that remained unconfirmed until late in the year. As early as the German round, the sight of new bits on his bike

11 ALVARO BAUTISTA
GO&FUN HONDA GRESINI

NATIONALITY
Spanish

DATE OF BIRTH
21 November 1984

2014 SEASON
1 rostrum, 1 fastest lap

TOTAL POINTS
89

Started the season with a string of three crashes but it looked like Alvaro had redeemed himself with a rostrum in France. Alas, his season got no better as he struggled with feeling at the front and grip at the rear. As the only team running Nissin brakes and Showa suspension, Gresini had no other bikes with which to compare data. It is difficult to say for sure how significant this was, but it certainly did not help. A tough season ended with the Gresini team in financial difficulties and losing its satellite Honda. For 2015 Aprilia will re-enter MotoGP and Gresini will become the factory's works team, with Alvaro staying on as one of two riders.

12 SCOTT REDDING
GO&FUN HONDA GRESINI

NATIONALITY
British

DATE OF BIRTH
4 January 1993

TOTAL POINTS
81

A tough rookie season on the under-powered customer Honda. Scott achieved his stated ambition – beating Nicky Hayden on the same bike – in the first race of the year and then had to pretend he was enjoying fighting for 12th place. He did not pretend very well but he did put in some great rides, notably at Indianapolis and Phillip Island. The other part of his task for the year – to be top customer Honda rider in the standings – was also achieved. Scott was due to stay with Gresini in 2015 and take over the satellite bike, but things have changed; he will still get the bike but it will be in the colours of Marc VDS, his old Moto2 team.

13 CAL CRUTCHLOW
DUCATI TEAM

NATIONALITY
British

DATE OF BIRTH
29 October 1985

2014 SEASON
1 rostrum

TOTAL POINTS
74

Cal's relationship with Ducati started with mechanical problems and injury, and then it got worse. By mid-season it was known that he would leave at the end of the year and it looked as if things were not going to get better. But from around Aragón things clicked. It started with a hold-your-breath qualifying lap that put Cal on the second row after awful free practice, and from there he was in position to take advantage of the misfortune of others to get on the rostrum. He nearly managed the same trick in Australia but crashed out of second place with a lap to go. Cal gets a factory Honda for 2015.

14 HIROSHI AOYAMA
DRIVE M7 ASPAR

NATIONALITY
Japanese

DATE OF BIRTH
25 October 1981

TOTAL POINTS
68

It was no surprise to see a Japanese rider on one of the new customer Hondas, but the reason Hiro got the job was probably because Takaaki Nakagami was misfiring in Moto2. The highlight of his season was finishing as top Open Class rider in Argentina, and he backed that up with two solid top-ten finishes in the tricky conditions of Aragón and Phillip Island. However, it was rare for Hiro to beat Scott Redding. As he ended up with very few options to stay in MotoGP, Hiro retired from racing at the end of the year – but he may be back from time to time as a wild card in his new position as HRC's test rider.

15 YONNY HERNANDEZ
ENERGY T.I. PRAMAC RACING

NATIONALITY
Colombian

DATE OF BIRTH
25 July 1988

TOTAL POINTS
53

Rode the 2013 model Ducati with his usual elan, frequently giving the slower satellite bikes from the Japanese factories a hard time. He livened up a few wet practice sessions, particularly at super-slippery Misano, and his career-best seventh place in Malaysia was a great ride. Yonny's obvious popularity at the Argentine GP showed why the World Championship needed to go back to South America. It was no surprise when he was signed up for 2015 to ride again for the Pramac team but on a contract with the Ducati factory. Fans everywhere of motorcycles going sideways will be very happy.

16 NICKY HAYDEN
DRIVE M7 ASPAR

NATIONALITY
American

DATE OF BIRTH
30 July 1981

TOTAL POINTS
47

Nicky's season was totally ruined by the injury to his right wrist that dates back to the first corner of the 2011 Valencian GP. Two operations this year made a total of five on the injury, the last one being a rather radical removal of three small bones. Not surprisingly, that kept Nicky out of four races and when he came back he was in obvious pain, albeit with increased mobility of the joint. However, his form was good enough to convince the Aspar team that he is going to be okay, so Nicky will be back on the new pneumatic-valve customer Honda, a bike hopefully more suited to one of Honda's ex-World Champions.

17 KAREL ABRAHAM
CARDION AB MOTORACING

NATIONALITY
Czech

DATE OF BIRTH
2 January 1990

TOTAL POINTS
33

Hampered at the start of the year by recovery from a major operation to repair his injured shoulder. Then things started to look up with two top customer Honda finishes and a highlight of top Open Class bike at Misano. Thereafter, however, Karel scored no more points. His last five races of the year were, in his words, a disaster. Retirement at Aragón was followed by three crashes, all related to brake problems. Neither team nor brake manufacturer were keen to discuss the issue, but Brembo's equipment was used by all the factory teams. Karel will be back with a customer Honda in 2015 but expect it to be using Nissin brakes.

18 HECTOR BARBERA
AVINTIA RACING

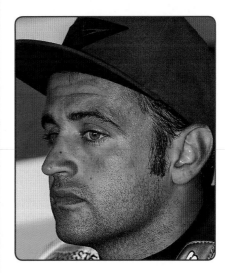

NATIONALITY
Spanish

DATE OF BIRTH
2 November 1986

TOTAL POINTS
26

Had a miserable time on the Avintia team's Kawasaki-based bike, which along with the ART Aprilias were the last remnants of the old CRT class. After getting a 2014 Ducati at Aragón, Hector reeled off four points-scoring rides at the final rounds, including a remarkable fifth place in Australia and another top Open Class finish in Malaysia. The bike was surplus to factory team requirements after the Desmosedici GP14.2 arrived but used Dorna's spec electronics, thus being eligible for the Open Class. The Ducati enabled the team to score enough points to ensure that Avintia will be back next year – with two Ducatis.

19 MICHELE PIRRO
DUCATI TEAM

NATIONALITY
Italian

DATE OF BIRTH
30 July 1981

TOTAL POINTS
18

Ducati's test rider rode as a wild card five times plus once as an injury replacement for Cal Crutchlow. The appearances were weighted heavily towards the start of the season as the factory's new racing boss, Gigi Dall'Igna, searched for a way forward. It was always difficult, therefore, to understand exactly the specification of the bike Pirro was riding; it was usually described as 'the test team's bike'. The man himself was well aware that his job was to collect data, not to win races. He was let off the leash at the final race of the year and scored a top-ten finish.

20 DANILO PETRUCCI
OCTO IODARACING TEAM

NATIONALITY
Italian

DATE OF BIRTH
24 October 1990

TOTAL POINTS
17

Danilo's season was ruined by a broken wrist sustained in Sunday-morning warm-up for the Spanish GP. At first it was not thought to be a serious injury but it ended up keeping him out of four races, and even when Danilo returned he was in pain and had little strength in his left arm. He described his Ioda Aprilia as a laboratory, not a motorcycle, but still put in some entertaining rides. Like the other Open Class machines made for the old CRT class, it was seriously out-gunned and Danilo's fight was with the Avintia and PBM bikes. He will be back in 2015 on a Pramac Ducati.

21 ALEX DE ANGELIS
NGM FORWARD RAING

NATIONALITY
Sammarinese

DATE OF BIRTH
26 February 1984

TOTAL POINTS
14

Alex started the season in Moto2 on the new Tasca team's Suter and scored a best finish of fifth at Assen, but after ten races he was only 14th in the championship. That disappointment no doubt helped him decide to join Forward Racing's MotoGP team after Indianapolis when Colin Edwards decided to bring forward his decision to retire. Alex rode eight races on the Yamaha, scoring points in four of them with a best finish of ninth at Phillip Island, where he brought all his experience to bear in the tricky conditions. It was enough to get him a ride for 2015 and Alex will return to the grid with the Ioda team.

22 COLIN EDWARDS
NGM FORWARD RACING

NATIONALITY
American

DATE OF BIRTH
27 February 1974

TOTAL POINTS
11

This was always going to be Colin's last season of racing. He used the Grand Prix of the Americas in his home state of Texas to announce that he would retire at the end of the season, but then decided to call it a day after Indianapolis, the second race on American soil. Why? His inability to alter his style to suit the bike combined with a very fast young team-mate who could. Fans and the paddock will miss his wit and wisdom, but Colin will not be totally lost to the sport as he has been signed by Yamaha to test the Michelin tyres that will become standard wear in MotoGP in 2016.

23 BROC PARKES
PAUL BIRD MOTORSPORT

NATIONALITY
Australian

DATE OF BIRTH
24 December 1981

TOTAL POINTS
9

The veteran Australian supersport rider joined Paul Bird Motorsport and scored the best result of the team's Grand Prix adventure with 11th place at Assen. He also had three more points-scoring rides – not bad for a rookie in his 30s. Like his team-mate, Michael Laverty, Broc frequently struggled to get the tyres working, and a big crash in practice for his home race at Phillip Island affected the end of his season. Developed a lucrative and successful sideline in endurance racing for Yamaha that saw him just miss a podium finish in the Suzuka 8 Hours.

24 MICHAEL LAVERTY
PAUL BIRD MOTORSPORT

NATIONALITY British
DATE OF BIRTH 7 June 1981
TOTAL POINTS 9

Finished his two-year adventure in MotoGP with three points-scoring rides and his usual full-on effort. Failed to conceal his frustration with the ageism of the MotoGP paddock and will return to BSB in 2015.

25 MIKE DI MEGLIO
AVINTIA RACING

NATIONALITY French
DATE OF BIRTH 17 January 1988
TOTAL POINTS 9

Struggled all year with the Kawasaki, not helped by a nasty double fracture of the right hand sustained at the first corner of Misano. Will be back with Avintia in 2015 on a Ducati.

26 KATS NAKASUGA
YAMALUBE RACING TEAM WITH YSP

NATIONALITY Japanese
DATE OF BIRTH 9 August 1981
TOTAL POINTS 4

Yamaha's factory test rider made his usual wild-card appearance at Motegi to test some new parts for the M1. His job was to finish the race, which he did in 12th place.

27 LEON CAMIER
DRIVE M7 ASPAR

NATIONALITY British
DATE OF BIRTH 4 August 1986
TOTAL POINTS 1

Replaced Nicky Hayden for four races when the American was recovering from his wrist operation. Impressed everyone but the team management deemed Leon too tall for future employment.

MICHEL FABRIZIO
OCTO IODARACING TEAM

NATIONALITY Italian
DATE OF BIRTH 17 September 1984

Second-choice replacement for Petrucci after his Jerez accident. Not surprisingly, Michel could not get the Ioda team's quirky Aprilia into the points in either of the races he started.

RANDY DE PUNIET
TEAM SUZUKI MOTOGP

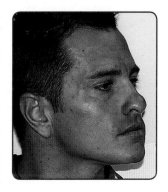

NATIONALITY French
DATE OF BIRTH 14 February 1981

For the final race of the year Randy was given the honour of riding the 2015 Suzuki on its début outing as a 'thank you' for his work as development rider – Valencia was probably his last Grand Prix.

R-S2 EVO
BORN TO RACE.

TITO RABAT
Moto2

MOTO 2 CHAMPION 2014

CERTIFICATION
EN13634:2010

THE MOST EVOLVED SPECIES IN SAFETY AND PRECISE FIT.

FASTEN FIT CONTROL

P.A.F.S. PRECISE AIR FIT SYSTEM

T.C.S. TORSION CONTROL SYSTEM®

M.C.S. METATARSAL CONTROL SYSTEM®

INSIDE LACING SYSTEM

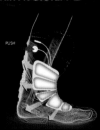

BUILT-IN AIR CHAMBER
ADJUSTABLE FIT SYSTEM

The **R-S2 EVO** has enhanced the superior performance levels of the exclusive safety systems, which have always distinguished TCX boots, with an adjustable fit providing enhanced precision. The new Fasten Fit Control fastening system works in sync with the Precise Air Fit - a special differentiated thickness air chamber, to increase comfort, wearability and riding response. Allowing the boot to adapt to the shape of the foot with the utmost precision.

tcxboots.com

TCX
FOCUS ON BOOTS

COMMERCIAL BANK GRAND PRIX OF QATAR
LOSAIL INTERNATIONAL CIRCUIT

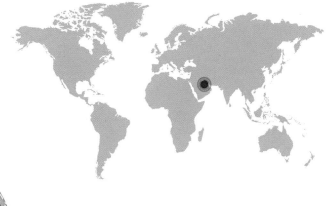

STRANGELY NORMAL

Despite all the rule changes, the first race of 2014 felt much like most of those of 2013

It has become a truism in the paddock: the Qatar race is not a good guide to what is going to happen for the rest of the year. This time, however, it turned out to be a good indicator, at least for the first half-a-dozen races.

The run-up to the race was dominated by a flurry of new and revised regulations as the opposing forces of Dorna and the manufacturers edged towards the goal of one common set of regulations for all MotoGP bikes. The final announcement – that all bikes would be using common software by the 2016 season – came as a shock and felt like a mildly surprising victory for the Dorna side of the argument, with the factories saving face by retaining the right to develop software.

For this season, there was more attention on the new definitions of the two types of bikes running in MotoGP: Factory and Open (see panel on page 49). Much attention centred on the fact that bikes in the Open Class could use a tyre a grade softer than those in the Factory Class. Surely this would be a major advantage to the Forward Team (basically with last year's satellite Yamaha) and the Ducatis? It certainly looked like it when Aleix Espargaro was fastest over the first two days on the Forward Yamaha. Then things started looking a little more normal.

Marc Marquez arrived at the first race of the year having missed most of pre-season testing thanks to a broken fibula, sustained in a training accident. He had only been putting weight on the injured leg for a week. Did it slow him down? Of course not. True, his pole position was taken with a last-gasp attack but his fight for the win with Valentino Rossi betrayed no problems. And it was a fight, one that the participants gave

'THE BATTLE WITH VALENTINO
WAS THE BEST PART OF THE
RACE BESIDES THE WIN.
I REALLY ENJOYED IT!'
MARC MARQUEZ

every sign of enjoying hugely. Flurries of passing and repassing, often in unlikely places, resulted in Marquez winning by a quarter of a second, although the fact that the two were able to have a clean fight was down to a lot of crashes.

Stefan Bradl led for the first eight laps, only to lose the front. Alvaro Bautista suffered a similar fate while shaping up to put in a late attack for a rostrum position. Late on Bradley Smith was on the tail of the leading group when he too lost the front. But the biggest loser was Jorge Lorenzo.

The man who lost the 2013 title by only four points was in trouble before the race started. Three operations in short order to remove old metalwork and repair his back had ruined his fitness, and winter testing had shown that the new Bridgestone front tyre's emphasis on longevity at the expense of side grip was just what his style did not need. Jorge looked out of sorts in practice and qualified in the middle of the second row.

Lorenzo looked to have redeemed himself when he got the holeshot, only to be the first to lose the front halfway round the first lap. It was, he admitted, a rookie error. It was also a disaster for Jorge's championship aspirations. Handing as implacable an opponent as Marquez 25 points at the first race of the year, when added to Jorge's other problems, looked to have ended his challenge before it had effectively started. Another Spaniard, Dani Pedrosa, came in third and looked slightly surprised to be on the rostrum at a track where he has never won.

As for the Open Class challenge, Aleix Espargaro finished an impressive fourth but he was over 11

OPPOSITE Alvaro Bautista qualified second but was the last of half a dozen fallers.

LEFT Jorge Lorenzo leads into the first corner, but he did not finish the lap. Smith in third and Bautista in fourth were also fallers.

ABOVE MotoGP rookie Scott Redding finished seventh and best of the new customer Honda RCV1000R riders.

not look much better than the previous year's, he was keen to point out – as evidence of the influence of new Ducati Corse boss Luigi 'Gigi' Dall'Igna – that the gap to the winner had been halved.

Behind the Ducatis, the new Open Class Honda RCV1000R – a true customer bike – proved a disappointment. Although they beat the likes of the Aprilia, the Avintias and the PBM bikes, these Hondas were simply too slow to compete with the Forward Yamahas or the factory satellite bikes. Scott Redding impressively held off Nicky Hayden to be the first man home on one in seventh place – not bad for a débutant.

The Rossi/Marquez dice was a repeat of last year's fight for second place, only with a different outcome. The question now was whether the rest of the season would pan out the same way? In 2013 Rossi had been fast in Qatar and, with hindsight, it was probably his best race of the year, Assen notwithstanding. Was this another false dawn for Valentino?

One notable conclusion could be drawn. The Honda did not have a major advantage over the Yamaha on the front straight. The 1-litre reduction in fuel-tank capacity should have affected the Yamaha on a fuel-heavy track, but there was no evidence of that. Rossi professed himself seriously impressed by the work done by the factory's engineers in keeping the engine useable. When Pedrosa let slip the fact that he had finished a few races on petrol fumes the previous season, it seemed fair to draw the conclusion that the new rule had slowed Honda, not Yamaha.

Not that it appeared to affect Marc Marquez. If that's what he could do with a partly healed broken leg, what could he do when fully fit?

ABOVE Bradley Smith started from third on the grid and was fighting for fourth when he fell.

BELOW Aleix Espargaro and the Forward Yamaha dominated free practice then finished a strong fourth in front of the factory Ducatis.

OPPOSITE Valentino Rossi and Marc Marquez enjoyed the fight and seeing each other on the podium.

seconds behind the winner – not quite the revolution some people were predicting. The two factory Ducatis finished fifth and sixth, Andrea Dovizioso just behind Espargaro but new recruit Cal Crutchlow trailing by 16 seconds, his patience severely tried by a major electronics glitch in the race on the back of a couple of crashes in practice. While Dovi's finishing position did

OPEN AND CLOSED

The major rule changes for 2014 were the reduction in the year's engine allocation from six to five and the reduction in fuel allowed for a race from 21 litres to 20. These rules applied to the Factory bikes and their satellite teams. All bikes had to run Dorna's ECU hardware but Factory bikes could write their own software.

The CRT (Claiming Rule Team) class was gone, having lasted just two years. In came the new designation of Open Class, with a simple definition of what an Open bike is: one that uses software of Dorna's specification. The reward for following that cost-cutting route was a fuel allowance of 24 litres per race and an engine allowance of 12 for the year. In addition Open entries do not have to respect the engine-development freeze and severely restricted test programme. As was the case with the CRT class, the Open bikes' tyre allocation is one grade softer than for the Factory teams.

A manufacturer can enter its bikes in the Open Class if it runs the standard software, and this is a route that Ducati Corse was rumoured to be contemplating because the team certainly needed to be able to develop and test its engine. To keep Ducati in the Factory class an old idea was resurrected: a manufacturer that had not won a dry race in two years (ie, Ducati) was allowed to start the year running to Open rules with the proviso that fuel allowance and engine allocation would be progressively trimmed after three third places, two second places, or a win. This tactic had previously been used to encourage Dunlop's participation when there was no control tyre and also to try to prevent Suzuki's withdrawal.

All of which sounds very reasonable.

Of course, things are never that simple for long. Forward Racing's Open Class bike, originally intended to be a leased Yamaha M1 engine in an FTR frame, ended up being last year's satellite Yamaha. That, and the arrival of a massive upgrade for the specification software just before the start of the season, did not amuse Honda, who wondered – with some justification – why Factory bikes should be admitted to a class that was supposed to cut costs for private teams.

COMMERCIAL BANK
GRAND PRIX OF QATAR
LOSAIL INTERNATIONAL CIRCUIT

ROUND 1
MARCH 23

OFFICIAL TIMEKEEPER

RACE RESULTS

CIRCUIT LENGTH 3.343 miles

NO. OF LAPS 22

RACE DISTANCE 73.546 miles

WEATHER Dry, 20°C

TRACK TEMPERATURE 18°C

WINNER Marc Marquez

FASTEST LAP 1m 55.575s, 104.080mph, Alvaro Bautista

LAP RECORD 1m 55.135s, 104.452mph, Casey Stoner, 2008

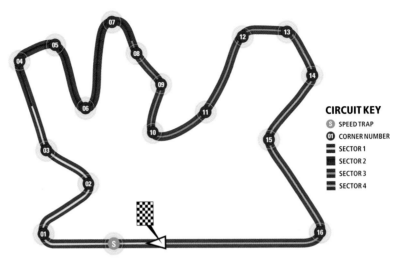

CIRCUIT KEY
- (S) SPEED TRAP
- (01) CORNER NUMBER
- SECTOR 1
- SECTOR 2
- SECTOR 3
- SECTOR 4

QUALIFYING

	Rider	Nation	Motorcycle	Team	Time	Pole +
1	Marquez	SPA	Honda	Repsol Honda Team	1m 54.507s	
2	Bautista	SPA	Honda	GO&FUN Honda Gresini	1m 54.564s	0.057s
3	Smith	GBR	Yamaha	Monster Yamaha Tech3	1m 54.601s	0.094s
4	Dovizioso	ITA	Ducati	Ducati Team	1m 54.644s	0.137s
5	Lorenzo	SPA	Yamaha	Movistar Yamaha MotoGP	1m 54.661s	0.154s
6	Pedrosa	SPA	Honda	Repsol Honda Team	1m 54.703s	0.196s
7	Bradl	GER	Honda	LCR Honda MotoGP	1m 54.871s	0.364s
8	Crutchlow	GBR	Ducati	Ducati Team	1m 54.888s	0.381s
9	Espargaro A	SPA	Yamaha	NGM Forward Racing	1m 54.986s	0.479s
10	Rossi	ITA	Yamaha	Movistar Yamaha MotoGP	1m 55.096s	0.589s
11	Iannone	ITA	Ducati	Pramac Racing	1m 55.127s	0.620s
12	Espargaro P	SPA	Yamaha	Monster Yamaha Tech3	1m 55.152s	0.645s
13	Hayden	USA	Honda	Drive M7 Aspar	1m 55.894s	Q1
14	Edwards	USA	Yamaha	NGM Forward Racing	1m 56.042s	Q1
15	Aoyama	JPN	Honda	Drive M7 Aspar	1m 56.479s	Q1
16	Redding	GBR	Honda	GO&FUN Honda Gresini	1m 56.555s	Q1
17	Hernandez	COL	Ducati	Energy T.I. Pramac Racing	1m 56.648s	Q1
18	Abraham	CZE	Honda	Cardion AB Motoracing	1m 56.715s	Q1
19	Barbera	SPA	Avintia	Avintia Racing	1m 57.006s	Q1
20	Petrucci	ITA	ART	Ioda Racing Project	1m 57.513s	Q1
21	Parkes	AUS	PBM	Paul Bird Motorsport	1m 57.574s	Q1
22	Di Meglio	FRA	Avintia	Avintia Racing	1m 57.667s	Q1
23	Laverty	GBR	PBM	Paul Bird Motorsport	1m 58.254s	Q1

1 MARC MARQUEZ
After missing most of pre-season with a broken fibula, the 2013 champion won from pole (his 10th pole in 19 premier-class races) after a fantastic battle with Rossi all the way. It was Honda's 250th win in the premier class of MotoGP.

2 VALENTINO ROSSI
A superb start to the season after a lacklustre qualifying – to put it mildly. Fought for the win and only missed out by a quarter of a second. But – and it is a big 'but' – he did the same here last year and did not take that form into the rest of the year.

3 DANI PEDROSA
More contented than you would have expected with third place, probably because he has never won the opening race of the year since he moved up to MotoGP. Maintained he was just happy to be on the rostrum in tricky conditions.

4 ALEIX ESPARGARO
Brilliant in free practice, where he topped the first three sessions, but then got a little excited in qualifying and wrecked both of his motorcycles. After a heroic stint by his crew, he followed the Ducatis for much of the race before picking his moment to pass.

5 ANDREA DOVIZIOSO
There were signs of improvements compared with the previous year's Ducati. Dovi had an understandably cautious race but the gap to the winner was halved compared with the 2013 Qatar race. However, the old problem of understeer remained.

6 CAL CRUTCHLOW
His first race as a factory rider, with Ducati, was disrupted by a problem with the electronics. The transponder did not know where the bike was on circuit and Cal ended up coasting over the line.

7 SCOTT REDDING
Top Open Class Honda and finishing in front of Hayden – the season's objective achieved on his MotoGP début. Used the soft tyre to put in some tough moves early on then followed Hayden, exchanged places, and then made the decisive move two laps from the flag.

8 NICKY HAYDEN
Wore out the left side of his front tyre chasing Pol Espargaro and ran off track, which put him in a dice with Redding. Not impressed with the performance of the new Honda.

9 COLIN EDWARDS
Struggled with grip and with getting the bike to turn – not what you would expect from Colin on what is essentially a satellite Yamaha.

10 ANDREA IANNONE
Crashed on the second lap, remounted and put in a comeback with lap times comparable to the factory Ducatis.

11 HIROSHI AOYAMA
Used the softest option tyre but found it difficult to adapt to the track conditions. Could not escape from Hernandez, even though he felt he had better pace.

LAP CHART

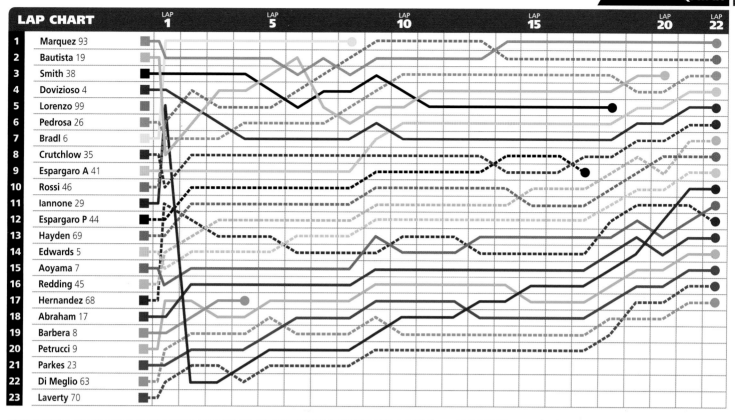

	Rider	LAP 1	LAP 5	LAP 10	LAP 15	LAP 20	LAP 22
1	Marquez 93						
2	Bautista 19						
3	Smith 38						
4	Dovizioso 4						
5	Lorenzo 99						
6	Pedrosa 26						
7	Bradl 6						
8	Crutchlow 35						
9	Espargaro A 41						
10	Rossi 46						
11	Iannone 29						
12	Espargaro P 44						
13	Hayden 69						
14	Edwards 5						
15	Aoyama 7						
16	Redding 45						
17	Hernandez 68						
18	Abraham 17						
19	Barbera 8						
20	Petrucci 9						
21	Parkes 23						
22	Di Meglio 63						
23	Laverty 70						

RACE

	Rider	Motorcycle	Race time	Time +	Fastest lap	Avg. speed	🅱
1	Marquez	Honda	42m 40.561s		1m 55.710s	103.4mph	H/H
2	Rossi	Yamaha	42m 40.820s	0.259s	1m 55.621s	103.3mph	H/M
3	Pedrosa	Honda	42m 43.931s	3.370s	1m 55.843s	103.2mph	H/M
4	Espargaro A	Yamaha	42m 52.184s	11.623s	1m 56.192s	102.9mph	H/M
5	Dovizioso	Ducati	42m 52.720s	12.159s	1m 56.285s	102.9mph	H/M
6	Crutchlow	Ducati	43m 09.087s	28.526s	1m 56.064s	102.2mph	H/M
7	Redding	Honda	43m 13.154s	32.593s	1m 56.416s	102.1mph	H/S
8	Hayden	Honda	43m 13.189s	32.628s	1m 56.428s	102.1mph	H/S
9	Edwards	Yamaha	43m 20.108s	39.547s	1m 57.119s	101.8mph	H/M
10	Iannone	Ducati	43m 23.921s	43.360s	1m 56.280s	101.7mph	H/M
11	Aoyama	Honda	43m 27.156s	46.595s	1m 57.396s	101.5mph	S/S
12	Hernandez	Ducati	43m 27.249s	46.688s	1m 57.625s	101.5mph	S/M
13	Abraham	Honda	43m 31.142s	50.581s	1m 57.293s	101.3mph	H/S
14	Petrucci	ART	43m 43.688s	1m 03.127s	1m 58.322s	100.9mph	H/S
15	Parkes	PBM	43m 54.947s	1m 14.386s	1m 58.470s	100.5mph	H/M
16	Laverty	PBM	44m 13.154s	1m 32.593s	1m 58.396s	99.7mph	H/S
17	Di Meglio	Avintia	44m 16.646s	1m 36.085s	1m 58.164s	99.6mph	H/S
NF	Bautista	Honda	38m 49.998s	2 laps	1m 55.575s	103.3mph	H/M
NF	Smith	Yamaha	34m 58.777s	4 laps	1m 55.871s	103.2mph	H/M
NF	Espargaro P	Yamaha	33m 15.444s	5 laps	1m 56.345s	102.5mph	H/M
NF	Bradl	Honda	15m 35.351s	14 laps	1m 55.937s	102.9mph	H/M
NF	Barbera	Avintia	8m 01.944s	18 laps	1m 57.822s	99.9mph	H/M
NF	Lorenzo	Yamaha	–	–	–	–	H/M

CHAMPIONSHIP

	Rider	Nation	Team	Points
1	Marquez	SPA	Repsol Honda Team	25
2	Rossi	ITA	Movistar Yamaha MotoGP	20
3	Pedrosa	SPA	Repsol Honda Team	16
4	Espargaro A	SPA	NGM Forward Racing	13
5	Dovizioso	ITA	Ducati Team	11
6	Crutchlow	GBR	Ducati Team	10
7	Redding	GBR	GO&FUN Honda Gresini	9
8	Hayden	USA	Drive M7 Aspar	8
9	Edwards	USA	NGM Forward Racing	7
10	Iannone	ITA	Pramac Racing	6
11	Aoyama	JPN	Drive M7 Aspar	5
12	Hernandez	COL	Energy T.I. Pramac Racing	4
13	Abraham	CZE	Cardion AB Motoracing	3
14	Petrucci	ITA	Ioda Racing Project	2
15	Parkes	AUS	Paul Bird Motorsport	1

12 YONNY HERNANDEZ
Became the first crasher of the year in free practice but had a good race with Aoyama and Abraham. Lost out to the Japanese rider on the last lap when he missed a gear.

13 KAREL ABRAHAM
Still in severe pain from the shoulder he had repaired at the end of last season. The second half of the race was a matter of hanging on and hoping.

14 DANILO PETRUCCI
Happy to score points for the first time in three years at Qatar. Despite his lack of testing, he was able to ride 'more softly' and learn a lot about the bike.

15 BROC PARKES
A point on his Grand Prix début for the Aussie all-rounder.

16 MICHAEL LAVERTY
Penalised for a jump-start yet rode up to 16th place and was not lapped – not bad on a track that Michael regards as the most difficult for his bike.

17 MIKE DI MEGLIO
Found his MotoGP début difficult – unsurprising after the lack of pre-season testing. Crashed twice in practice and was not confident in qualifying. Respectably quick at the start but not on worn tyres. Tough début.

DID NOT FINISH

ALVARO BAUTISTA
Started from second, set the fastest lap, and ran in the leading group until crashing out two laps from home.

POL ESPARGARO
Put out by a gearbox problem only four laps from the flag while closing in on his brother and Dovizioso.

BRADLEY SMITH
On the front row for the first time, ran with the leaders until he crashed at Turn 6 while running a close fifth.

STEFAN BRADL
Led the race from a third-row start but crashed at Turn 6 on the eighth lap.

HECTOR BARBERA
Broke the gearshift after three laps but pleased to have made a lot of progress with the new Avintia bike.

JORGE LORENZO
Failed to qualify on the front row for the first time at Losail, but got a great start and took the lead only to lose the front and crash on the first lap.

TEXAS
ROUND 2

RED BULL GRAND PRIX OF THE AMERICAS
CIRCUIT OF THE AMERICAS

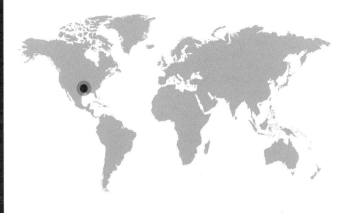

ANNIVERSARY WALTZ

One year after his first MotoGP victory, Marc Marquez led a race from flag to flag for the first time

Marc Marquez's seemingly inevitable progress to another victory from pole position was remarkable only for the lack of surprise it generated. It was, after all, at this race a year previously that he won his first MotoGP race, yet in only 12 months he has attained an aura of invincibility that would have done credit to Mick Doohan at the peak of his powers. Two incidents in the TV commentary box illustrated this perfectly.

One involved Kevin Schwantz, a guest in the BT Sport commentary box. He had sat in on qualifying, offering the viewers a few well-honed, uber-insightful snippets. At the end of the broadcast, a super-slo-mo of Marc Marquez in a right-hander was replayed. Kevin took over with Marc a little wide on entry: 'I need a bit of that paint... so I'll spin the rear up... [Marc's front tyre duly clips the painted curb]... that's where I wanna be.' There followed a short pause, perfectly timed for effect: 'Only Marc Marquez can do this.'

Ben Spies had hardly been less effusive on Friday. At the end of free practice, he also took over the broadcast: 'I need to explain a couple of things.' He'd already talked about his retirement and the shoulder, so what did he have on his mind? 'When I was riding I was maybe in the top six in the world, maybe towards the top on a good day.' No arguing with that. 'If Jorge or Valentino went past I could look and see what they were doing, maybe see they were a little smoother than me, but I understood. When Casey Stoner or Marc Marquez went past, I had no idea how they could do that stuff.'

So there you have it. On the best possible authority, we are watching an all-time great.

The only time Marc looked remotely worried was

ABOVE The Tech 3 Yamahas close on Rossi, who had front-tyre problems. Bradley Smith was fourth, Pol Espargaro sixth.

RIGHT Not just a jump start – a massive, super de luxe, world-class jump start. Jorge Lorenzo leads through Turn 1 by an improbable distance.

OPPOSITE After announcing his impending retirement, Colin Edwards did not get to finish his last GP in Texas.

at the very last corner when he had a big moment as he was lining up his wheelie. It was, he explained, to alleviate his mechanics' boredom. He also admitted that leading from flag to flag did require a real effort in concentration.

Behind him Dani Pedrosa again did a decent job in second place and Andrea Dovizioso gave Ducati an unexpected rostrum position. Dovi was suffering from flu and knew he would not have the strength for a last-lap braking duel, and his judgement of his pace proved just right as he did not run into the serious tyre problems that afflicted much of the field.

Bridgestone had underestimated the strain the Texas track would put on the right side of the front tyre. Valentino Rossi was the most high-profile victim: he was pretty sure he could have been a contender for a rostrum finish but, like the rest of us, still seemed a little unsure of his potential this year.

Vale's team-mate was a lot worse off. After his first-lap crash in the first race, it did not seem as if things could get worse for Jorge Lorenzo, but they did – he made a world-class false start. What on earth caused Jorge to jump before Bradley Smith, who was right behind him? The answer would appear to be insects. He collected a few 'mosquitos' on his visor on the warm-up lap and so removed a tear-off on the grid – 'I don't normally do this.' Evidently this was enough to disconcert Jorge and he was still rattled by this deviation from his routine when the starting lights went on. A Grand Prix starts when the lights go off but unfortunately a mildly anxious Jorge just noticed a change in the lights – and went when they came on.

'2014 WILL BE MY LAST YEAR OF RACING MOTORCYCLES...'
COLIN EDWARDS

ABOVE Andrea Dovizioso held off Stefan Bradl for an unexpected third place – another sign of Ducati's steady progress.

BELOW Selfie time on the podium. Andrea Dovizioso did his best to spoil the picture.

Quite a few riders could not believe their eyes. Aleix Espargaro was one; he forgot to start. Valentino Rossi was another; he was confused. And Marc Marquez, on pole, thought he had been beaten off the line again, until he saw Jorge shaking his head. This all sounds a little far-fetched, but the view of other riders is instructive.

Most riders have a set routine for the start. It is part of getting in the zone, and, yes, it can look a little like 'OCD' to us outsiders. If you hang around with riders or visit their homes, you tend to see neatness going from the, well, neat to the utterly obsessive, where a kitchen implement not at 90 degrees to the counter top is an offence against the order of the universe. Watch them at breakfast in a hotel – the salt and pepper gets rearranged just so. Things have to be ordered in a sportsman's life. So, yes, Jorge's reason for his jump-start sounds crazy, but very few people thought it was nonsense. Bradley Smith said that if his bike had been in gear, he would have gone too; Bradley also has a strict routine that includes putting the bike in gear as the lights come on.

Marc's remark about being disappointed that he was beaten off the line was not just a joke at Jorge's expense. Just about the only weakness Marquez showed last year was at the start and sometimes Lorenzo took full advantage and escaped. So Marc did a lot of work in the tests, particularly at Valencia, on eliminating that weakness. As it turned out, he need not have worried. If he now has his starts sorted, the rest can start worrying even more.

If that were possible.

THE TORNADO BOWS OUT

Colin Edwards used the pre-event press conference at what is very much his home Grand Prix to announce that he would retire from racing at the end of the season. He looked nervous but calmly and clearly announced that 2014 would be his last season as a motorcycle racer. He did not get much further before a prolonged round of applause interrupted him.

Colin is 40 and has three kids, but he had not been planning this move for long. He made up his mind only a month or so earlier. What seemed to have bought on retirement was the knowledge that his Forward Yamaha needed a certain riding style and the equally certain knowledge that he could not adapt any more.

The announcement produced fulsome tributes, a good laugh and a couple of charming moments. Valentino Rossi declared Colin his best friend in the paddock and reminisced about their times as team-mates. Marc Marquez was trying so hard to be respectful when he said 'He started the World Championship when I was two years old' and ended up wondering why everyone, including Colin, was laughing. Nicky Hayden was his usual self: he looked over towards Colin's wife

and kids and said 'He's got a lot to look forward to.' Colin looked as if that might have sent him over the top but he kept control.

Stopping something you have been doing since you were four is never going to be easy, but Colin has been clever with his investments, with his Boot Camp and other ventures, while his son is a keen dirt-tracker and baseball player. He will

have plenty to do and you know he will do it well.

He will leave with only one thing missing from his CV – that elusive MotoGP win. He was American 250cc champion in his first year as a professional, twice World Superbike Champion, then joined the Grand Prix paddock in 2003. He set three pole positions, three fastest laps and finished on the podium 12 times.

BELOW Yonny Hernandez and Scott Redding fought over some points until the Briton fell late on, another victim of a badly worn front tyre.

RED BULL GRAND PRIX OF THE AMERICAS
CIRCUIT OF THE AMERICAS

ROUND 2
APRIL 13

OFFICIAL TIMEKEEPER

RACE RESULTS

CIRCUIT LENGTH 3.427 miles

NO. OF LAPS 21

RACE DISTANCE 71.967 miles

WEATHER Dry, 26°C

TRACK TEMPERATURE 32°C

WINNER Marc Marquez

FASTEST LAP 2m 03.575s,
99.792mph, Marc Marquez (record)

PREVIOUS LAP RECORD 2m 04.242s,
99.233mph, Marc Marquez, 2013

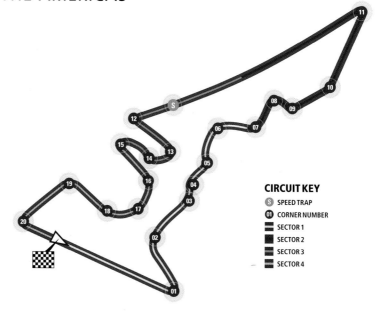

CIRCUIT KEY
- **S** SPEED TRAP
- **01** CORNER NUMBER
- SECTOR 1
- SECTOR 2
- SECTOR 3
- SECTOR 4

TYRE OPTIONS

CENTRE
LEFT · RIGHT
FRONT

FRONT COMPOUNDS
SOFT (**S**), MEDIUM (**M**)

CENTRE
LEFT · RIGHT
REAR

REAR COMPOUNDS
SOFT (**S**), MEDIUM (**M**),
HARD (**H**)

SEVERITY RATING
<MILD   SEVERE>

BRIDGESTONE

QUALIFYING

	Rider	Nation	Motorcycle	Team	Time	Pole +
1	Marquez	SPA	Honda	Repsol Honda Team	2m 02.773s	
2	Pedrosa	SPA	Honda	Repsol Honda Team	2m 03.062s	0.289s
3	Bradl	GER	Honda	LCR Honda MotoGP	2m 03.196s	0.423s
4	Espargaro A	SPA	Yamaha	NGM Forward Racing	2m 03.240s	0.467s
5	Lorenzo	SPA	Yamaha	Movistar Yamaha MotoGP	2m 03.243s	0.470s
6	Rossi	ITA	Yamaha	Movistar Yamaha MotoGP	2m 03.244s	0.471s
7	Crutchlow	GBR	Ducati	Ducati Team	2m 03.780s	1.007s
8	Smith	GBR	Yamaha	Monster Yamaha Tech3	2m 03.800s	1.027s
9	Iannone	ITA	Ducati	Pramac Racing	2m 03.842s	1.069s
10	Dovizioso	ITA	Ducati	Ducati Team	2m 03.846s	1.073s
11	Espargaro P	SPA	Yamaha	Monster Yamaha Tech3	2m 03.913s	1.140s
12	Bautista	SPA	Honda	GO&FUN Honda Gresini	2m 03.923s	1.150s
13	Redding	GBR	Honda	GO&FUN Honda Gresini	2m 04.617s	Q1
14	Hayden	USA	Honda	Drive M7 Aspar	2m 05.062s	Q1
15	Hernandez	COL	Ducati	Energy T.I. Pramac Racing	2m 05.677s	Q1
16	Aoyama	JPN	Honda	Drive M7 Aspar	2m 05.788s	Q1
17	Abraham	CZE	Honda	Cardion AB Motoracing	2m 06.239s	Q1
18	Barbera	SPA	Avintia	Avintia Racing	2m 06.270s	Q1
19	Edwards	USA	Yamaha	NGM Forward Racing	2m 06.741s	Q1
20	Laverty	GBR	PBM	Paul Bird Motorsport	2m 06.939s	Q1
21	Parkes	AUS	PBM	Paul Bird Motorsport	2m 07.403s	Q1
22	Petrucci	ITA	ART	Ioda Racing Project	2m 07.745s	Q1
23	Di Meglio	FRA	Avintia	Avintia Racing	2m 07.761s	Q1

1 MARC MARQUEZ
Fastest in every session, and led every lap for the first time in a MotoGP race. The only times he was worried were when Lorenzo went past him off the start and when he wobbled at the last corner. The only rider to race on the hard rear tyre.

2 DANI PEDROSA
Followed his team-mate for the whole race, knowing full well that Marc was fractionally faster than him everywhere – difficult to know what more he could have done.

3 ANDREA DOVIZIOSO
Did not panic at the start as he was suffering from flu and knew he would not have much strength at the end of the race, so needed to pull away from any opposition and avoid a fight on the brakes. That gave the tyres an easy time and Dovi his first rostrum on a Ducati.

4 STEFAN BRADL
Started from the front row for the first time since Laguna Seca 2013 but could not hold on to a rostrum place as his front tyre went off. Like most of the other victims of this problem, he was unsure as to why it had happened.

5 BRADLEY SMITH
Career-best finish and top Yamaha for the first time. Overheated his brakes and the front tyre so backed off for three or four laps, then pushed in the second half and had a good fight with Bradl during the final laps.

6 POL ESPARGARO
Delighted to finish a MotoGP race for the first time and to do it in front of the factory Yamahas. Got in front of Iannone on the last lap despite pain from the shoulder he broke pre-season.

7 ANDREA IANNONE
A career best in MotoGP despite being a victim of serious front-tyre degradation that slowed him over the last six laps. Ran in third early on, and described this as his first good race for Ducati.

8 VALENTINO ROSSI
One of several riders to destroy the right side of his front tyre – his lap times went up by three seconds after seven laps! Convinced he could have fought for the rostrum.

9 ALEIX ESPARGARO
Suffered from serious chatter on Sunday and could not back up an impressive qualifying position.

10 JORGE LORENZO
Just when you thought things could not get worse for Jorge, he jumped the start. Took his ride-through penalty immediately then worked his way through the field for a few points.

11 NICKY HAYDEN
Did not enjoy being so far off the pace, but saved his best for Sunday and finished as top customer Honda rider.

LAP CHART

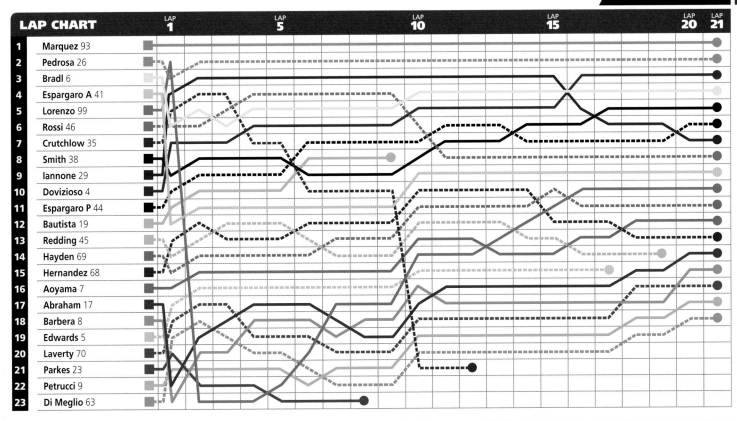

	Rider	LAP 1	LAP 5	LAP 10	LAP 15	LAP 20	LAP 21
1	Marquez 93						
2	Pedrosa 26						
3	Bradl 6						
4	Espargaro A 41						
5	Lorenzo 99						
6	Rossi 46						
7	Crutchlow 35						
8	Smith 38						
9	Iannone 29						
10	Dovizioso 4						
11	Espargaro P 44						
12	Bautista 19						
13	Redding 45						
14	Hayden 69						
15	Hernandez 68						
16	Aoyama 7						
17	Abraham 17						
18	Barbera 8						
19	Edwards 5						
20	Laverty 70						
21	Parkes 23						
22	Petrucci 9						
23	Di Meglio 63						

RACE

	Rider	Motorcycle	Race time	Time +	Fastest lap	Avg. speed	🏁
1	Marquez	Honda	43m 33.430s		2m 03.575s	99.0mph	M/H
2	Pedrosa	Honda	43m 37.554s	4.124s	2m 03.587s	98.9mph	M/M
3	Dovizioso	Ducati	43m 54.406s	20.976s	2m 04.655s	98.3mph	M/M
4	Bradl	Honda	43m 56.220s	22.790s	2m 04.462s	98.2mph	M/M
5	Smith	Yamaha	43m 56.393s	22.963s	2m 04.567s	98.2mph	M/M
6	Espargaro P	Yamaha	43m 59.997s	26.567s	2m 04.562s	98.1mph	M/M
7	Iannone	Ducati	44m 01.687s	28.257s	2m 03.978s	98.0mph	M/M
8	Rossi	Yamaha	44m 18.949s	45.519s	2m 04.152s	97.4mph	M/M
9	Espargaro A	Yamaha	44m 21.035s	47.605s	2m 05.519s	97.3mph	M/M
10	Lorenzo	Yamaha	44m 22.541s	49.111s	2m 04.871s	97.2mph	M/M
11	Hayden	Honda	44m 34.165s	1m 00.735s	2m 06.165s	96.8mph	M/M
12	Aoyama	Honda	44m 37.384s	1m 03.954s	2m 06.598s	96.7mph	M/M
13	Hernandez	Ducati	44m 40.763s	1m 07.333s	2m 06.098s	96.6mph	M/M
14	Abraham	Honda	45m 01.402s	1m 27.972s	2m 07.016s	95.8mph	M/S
15	Barbera	Avintia	45m 05.806s	1m 32.376s	2m 06.725s	95.7mph	M/S
16	Laverty	PBM	45m 05.973s	1m 32.543s	2m 07.922s	95.7mph	M/S
17	Petrucci	ART	45m 12.606s	1m 39.176s	2m 08.157s	95.4mph	M/S
18	Di Meglio	Avintia	45m 25.392s	1m 51.962s	2m 07.941s	95.0mph	M/S
NF	Redding	Honda	40m 28.681s	2 laps	2m 05.996s	96.4mph	M/M
NF	Edwards	Yamaha	36m 17.593s	4 laps	2m 07.049s	96.3mph	M/M
NF	Crutchlow	Ducati	26m 02.114s	9 laps	2m 04.041s	94.7mph	M/M
NF	Bautista	Honda	18m 47.805s	12 laps	2m 04.373s	98.4mph	M/M
NF	Parkes	PBM	17m 29.053s	13 laps	2m 08.632s	94.0mph	M/S

CHAMPIONSHIP

	Rider	Nation	Team	Points
1	Marquez	SPA	Repsol Honda Team	50
2	Pedrosa	SPA	Repsol Honda Team	36
3	Rossi	ITA	Movistar Yamaha MotoGP	28
4	Dovizioso	ITA	Ducati Team	27
5	Espargaro A	SPA	NGM Forward Racing	20
6	Iannone	ITA	Pramac Racing	15
7	Bradl	GER	LCR Honda MotoGP	13
	Hayden	USA	Drive M7 Aspar	13
9	Smith	GBR	Monster Yamaha Tech3	11
10	Espargaro P	SPA	Monster Yamaha Tech3	10
	Crutchlow	GBR	Ducati Team	10
12	Redding	GBR	GO&FUN Honda Gresini	9
	Aoyama	JPN	Drive M7 Aspar	9
14	Edwards	USA	NGM Forward Racing	7
	Hernandez	COL	Energy T.I. Pramac Racing	7
16	Lorenzo	SPA	Movistar Yamaha MotoGP	6
17	Abraham	CZE	Cardion AB Motoracing	5
18	Petrucci	ITA	Ioda Racing Project	2
19	Barbera	SPA	Avintia Racing	1
	Parkes	AUS	Paul Bird Motorsport	1

12 HIROSHI AOYAMA
Happier with the front of the bike than in Qatar and a lot closer to team-mate Hayden.

13 YONNY HERNANDEZ
Pleased to run with Hayden and Aoyama for much of the race, and to achieve his goal of scoring points in every race.

14 KAREL ABRAHAM
Still suffering with his shoulder and with the front tyre after ten laps. Stayed out because points were on offer.

15 HECTOR BARBERA
Noticed serious front-tyre problems after just three laps and felt he might crash on every right-hander, but kept going 'out of respect for my team'.

16 MICHAEL LAVERTY
Just missed out on a point. A worn front tyre prevented Michael pressing his attack on Barbera on the last lap.

17 DANILO PETRUCCI
Banged into both Parkes and Barbera off the start, after which Danilo felt a strong vibration and assumed he had

damaged something or dislodged a sensor. It turned out all was okay and he was able to finish the race.

18 MIKE DI MEGLIO
Much the same story as in the first race of the year: lack of testing meant he could not get comfortable with the bike.

DID NOT FINISH

SCOTT REDDING
Had problems with the front tyre after lap seven, resulting in his crash late in the race. Diced with Hernandez, who regularly passed him on the straights, thus messing up Scott's rhythm and preventing him catching the group in front.

COLIN EDWARDS
Front-tyre problems followed by fuel starvation four laps from the flag meant Colin's last race in Texas was not as he would have wanted.

CAL CRUTCHLOW
In trouble with the rear tyre from the start, so stopped and changed to the soft option. Crashed at Turn 11 and did some serious damage to the little finger on his right hand.

ALVARO BAUTISTA
Crashed on lap six when he lost the front while battling for third place.

BROC PARKES
Forced to retire with front-tyre problems, no grip and lots of chatter.

ARGENTINA
ROUND 3

G.P. RED BULL DE LA REPÚBLICA ARGENTINA
AUTÓDROMO TERMAS DE RÍO HONDO

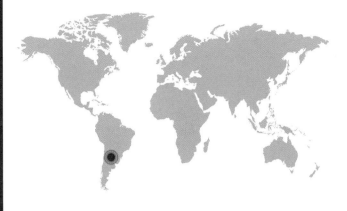

SOUTH OF THE BORDER

MotoGP returned to South America and everyone had fun, especially Marc Marquez

It felt like a Grand Prix for a continent, not a country. World Championship motorcycle racing returned to South America for the first time in 10 years – the Rio race of 2004 was the last occasion – and to Argentina for the first time in 15 years.

Not surprisingly, local hero Sebastian Porto, making a comeback in the Moto2 class, could not put his nose outside his pit without being mobbed, while Yonny Hernandez was permanently posing with excited groups of Colombian fans, much like Eric Granado, the teenage Brazilian, was doing in Moto3. The flags and number plates of every South American country were in the stands and the massive campsites that surround the Termas de Rio Hondo circuit.

There was a splendidly retro feel about the whole event, which, to older observers, was reminiscent of the Bol d'Or circa 1980 or the Spanish Grand Prix at Jarama in the '70s. Long-nosed Mercedes buses – looking as if they had come straight from Woodstock – and air-cooled motorcycles fitted in perfectly with the roadside bars with their smoky barbecues and mangy dogs.

Termas de Rio Hondo is a small spa town a very long way from anywhere else and you are well aware that you are in a very big country. It is a two-day drive from Buenos Aires or a two-hour flight from there to Tucumán followed by an interesting drive, which seemed to involve many MotoGP people being fined by the police for unspecified offences. Those minor gripes aside, the town was patently delighted to host the event. Anyone who thought the locals would not know who or what was going on was soon disabused of that notion. Before practice had started, Valentino Rossi and Marc Marquez had needed the help of their retinues to escape from a

ABOVE Andrea Iannone was top Ducati rider in sixth place, underlining his impressive form and consistency.

RIGHT Jorge Lorenzo rediscovered his mojo and led most of the race before being overhauled by the Repsol Hondas.

town-centre restaurant, although Marc said nobody had noticed him until Rossi left. South America, best described as one country broken up into ten parts, was ready and waiting for its race.

There were, of course, teething problems with the redesigned track and it took some all-nighters from IRTA and Dorna staff to get everything ready in time. Sure, the paint was still wet on some buildings, the Wi-Fi was flaky, and post-race traffic was challenging – but the event was a success.

The track layout was universally popular, with fast corners, a variety of cambers, and a decidedly tricky pair of corners to end the lap. However, the tarmac was very 'green' and there was so much dust on it that on Friday Andrea Dovizioso said that no traction-control system ever devised could have coped. By race day things had improved considerably, although it was still unwise to venture off-line.

Bridgestone guarded against a repeat of the problems of the previous race by bringing three types of front tyre rather than two. A test the previous year had been inconclusive thanks to first dust and then rain, so it was agreed that hard, medium and soft would be available for this race. Not that it appeared to make any difference to Marc Marquez. He happily destroyed a rear tyre in a handful of laps in the first session and in qualifying took his third pole in three races by the massive margin of three-quarters of a second.

The Yamahas, however, made the early running in the race, with Jorge Lorenzo looking like his old self after the traumas of Qatar and Texas. Rossi, still seeking assurance that he could be competitive, chased him with Andrea

'THIS IS PROBABLY
THE MOST SWEET THIRD
PLACE IN MY CAREER IN MOTOGP'

JORGE LORENZO

Iannone again impressive in third. The MotoGP field did a good impersonation of a Moto3 race for the first couple of laps, running four abreast out of the final corner on the first lap.

Marquez worked his way up to second place, aided by the occasional mistake by Rossi and the Italian being firmly shoved out of the way by Stefan Bradl. That put Valentino back to sixth and effectively ended his chances of a rostrum finish. Rossi did fight back but Dani Pedrosa, quiet in the opening laps, got past him in the aftermath of the Bradl barge and then passed Iannone for third place.

Marquez, still shadowing race leader Lorenzo, was four seconds ahead of Dani at this point and that gap stayed constant for a few more laps until, ten laps from the flag, Pedrosa started to motor. It did not take Marquez long to react and he took the lead with eight laps to go, but Pedrosa kept on coming. On lap 22 of 25 Dani set the fastest lap of the race and next time round aggressively pushed past Lorenzo. It was too late to catch Marquez, who had opened up a two-and-a-half-second gap, but Dani had shown he still had it in him to challenge his team-mate. Not that the man himself seemed impressed: 'With the pace we had we could have pushed for the win.' On reflection, he blamed himself for being too keen to preserve his tyres.

So Marquez continued his run of victories from pole – the last man to do that in the first three races of a season was the great Giacomo Agostini on the MV Agusta in 1971. There were now two topics of conversation in the paddock. Could Marc really win them all this year? And would everything and everybody really get from the depths of Argentina to Jerez for the Spanish race the following weekend?

ABOVE Hiro Aoyama was delighted to be top Open Class finisher after passing his team-mate Nicky Hayden on the last corner.

BELOW Scott Redding leads Aoyama in the battle of the customer Hondas.

OPPOSITE Stefan Bradl had a good race after a big crash in qualifying and a barging match with Valentino Rossi early in the race.

INSIDE TRACK

Fast tracks usually provide good racing, and the Termas de Rio Hondo circuit was expected to become the fastest on the calendar. The simulations of the designer – Jarno Zaffelli of the Italian company Dromo – projected an average lap speed of nearly 117mph (188kph), which would have been considerably quicker than Phillip Island, the fastest track on the calendar at 112.9mph (181kph). Dani Pedrosa's lap record, however, proved to be considerably slower: 108.3mph (174.3kph) made the South American circuit slower than Mugello as well as Phillip Island, and only fractionally faster than Assen and Silverstone.

But Termas de Rio Honda is not only quick – it provides great racing. The Moto3 race saw overtaking on every corner of the track, and riders from all three classes universally praised it.

Much credit must go to Zaffelli, who completely rejigged the 2007 layout that had been deemed unsuitable for MotoGP. Clever use of camber – or lack of it – and gradients that are not readily apparent on TV pictures provided 14 corners, all of which were the result of much computer analysis of thousands of

crashes. Dromo's dimensioning of run-off areas and risk assessments were carried out with their own software systems, which are also being applied to ski racing in conjunction with Dainese. The company has also worked for Mugello, Imola and Misano on accurate surveying and repaving.

Without doubt, the fact that the

circuit was designed specifically for motorcycle racing helped enormously, as did the support of a local government that is keen to open up the area to tourism. The future of the circuit, at least in the short term, seems safe and MotoGP will return to Argentina in 2015 and beyond. It will be interesting to see how much faster the track is next time.

G.P. RED BULL DE LA REPÚBLICA ARGENTINA
AUTÓDROMO TERMAS DE RÍO HONDO

ROUND 3
APRIL 27

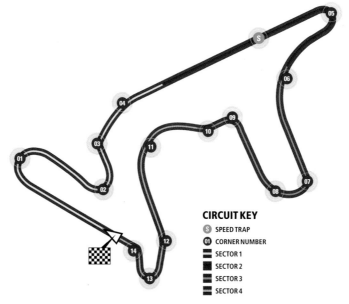

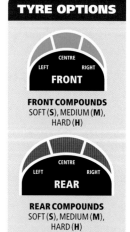

TYRE OPTIONS

FRONT

FRONT COMPOUNDS
SOFT (**S**), MEDIUM (**M**), HARD (**H**)

REAR

REAR COMPOUNDS
SOFT (**S**), MEDIUM (**M**), HARD (**H**)

SEVERITY RATING

<MILD   SEVERE>

RACE RESULTS

CIRCUIT LENGTH 2.986 miles
NO. OF LAPS 25
RACE DISTANCE 74.650 miles
WEATHER Dry, 24°C
TRACK TEMPERATURE 21°C
WINNER Marc Marquez
FASTEST LAP 1m 39.233s, 108.305mph, Dani Pedrosa (record)
LAP RECORD 1m 39.233s, 108.305mph, Dani Pedrosa, 2014

CIRCUIT KEY
- **S** SPEED TRAP
- **01** CORNER NUMBER
- SECTOR 1
- SECTOR 2
- SECTOR 3
- SECTOR 4

QUALIFYING

	Rider	Nation	Motorcycle	Team	Time	Pole +
1	Marquez	SPA	Honda	Repsol Honda Team	1m 37.683s	
2	Lorenzo	SPA	Yamaha	Movistar Yamaha MotoGP	1m 38.425s	0.742s
3	Pedrosa	SPA	Honda	Repsol Honda Team	1m 38.651s	0.968s
4	Espargaro A	SPA	Yamaha	NGM Forward Racing	1m 38.794s	1.111s
5	Dovizioso	ITA	Ducati	Ducati Team	1m 38.856s	1.173s
6	Rossi	ITA	Yamaha	Movistar Yamaha MotoGP	1m 38.949s	1.266s
7	Smith	GBR	Yamaha	Monster Yamaha Tech3	1m 38.958s	1.275s
8	Iannone	ITA	Ducati	Pramac Racing	1m 39.237s	1.554s
9	Bradl	GER	Honda	LCR Honda MotoGP	1m 39.297s	1.614s
10	Bautista	SPA	Honda	GO&FUN Honda Gresini	1m 39.429s	1.746s
11	Espargaro P	SPA	Yamaha	Monster Yamaha Tech3	1m 39.822s	2.139s
12	Hayden	USA	Honda	Drive M7 Aspar	1m 40.541s	2.858s
13	Redding	GBR	Honda	GO&FUN Honda Gresini	1m 40.238s	Q1
14	Edwards	USA	Yamaha	NGM Forward Racing	1m 40.476s	Q1
15	Abraham	CZE	Honda	Cardion AB Motoracing	1m 40.615s	Q1
16	Aoyama	JPN	Honda	Drive M7 Aspar	1m 40.616s	Q1
17	Hernandez	COL	Ducati	Energy T.I. Pramac Racing	1m 40.691s	Q1
18	Parkes	AUS	PBM	Paul Bird Motorsport	1m 40.981s	Q1
19	Pirro	ITA	Ducati	Ducati Team	1m 41.018s	Q1
20	Laverty	GBR	PBM	Paul Bird Motorsport	1m 41.103s	Q1
21	Barbera	SPA	Avintia	Avintia Racing	1m 41.129s	Q1
22	Di Meglio	FRA	Avintia	Avintia Racing	1m 41.267s	Q1
23	Petrucci	ITA	ART	Ioda Racing Project	1m 41.686s	Q1

1 MARC MARQUEZ
The third win in a row, and again from pole. Tangled up in early fairing-bashing but worked his way up to second behind Lorenzo by lap five. Followed the Yamaha until Pedrosa started closing, when he passed and went for the hat trick.

2 DANI PEDROSA
Paid the price for a cautious opening to the race. Set the fastest lap with a late charge past Lorenzo and closed to within a couple of seconds of his team-mate.

3 JORGE LORENZO
Looked much more like his old self when he got the holeshot and led for 16 laps. Last year, that would have been it. But the ease with which Marquez passed Jorge and then pulled away, and Pedrosa's late pass, showed graphically how things have changed from 2013.

4 VALENTINO ROSSI
Vale and his crew were fuming, just as they were after the previous race. They were convinced they had the pace for a rostrum finish but a lunge from Bradl and some mistakes of his own kept Valentino back in fourth.

5 STEFAN BRADL
Fifth place was a good comeback after a heavy crash in qualifying. Involved in some frantic action early on, including a lunge up the inside that Rossi blamed for ruining his rostrum chances. Lost confidence in his front tyre in the closing stages.

6 ANDREA IANNONE
Another very impressive weekend, with his second career-best result in a row. Ran in third place early on while dicing with Bradl, and ended the race as top Ducati.

7 BRADLEY SMITH
As in Texas, not confident on a full tank at the start of the race but picked up the pace towards the end, setting his personal fastest lap late on.

8 POL ESPARGARO
Like his team-mate Smith, Pol did not feel good with a full tank. Tried to stay with Bradley but could not in the later stages as the Brit got faster and Pol lost confidence in his rear tyre.

9 ANDREA DOVIZIOSO
Started well but soon ran into trouble with his front tyre both on corner entry and the brakes. Thought he might have chosen the wrong tyre, but it was the same one used by Iannone. Also complained of some engine problems.

10 HIROSHI AOYAMA
More like his old self: top RCV1000R rider with a last-lap pass and a crossed-up wheelie over the line. Not bad for a guy with serious digestive problems.

11 NICKY HAYDEN
Looked like he had won an entertaining four-bike dice but Nicky's team-mate got him at the penultimate corner.

LAP CHART

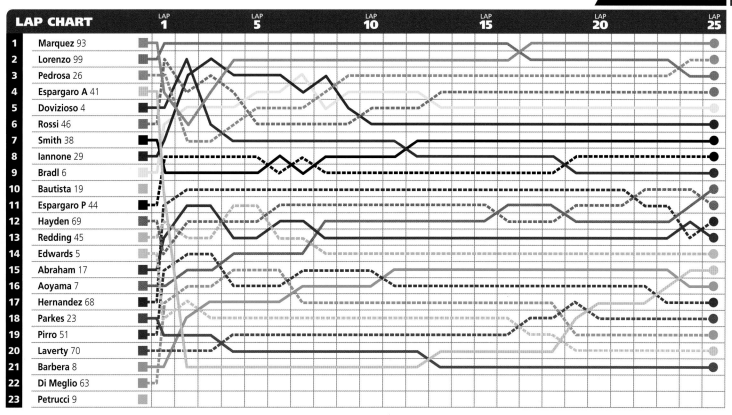

	LAP 1	LAP 5	LAP 10	LAP 15	LAP 20	LAP 25
1	Marquez 93					
2	Lorenzo 99					
3	Pedrosa 26					
4	Espargaro A 41					
5	Dovizioso 4					
6	Rossi 46					
7	Smith 38					
8	Iannone 29					
9	Bradl 6					
10	Bautista 19					
11	Espargaro P 44					
12	Hayden 69					
13	Redding 45					
14	Edwards 5					
15	Abraham 17					
16	Aoyama 7					
17	Hernandez 68					
18	Parkes 23					
19	Pirro 51					
20	Laverty 70					
21	Barbera 8					
22	Di Meglio 63					
23	Petrucci 9					

RACE

	Rider	Motorcycle	Race time	Time +	Fastest lap	Avg. speed	
1	Marquez	Honda	41m 39.821s		1m 39.264s	107.5mph	H/H
2	Pedrosa	Honda	41m 41.658s	1.837s	1m 39.233s	107.4mph	M/H
3	Lorenzo	Yamaha	41m 43.022s	3.201s	1m 39.603s	107.4mph	M/H
4	Rossi	Yamaha	41m 44.719s	4.898s	1m 39.339s	107.2mph	H/H
5	Bradl	Honda	41m 54.850s	15.029s	1m 40.093s	106.8mph	M/H
6	Iannone	Ducati	41m 59.268s	19.447s	1m 40.160s	106.6mph	M/M
7	Smith	Yamaha	42m 04.013s	24.192s	1m 40.049s	106.4mph	H/H
8	Espargaro P	Yamaha	42m 08.939s	29.118s	1m 40.340s	106.3mph	M/H
9	Dovizioso	Ducati	42m 13.494s	33.673s	1m 40.290s	106.1mph	H/M
10	Aoyama	Honda	42m 23.100s	43.279s	1m 40.904s	105.6mph	M/M
11	Hayden	Honda	42m 23.173s	43.352s	1m 41.020s	105.6mph	M/M
12	Hernandez	Ducati	42m 24.640s	44.819s	1m 41.171s	105.6mph	M/M
13	Abraham	Honda	42m 24.999s	45.178s	1m 41.296s	105.6mph	M/M
14	Redding	Honda	42m 28.477s	48.656s	1m 41.296s	105.4mph	M/M
15	Espargaro A	Yamaha	42m 32.071s	52.250s	1m 40.602s	105.3mph	H/M
16	Barbera	Avintia	42m 33.326s	53.505s	1m 41.480s	105.3mph	M/M
17	Pirro	Ducati	42m 33.490s	53.669s	1m 41.266s	105.2mph	M/M
18	Laverty	PBM	42m 36.391s	56.570s	1m 41.506s	105.1mph	M/M
19	Di Meglio	Avintia	42m 42.961s	1m 03.140s	1m 41.776s	104.8mph	M/M
20	Edwards	Yamaha	42m 45.581s	1m 05.760s	1m 41.720s	104.7mph	H/M
21	Parkes	PBM	42m 56.543s	1m 16.722s	1m 42.534s	104.3mph	M/M
NF	Bautista	Honda	–	–	–	–	M/H
NF	Petrucci	ART	–	–	–	–	M/M

CHAMPIONSHIP

	Rider	Nation	Team	Points
1	Marquez	SPA	Repsol Honda Team	75
2	Pedrosa	SPA	Repsol Honda Team	56
3	Rossi	ITA	Movistar Yamaha MotoGP	41
4	Dovizioso	ITA	Ducati Team	34
5	Iannone	ITA	Pramac Racing	25
6	Bradl	GER	LCR Honda MotoGP	24
7	Lorenzo	SPA	Movistar Yamaha MotoGP	22
8	Espargaro A	SPA	NGM Forward Racing	21
9	Smith	GBR	Monster Yamaha Tech3	20
10	Espargaro P	SPA	Monster Yamaha Tech3	18
11	Hayden	USA	Drive M7 Aspar	18
12	Aoyama	JPN	Drive M7 Aspar	15
13	Redding	GBR	GO&FUN Honda Gresini	11
14	Hernandez	COL	Energy T.I. Pramac Racing	11
15	Crutchlow	GBR	Ducati Team	10
16	Abraham	CZE	Cardion AB Motoracing	8
17	Edwards	USA	NGM Forward Racing	7
18	Petrucci	ITA	Ioda Racing Project	2
19	Barbera	SPA	Avintia Racing	1
20	Parkes	AUS	Paul Bird Motorsport	1

12 YONNY HERNANDEZ
Thoroughly enjoyed racing at home in South America. He was part of the dice for tenth place but had to concede places late on when his tyres went off.

13 KAREL ABRAHAM
Much happier with his fitness and the ability to race with and beat Redding.

14 SCOTT REDDING
One of those races that rookies have to go through as part of the learning process. Struggled both with front grip under braking and with his physical condition – cold symptoms.

15 ALEIX ESPARGARO
Lost the front and crashed on the second lap, then remounted and scored a point. Like the satellite Yamaha riders, he had trouble with the bike on a full tank.

16 HECTOR BARBERA
Used the team's new chassis in free practice but the inevitable lack of testing had an effect.

17 MICHELE PIRRO
The Ducati factory test rider replaced the injured Cal Crutchlow but was never happy with the bike and had a lacklustre weekend.

18 MICHAEL LAVERTY
Finished under a minute behind the winner for the first time in his MotoGP career.

19 MIKE DI MEGLIO
Impressive in free practice and competitive with other Open Class bikes in the race.

20 COLIN EDWARDS
A horrible weekend. Colin qualified badly and struggled for the whole race.

21 BROC PARKES
Qualified well but struggled in the race with lack of grip.

DID NOT FINISH

ALVARO BAUTISTA
Crashed on the first lap after contact with Aleix Espargaro, making it three crashes in the first three races of the year.

DANILO PETRUCCI
Crashed on the first lap trying to make up for his qualifying by going inside Barbera at Turn 4. Got squeezed and fell.

DID NOT START

CAL CRUTCHLOW
Missed the race because his finger injury from Texas was found to be more serious than first thought and required an operation. Replaced by Pirro.

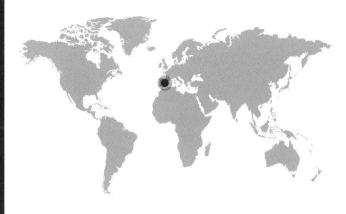

GRAN PREMIO bwin
DE ESPAÑA
CIRCUITO DE JEREZ

STILL PERFECT

Back to Europe and Marc Marquez won again, but Valentino Rossi gave him a good fight

There is always that feeling that you do not really understand what is going on in the championship until it gets back to Europe. Sure, Marquez is going to be almost unbeatable but just how serious will Rossi's challenge be? Is Jorge Lorenzo really that confused? What is bothering Dani Pedrosa? The first three races of the year raised all those questions without really providing answers.

The question of Rossi's form was particularly frustrating: yes, he had a good race in Qatar but 12 months previously that had been no indicator of his performances over the season; then there were tyre problems in Texas and mistakes in Argentina. Valentino arrived back in Europe third in the championship, already 34 points behind Marquez and 15 behind second-placed Pedrosa, and only seven in front of Dovizioso. This was not a position that accurately reflected his form, but Valentino was a little tense in the knowledge that the factories would be making decisions on contracts over the next two or three races. The Spanish race would prove that Valentino was indeed back to form and seemed to be the only man in the field with the confidence to take on Mighty Marc.

Rossi's status as Yamaha's top man was underlined by his enthusiastic use of a new chassis that Lorenzo did not see as an improvement. Valentino said before the race that the way to get to Marquez was to break his rhythm by harassing him. This is easier said than done, of course, but Valentino's first couple of laps were certainly aggressive enough to demonstrate that he meant what he said. He led briefly but it did not take long for Marquez to get back past, the start of the second lap to be precise, and then he could not shake off the Yamaha for the rest of the race. Here was the answer to the question everyone, including Valentino, had been asking since Qatar: yes, he was faster than he had been since 2009; and yes, he looked like a championship contender.

There was also the small matter of beating his team-mate. Jerez was the first time Rossi had achieved this in what was effectively a fair fight – with no injuries or mechanical issues – since he and Lorenzo were reunited for the 2013 season. After the race there was a definite sense of relief and an undercurrent of the old certainty. Once again we had to pay close attention to Vale's pronouncements and do a little decoding. What did he mean by, 'My team is working very well… I am very happy with the way the bike is being developed?' It could be taken as a dig at his old crew chief, Jerry Burgess, but that would be simplistic. It was more like a lecture to the media people who doubted his judgement: he was saying, 'See? I was right.'

Rossi's team-mate looked as if he was continuing his rehabilitation after the horrors of the first couple of races, but then it all went wrong. Second on the grid, he was a close third in the race until he was caught by Pedrosa and dropped back. A subdued Jorge laid some of the blame on his physical condition, referring to the three operations he had had before the start of the season. Pedrosa's race was nearly as puzzling; again, he did not appear to really find any pace until the final stages, when he ghosted past Lorenzo and closed right up on Rossi, later lamenting that he needed a few more corners to pass the Italian.

Jerez has never been kind to Ducati and that trend continued. Cal Crutchlow retired not because he had come back too early from his hand injury but because he had run out of brakes, leading to suggestions that bigger brake discs were needed, while it took all of

RIGHT Valentino Rossi did his best to disrupt Marc Marquez's progress in the early laps but the champion would not be denied.

BELOW Nicky Hayden had his best race so far on the Honda RCV1000R but, worryingly, his old wrist injury was playing up.

'I'M SURE THAT SOONER OR LATER
WILL COME A RACE WHICH WE
ARE UNABLE TO WIN'
MARC MARQUEZ

ABOVE Yonny
Hernandez was starting
to shed his reputation
as a crasher, finishing
every race so far.

BELOW Unsurprisingly
Marc and his fan club
were delighted with
his first win in any
class at Jerez.

OPPOSITE Two happy men
fighting for fifth: Bautista
because he finally finished a race
(in sixth), Dovizioso because Jerez
has never favoured the Ducati.

Andrea Dovizioso's experience to win the group fight for fifth place. Seventh-placed Aleix Espargaro was particularly exasperated after twice being passed in a straight line, Alvaro Bautista in sixth place was just pleased to finish for the first time this season, while eighth-placed Bradley Smith on a new chassis was happy to finish right with the trio ahead of him. Stefan Bradl dropped off the group with arm pump and was nearly caught by Nicky Hayden's customer Honda, running the softest tyres on offer against Bridgestone's advice.

Marc Marquez's win could hardly be called unexpected, but this time it was his qualifying that was startling. Marc has already invented new ways to ride a motorcycle, and now he invented a new way to qualify. Marc himself had the idea and suggested it to his crew chief Santi Hernandez, who did the maths.

On a day hot enough for a soft rear tyre to last just one lap of qualifying, they hatched a plan to get three runs and therefore three flying laps in the 15-minute session. Bear in mind that Marc had not had things his own way so far that weekend, with both Pedrosa and Lorenzo heading him. Marc and Santi achieved their three runs by swapping bikes – not rear wheels. Marc went out on his number-one bike, did an out-lap, a flying lap and an in-lap. He then went out and did the same again on his second bike, so that his last run was back on the number-one bike, now shod with a new soft tyre and slightly cooler than it would otherwise have been. Marc promptly put it on pole and disposed of Lorenzo's absolute lap record that had stood since 2008, which was the last year, incidentally, when MotoGP featured qualifying tyres. Just when the opposition thought they had found a weakness, he does that.

RUBBER BAND

Bridgestone made two announcements over the weekend. The first was of minor significance: all three front-tyre compounds would now be available at every race to avoid the problems that had occurred in Texas. The second was of seismic importance: the company would not be extending its contract as MotoGP's spec-tyre supplier after two three-year contracts, the second running to the end of 2014, but Bridgestone did agree to stay on for a final season in 2015 in the interests of ensuring a smooth transition.

The Japanese company arrived in MotoGP in 2002, the year the four-stroke formula made its début, and became the official tyre supplier in 2009. Valentino Rossi commented that he last rode a MotoGP bike on another brand of tyre way back in 2007 and that the difference achieved by Bridgestone was breathtaking – could a new supplier come near those standards, he wondered? Asked what he wanted from a tyre supplier, Dani Pedrosa said first and foremost, 'a safe tyre, and then we complain for performance.' That neatly encapsulates the 'no-win' situation a

spec-tyre supplier is in; when they work, they are tyres; when they do not work, they are Bridgestones.

So who would be willing to pick up this particular poisoned chalice? Officially, Dorna issued tender documents with a three-week deadline for offers. However, it was an open

secret that the subject had been under discussion for a good while and that neither Dunlop and Pirelli were interested in putting in an offer. So it was no surprise when at the end of the three-week period Michelin was announced as the official tyre supplier from the start of the 2016 season.

GRAN PREMIO bwin DE ESPAÑA
CIRCUITO DE JEREZ
ROUND 4
MAY 4

OFFICIAL TIMEKEEPER

RACE RESULTS

CIRCUIT LENGTH 2.748 miles

NO. OF LAPS 27

RACE DISTANCE 74.205 miles

WEATHER Dry, 28°C

TRACK TEMPERATURE 50°C

WINNER Marc Marquez

FASTEST LAP 1m 39.841s, 99.047mph, Marc Marquez

LAP RECORD 1m 39.565s, 99.357mph, Jorge Lorenzo, 2013

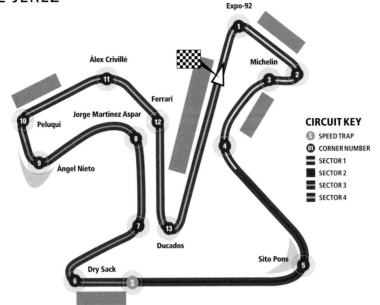

CIRCUIT KEY
- **S** SPEED TRAP
- **01** CORNER NUMBER
- SECTOR 1
- SECTOR 2
- SECTOR 3
- SECTOR 4

TYRE OPTIONS

FRONT

FRONT COMPOUNDS
SOFT (**S**), MEDIUM (**M**), HARD (**H**)

REAR

REAR COMPOUNDS
EXTRA SOFT (**XS**), SOFT (**S**), MEDIUM (**M**)

SEVERITY RATING

<MILD   SEVERE>

BRIDGESTONE

QUALIFYING

	Rider	Nation	Motorcycle	Team	Time	Pole +
1	Marquez	SPA	Honda	Repsol Honda Team	1m 38.120s	
2	Lorenzo	SPA	Yamaha	Movistar Yamaha MotoGP	1m 38.541s	0.421s
3	Pedrosa	SPA	Honda	Repsol Honda Team	1m 38.630s	0.510s
4	Rossi	ITA	Yamaha	Movistar Yamaha MotoGP	1m 38.857s	0.737s
5	Espargaro A	SPA	Yamaha	NGM Forward Racing	1m 39.007s	0.887s
6	Dovizioso	ITA	Ducati	Ducati Team	1m 39.222s	1.102s
7	Bradl	GER	Honda	LCR Honda MotoGP	1m 39.243s	1.123s
8	Espargaro P	SPA	Yamaha	Monster Yamaha Tech3	1m 39.293s	1.173s
9	Smith	GBR	Yamaha	Monster Yamaha Tech3	1m 39.390s	1.270s
10	Bautista	SPA	Honda	GO&FUN Honda Gresini	1m 39.751s	1.631s
11	Edwards	USA	Yamaha	NGM Forward Racing	1m 39.814s	1.694s
12	Hayden	USA	Honda	Drive M7 Aspar	1m 39.826s	1.706s
13	Aoyama	JPN	Honda	Drive M7 Aspar	1m 39.768s	Q1
14	Crutchlow	GBR	Ducati	Ducati Team	1m 39.849s	Q1
15	Iannone	ITA	Ducati	Pramac Racing	1m 40.118s	Q1
16	Abraham	CZE	Honda	Cardion AB Motoracing	1m 40.126s	Q1
17	Pirro	ITA	Ducati	Ducati Team	1m 40.239s	Q1
18	Redding	GBR	Honda	GO&FUN Honda Gresini	1m 40.453s	Q1
19	Hernandez	COL	Ducati	Energy T.I. Pramac Racing	1m 40.566s	Q1
20	Petrucci	ITA	ART	Ioda Racing Project	1m 41.009s	Q1
21	Laverty	GBR	PBM	Paul Bird Motorsport	1m 41.124s	Q1
22	Di Meglio	FRA	Avintia	Avintia Racing	1m 41.517s	Q1
23	Parkes	AUS	PBM	Paul Bird Motorsport	1m 41.702s	Q1
24	Barbera	SPA	Avintia	Avintia Racing	1m 42.052s	Q1

1 MARC MARQUEZ
His first win in any class at Jerez. Invented a new qualifying strategy to take pole, fought off Rossi's attempt to disrupt his race, took the lead at the end of the back straight and never looked back.

2 VALENTINO ROSSI
Vale's first podium at Jerez, one of his favourite tracks, since 2010. Showed that he would be a force to reckon with this season as he took the fight to Marquez in the early laps and fought off Pedrosa in the closing stages.

3 DANI PEDROSA
Knew he did not have his team-mate's pace because of problems with his front tyre. Followed the Yamahas for much of the race before mounting a late attack.

4 JORGE LORENZO
Not the way he wanted to celebrate his 200th GP. His race was compromised by a bad start and, said Jorge, his lack of fitness.

5 ANDREA DOVIZIOSO
Delighted with the result on a track that does not favour the Ducati. Rode brilliantly to hold off Espargaro.

6 ALVARO BAUTISTA
Relieved to finish a race for the first time this season. Problems at the start with the front tucking but enjoyed his dice with Dovizioso.

7 ALEIX ESPARGARO
Frustrated by the fact that every time he passed Dovizioso on the brakes the Ducati simply went back past on the straight. Had to be happy with finishing top Open Class bike once more.

8 BRADLEY SMITH
A better result than it looked on paper. Got a great start to go fourth, then

involved in the four-way battle for fifth. Finished the race less than half a second behind Dovizioso.

9 POL ESPARGARO
Did not make a good start and had to work himself and the tyres hard to get on to the back of the fifth-place group, but did not have the resources left to make a pass.

10 STEFAN BRADL
After a few laps he ran into a problem with arm pump that totally wrecked his race and required surgery after the post-race Monday test.

11 NICKY HAYDEN
Super-soft tyres and a track that does not reward top speed meant Nicky had his best race so far on the RCV1000R. Made a small mistake at Turn 4 that lost him the tow to Bradl. Worryingly, still in some discomfort from the hand he had operated on over winter. It was bad enough for him to miss the Monday test.

12 HIROSHI AOYAMA
Cautious at the start with the front tyre cold, got moving after seven laps and closed the gap to the group in front; but could not make a pass as he had failed to make use of the tyres while at their best.

LAP CHART

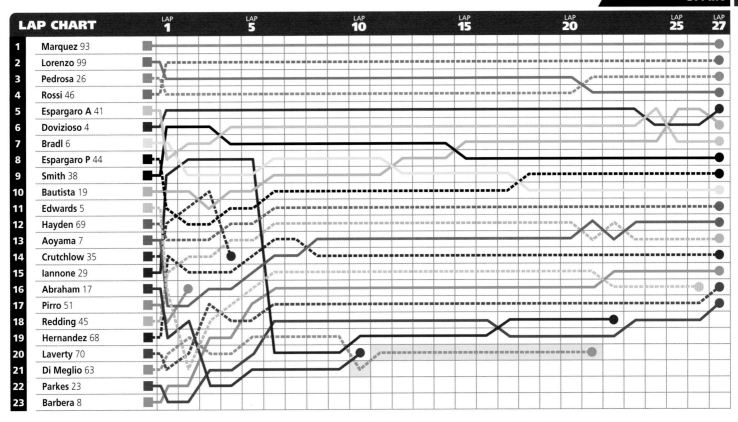

		LAP 1	LAP 5	LAP 10	LAP 15	LAP 20	LAP 25	LAP 27
1	Marquez 93							
2	Lorenzo 99							
3	Pedrosa 26							
4	Rossi 46							
5	Espargaro A 41							
6	Dovizioso 4							
7	Bradl 6							
8	Espargaro P 44							
9	Smith 38							
10	Bautista 19							
11	Edwards 5							
12	Hayden 69							
13	Aoyama 7							
14	Crutchlow 35							
15	Iannone 29							
16	Abraham 17							
17	Pirro 51							
18	Redding 45							
19	Hernandez 68							
20	Laverty 70							
21	Di Meglio 63							
22	Parkes 23							
23	Barbera 8							

RACE

	Rider	Motorcycle	Race time	Time +	Fastest lap	Avg. speed	
1	Marquez	Honda	45m 24.134s		1m 39.841s	98.1mph	M/M
2	Rossi	Yamaha	45m 25.565s	1.431s	1m 40.195s	98.0mph	H/M
3	Pedrosa	Honda	45m 25.663s	1.529s	1m 40.186s	98.0mph	M/M
4	Lorenzo	Yamaha	45m 32.675s	8.541s	1m 40.306s	97.7mph	M/M
5	Dovizioso	Ducati	45m 51.628s	27.494s	1m 41.062s	97.1mph	M/S
6	Bautista	Honda	45m 51.740s	27.606s	1m 41.153s	97.1mph	M/S
7	Espargaro A	Yamaha	45m 52.051s	27.917s	1m 40.937s	97.1mph	M/S
8	Smith	Yamaha	45m 52.081s	27.947s	1m 41.057s	97.1mph	M/S
9	Espargaro P	Yamaha	45m 53.553s	29.419s	1m 41.409s	97.0mph	H/M
10	Bradl	Honda	45m 57.006s	32.872s	1m 40.879s	96.9mph	M/M
11	Hayden	Honda	45m 59.624s	35.490s	1m 41.436s	96.7mph	M/XS
12	Aoyama	Honda	46m 04.217s	40.083s	1m 41.488s	96.6mph	M/XS
13	Redding	Honda	46m 07.964s	43.830s	1m 41.109s	96.5mph	H/XS
14	Hernandez	Ducati	46m 16.429s	52.295s	1m 41.850s	96.2mph	M/S
15	Barbera	Avintia	46m 19.007s	54.873s	1m 42.187s	96.1mph	M/XS
16	Laverty	PBM	46m 30.316s	1m 06.182s	1m 42.590s	95.7mph	M/XS
17	Parkes	PBM	46m 47.554s	1m 23.420s	1m 42.578s	95.1mph	M/XS
NF	Edwards	Yamaha	44m 38.537s	1 lap	1m 41.811s	96.0mph	M/XS
NF	Iannone	Ducati	37m 58.025s	5 laps	1m 40.783s	95.5mph	M/S
NF	Di Meglio	Avintia	38m 26.438s	6 laps	1m 42.957s	90.0mph	M/XS
NF	Abraham	Honda	17m 47.012s	17 laps	1m 42.024s	92.7mph	M/XS
NF	Crutchlow	Ducati	6m 53.854s	23 laps	1m 40.877s	95.6mph	M/S
NF	Pirro	Ducati	3m 30.646s	25 laps	1m 41.803s	93.9mph	M/XS

CHAMPIONSHIP

	Rider	Nation	Team	Points
1	Marquez	SPA	Repsol Honda Team	100
2	Pedrosa	SPA	Repsol Honda Team	72
3	Rossi	ITA	Movistar Yamaha MotoGP	61
4	Dovizioso	ITA	Ducati Team	45
5	Lorenzo	SPA	Movistar Yamaha MotoGP	35
6	Bradl	GER	LCR Honda MotoGP	30
	Espargaro A	SPA	NGM Forward Racing	30
8	Smith	GBR	Monster Yamaha Tech3	28
9	Iannone	ITA	Pramac Racing	25
	Espargaro P	SPA	Monster Yamaha Tech3	25
11	Hayden	USA	Drive M7 Aspar	23
12	Aoyama	JPN	Drive M7 Aspar	19
13	Redding	GBR	GO&FUN Honda Gresini	14
14	Hernandez	COL	Energy T.I. Pramac Racing	13
15	Bautista	SPA	GO&FUN Honda Gresini	10
	Crutchlow	GBR	Ducati Team	10
17	Abraham	CZE	Cardion AB Motoracing	8
18	Edwards	USA	NGM Forward Racing	7
19	Petrucci	ITA	Ioda Racing Project	2
	Barbera	SPA	Avintia Racing	2
21	Parkes	AUS	Paul Bird Motorsport	1

13 SCOTT REDDING
Enjoyed the race a lot more than practice and qualifying. Had to put an aggressive move on Crutchlow, who had problems, which lost him contact with Hayden. When he pushed to close the gap the front tucked and late in the race the rear lost grip.

14 YONNY HERNANDEZ
Points again but not happy with his race pace after a good warm-up – the reason was the usual Ducati problem of understeer.

15 HECTOR BARBERA
Another weekend of struggling with the electronics on what is basically a leftover CRT bike. Not happy at all but glad to score another point.

16 MICHAEL LAVERTY
A lonely race and 16th again, but finished closer to the winner than at the previous season's race.

17 BROC PARKES
Followed his team-mate home in a race where the PBM bikes did not match their practice pace in the race.

DID NOT FINISH

COLIN EDWARDS
Had his usual problem with turning the bike, then another fuelling problem stopped him on the last lap.

ANDREA IANNONE
Crashed out on the last corner of the fifth lap when he lost the front; got back on but was forced to retire.

MIKE DI MEGLIO
Suffered chronic traction problems. In the race he was lapping three seconds slower than in practice, so pulled in.

CAL CRUTCHLOW
Surprised everyone except himself by racing despite the injury to his right hand. Pulled in because his brakes overheated and boiled the fluid.

KAREL ABRAHAM
Suffered from front brake problems that eventually caused him to crash at Turn One.

MICHELE PIRRO
Riding as a wild card on the factory test team's bike. Lost the front on lap three.

DID NOT START

DANILO PETRUCCI
Broke a bone in his forearm in a Sunday morning warm-up crash. It did not look too serious but would result in Danilo missing the next three races.

FRANCE
ROUND 5

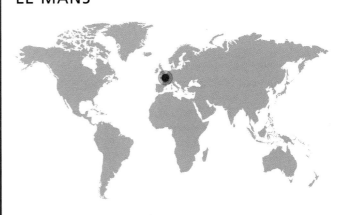

MONSTER ENERGY
GRAND PRIX DE FRANCE
LE MANS

MARC RIDES HIS LUCK

Marc Marquez won again despite early problems and with the help of a slip from Valentino Rossi

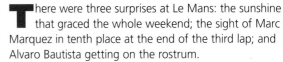

There were three surprises at Le Mans: the sunshine that graced the whole weekend; the sight of Marc Marquez in tenth place at the end of the third lap; and Alvaro Bautista getting on the rostrum.

Of the three, it may well be that the Go&Fun Gresini rider's third place was the most significant. After failing to score in the first three races of the year, achieving the Gresini team's first top-three finish with its new sponsor at last gave the team a reason to at least consider re-signing him.

This was one of those seasons when nearly every rider would be out of contract at the end of the year, the only exception being Cal Crutchlow. Needless to say, no-one was surprised when Honda announced before the race that it had re-signed Marc Marquez for another two years. Neither was there any surprise when Marquez produced another new way of taking pole position, and yet again it was demoralising for the rest of the field.

His Jerez strategy had been to use both bikes for three runs, but this time he did more than one flying lap on each of his two bikes. After a conventional first run, he parked the number-one bike and without any apparent hurry got on his number-two machine. He then went nearly half a second faster than he had done on the first bike to lead the field by 0.7sec. That is a ridiculous margin on a 1min 32sec lap.

Pol Espargaro got second with what he admitted was a banzai lap and Dovizioso took third thanks to clever use of the super-soft rear tyre that the regulations allow Ducati as part of the team's 'concessions' for not having won a race for two years. Where were Rossi and Lorenzo, the real contenders for race victory?

'THIS WEEKEND
HAS ACTUALLY BEEN
LIKE A SMALL DREAM'

POL ESPARGARO

Over 0.8sec slower – it felt like the illusions of Jerez were clearing.

Rossi did manage to give Marquez a race, after the young maestro made a lacklustre start and ran off track early on avoiding Lorenzo, who had outbraked himself. That put Marc back to tenth. Rossi tried to take advantage, moving to the front and opening up a small lead, but Marquez, with astonishing calmness, worked his way through the field: he was seventh after three laps, fourth after seven, set a new lap record eighth time round, and had third place after ten laps. A lap later he was past Pol Espargaro, busy backing up that superb qualifying performance, and into second place.

Rossi, by his own admission, then made it easy for Marc by running wide at a downhill right, gifting him the lead. Game over. Rossi did not claim that he would have won, just that he would have made life a little more difficult for Marquez.

Early front men Dovizioso and Bradl faded, the latter, like Pedrosa, suffering from the effects of an arm-pump operation. Dani had been quick right up to qualifying but said he had to take it easy thereafter. After the race he tweeted a photo of his right forearm with gruesome-looking staples from wrist to elbow.

Nicky Hayden was also suffering. His close-season operation to have metalwork removed from his right wrist did not seem to have cured the problem, leading Nicky to miss the post-Jerez test. In France a sideswipe from Iannone both ended his race early and aggravated the injury.

Troubles of another kind afflicted Bradley Smith, who had switched to a new chassis at Jerez. In first

LEFT Pol Espargaro was second on the grid and third for much of the race – not bad for a rookie.

ABOVE After an awful start to the year, Alvaro Bautista finished on the podium. Here he fights with Bradley Smith.

free practice another massive crash, his third on the new equipment, saw the old frame retrieved from the workshop. The new chassis had proved to be a distraction, and one that had put Bradley not just lower down the order than he had hoped and expected, but now behind his team-mate – who was a genuine contender for both pole position and the rostrum.

It was a very cheerful rostrum. Rossi and Marquez always seem pleased to see each other. Both patently enjoy racing motorcycles and have serious respect for each other. Marquez always manages to summon some polite respect when talking about Valentino, whether or not he is present.

When Rossi remarked, a little wistfully, that he wished he could have raced against Marc when he was 21 years old, the Spaniard came back with a cute remark about the next race in Italy: 'At Mugello, Valentino will be 21 again.' For the record, Marc was 21 years and 90 days old when he won at Le Mans, making him the youngest man ever to win five premier-class races in a row, taking that record from Mike Hailwood; Mike won the first five races of 1962 on an MV Agusta at the age of 22 years and 160 days. With all of Freddie Spencer's records from the 1980s having been eclipsed, the statisticians are now having to go back an extra 20 years to measure Marc's achievements.

And now there was open debate about a question that until this race had seemed like hyperbole. It now seemed reasonable to ask openly if Marquez really could win every race of the year. The consensus among the paddock's elder statesmen, who had seen riders like Spencer as well as Mick Doohan and the young Rossi, was that the next three races were vital: the trio of grand, old, high-speed tracks – Mugello, Catalunya and Assen.

And you did not have to have been around for very long at all to know that only one man looked like he could stop the run, and that was Valentino Rossi. More importantly, after the confusing start to his year, Valentino also now clearly believed that he was the man to stop Marquez.

TOP STOPPERS

Cal Crutchlow's brake problems at Jerez highlighted the growing feeling that the standard 320mm discs were no longer up to the job. The regulations require the use of the larger 340mm size at Motegi, while the teams are given the option to use either size at Catalunya and Sepang. However, the riders' concerns, voiced at the Safety Commission, and consultation with the manufacturers, Brembo and Nissin, led to the rule being modified.

The Grand Prix Commission met the week after Le Mans – and before Mugello – and decided that the option to use either size should be extended to all tracks except Motegi, where the larger size would continue to be mandatory.

The problem arose because brake disc size (and mass) was standardised at the end of 2011 as a cost-cutting measure, but the 1,000cc bikes that arrived in 2012 were heavier than the 800s. Moreover, the weight of the 1,000s grew a year later to 160kg (over 350lb), which was 12kg (over 26lb) above the minimum weight limit for 800s.

Engineers being what they are, it was soon apparent that the 320mm discs

were marginal for the Japanese race at Motegi, leading to the decision to use a larger size for that race. A couple of years further on and those engineers have pushed the bikes onwards to the point where the brakes are now at the edge of their performance envelope at several tracks – hence the decision.

It should be noted that the bigger brakes do not provide any increase in stopping power as the pad-to-disc swept area is unchanged. However, the extra material in the discs acts as a heat sink and is able to store the heat energy generated without the discs exceeding their safe operating temperature limit.

ABOVE AND RIGHT
All smiles on the podium from regulars Marquez and Rossi plus Alvaro Bautista enjoying just his third visit.

MONSTER ENERGY GRAND PRIX DE FRANCE
LE MANS
ROUND 5
MAY 18

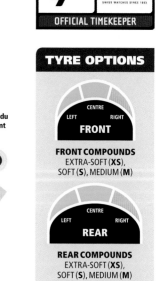

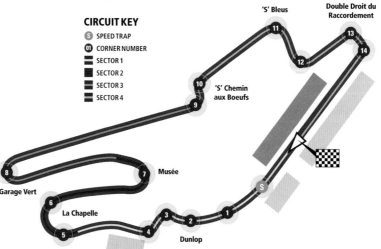

CIRCUIT KEY
- Ⓢ SPEED TRAP
- ⓪① CORNER NUMBER
- ▬ SECTOR 1
- ▬ SECTOR 2
- ▬ SECTOR 3
- ▬ SECTOR 4

'S' Bleus
Double Droit du Raccordement
'S' Chemin aux Boeufs
Musée
Garage Vert
La Chapelle
Dunlop

TYRE OPTIONS

FRONT
CENTRE
LEFT RIGHT

FRONT COMPOUNDS
EXTRA-SOFT (**XS**),
SOFT (**S**), MEDIUM (**M**)

REAR
CENTRE
LEFT RIGHT

REAR COMPOUNDS
EXTRA-SOFT (**XS**),
SOFT (**S**), MEDIUM (**M**)

SEVERITY RATING
<MILD   SEVERE>

BRIDGESTONE

RACE RESULTS

CIRCUIT LENGTH 2.597 miles
NO. OF LAPS 28
RACE DISTANCE 72.812 miles
WEATHER Dry, 23°C
TRACK TEMPERATURE 42°C
WINNER Marc Marquez
FASTEST LAP 1m 33.548s,
100.041mph, Marc Marquez (record)
PREVIOUS LAP RECORD 1m 33.617s,
99.979mph, Dani Pedrosa, 2011

QUALIFYING

	Rider	Nation	Motorcycle	Team	Time	Pole +
1	Marquez	SPA	Honda	Repsol Honda Team	1m 32.042s	
2	Espargaro P	SPA	Yamaha	Monster Yamaha Tech3	1m 32.734s	0.692s
3	Dovizioso	ITA	Ducati	Ducati Team	1m 32.755s	0.831s
4	Bradl	GER	Honda	LCR Honda MotoGP	1m 32.846s	0.804s
5	Rossi	ITA	Yamaha	Movistar Yamaha MotoGP	1m 32.873s	0.831s
6	Lorenzo	SPA	Yamaha	Movistar Yamaha MotoGP	1m 32.899s	0.857s
7	Bautista	SPA	Honda	GO&FUN Honda Gresini	1m 33.006s	0.964s
8	Espargaro A	SPA	Yamaha	NGM Forward Racing	1m 33.015s	0.973s
9	Pedrosa	SPA	Honda	Repsol Honda Team	1m 33.023s	0.981s
10	Smith	GBR	Yamaha	Monster Yamaha Tech3	1m 33.058s	1.016s
11	Iannone	ITA	Ducati	Pramac Racing	1m 33.102s	1.060s
12	Crutchlow	GBR	Ducati	Ducati Team	1m 33.315s	1.273s
13	Hayden	USA	Honda	Drive M7 Aspar	1m 33.859s	Q1
14	Hernandez	COL	Ducati	Energy T.I. Pramac Racing	1m 33.999s	Q1
15	Edwards	USA	Yamaha	NGM Forward Racing	1m 34.203s	Q1
16	Redding	GBR	Honda	GO&FUN Honda Gresini	1m 34.233s	Q1
17	Aoyama	JPN	Honda	Drive M7 Aspar	1m 34.457s	Q1
18	Abraham	CZE	Honda	Cardion AB Motoracing	1m 34.880s	Q1
19	Barbera	SPA	Avintia	Avintia Racing	1m 35.499s	Q1
20	Parkes	AUS	PBM	Paul Bird Motorsport	1m 35.795s	Q1
21	Laverty	GBR	PBM	Paul Bird Motorsport	1m 35.932s	Q1
22	Di Meglio	FRA	Avintia	Avintia Racing	1m 36.163s	Q1

1 MARC MARQUEZ
It looked as if Marc was in trouble when he ran off the track avoiding Lorenzo on the first lap and dropped back to 10th, but he calmly worked his way to the front of the pack. He took the lead when Rossi made an error and never gave him a chance to repass.

2 VALENTINO ROSSI
Took the lead on the fourth lap and opened up a one-second lead. When Marquez caught him, Rossi ran wide and gifted the Spaniard the lead. Annoyed at his mistake but looked and sounded more like his old self.

3 ALVARO BAUTISTA
Just when you thought he was a safe bet for unemployment, Alvaro got his first rostrum since Misano 2012 – and Team Gresini's first in the colours of its current sponsor.

4 POL ESPARGARO
The outstanding satellite team performance of the season so far. Qualified on the front row for the first time, ran second for five laps and third for seven laps, then held off Pedrosa in the closing stages and beat his team-mate handily. A massive confidence booster.

5 DANI PEDROSA
Had surgery on his right arm to relieve arm pump after Jerez. It did not look a problem until qualifying, where Dani finished ninth and said he could not push because of the operation. After the race, his team blamed the surgery while Dani blamed the front tyre.

6 JORGE LORENZO
Another unpleasant weekend. Jorge could not do the lap times that practice and qualifying indicated were possible. Beaten in the race not just by his team-mate but also by a satellite team Yamaha.

7 STEFAN BRADL
His race was compromised by a rear-suspension change to improve edge grip, but after six laps he found they had gone in the wrong direction.

8 ANDREA DOVIZIOSO
Brilliant in qualifying and at the start of the race, but reality intruded and he faded mid-race – as expected.

9 ALEIX ESPARGARO
Expected more but still finished as top Open bike. His main problem was set-up of the electronics.

10 BRADLEY SMITH
He made a brave charge round the outside at the first corner, but was again compromised by a lack of side grip. Made a big change to the rear of the bike for the race, and took a while to come to terms with it.

11 CAL CRUTCHLOW
Much happier than you might expect. Needed a finish and pleasantly surprised by the race pace he could run. Only three seconds behind his team-mate.

LAP CHART

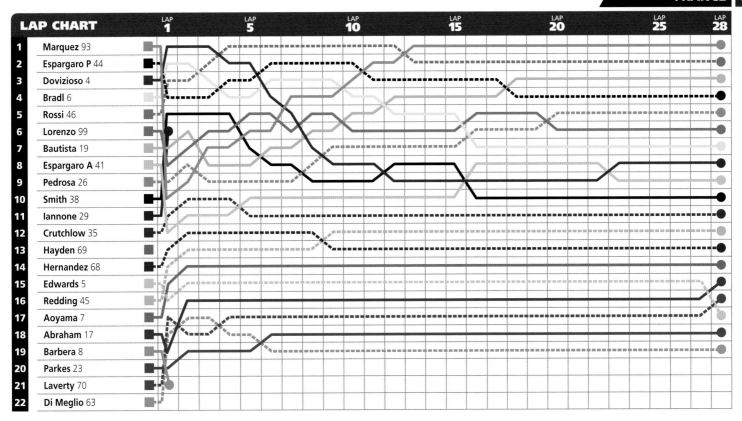

		LAP 1	LAP 5	LAP 10	LAP 15	LAP 20	LAP 25	LAP 28
1	Marquez 93							
2	Espargaro P 44							
3	Dovizioso 4							
4	Bradl 6							
5	Rossi 46							
6	Lorenzo 99							
7	Bautista 19							
8	Espargaro A 41							
9	Pedrosa 26							
10	Smith 38							
11	Iannone 29							
12	Crutchlow 35							
13	Hayden 69							
14	Hernandez 68							
15	Edwards 5							
16	Redding 45							
17	Aoyama 7							
18	Abraham 17							
19	Barbera 8							
20	Parkes 23							
21	Laverty 70							
22	Di Meglio 63							

RACE

	Rider	Motorcycle	Race time	Time +	Fastest lap	Avg. speed	
1	Marquez	Honda	44m 03.925s		1m 33.548s	99.1mph	S/S
2	Rossi	Yamaha	44m 05.411s	1.486s	1m 33.878s	99.0mph	S/S
3	Bautista	Honda	44m 07.069s	3.144s	1m 33.900s	99.0mph	S/S
4	Espargaro P	Yamaha	44m 07.642s	3.717s	1m 33.970s	99.0mph	S/S
5	Pedrosa	Honda	44m 08.002s	4.077s	1m 33.668s	99.0mph	S/S
6	Lorenzo	Yamaha	44m 11.013s	7.088s	1m 33.977s	98.9mph	S/S
7	Bradl	Honda	44m 15.452s	11.527s	1m 34.017s	98.7mph	S/S
8	Dovizioso	Ducati	44m 26.028s	22.103s	1m 34.172s	98.3mph	S/S
9	Espargaro A	Yamaha	44m 26.551s	22.626s	1m 34.426s	98.2mph	S/S
10	Smith	Yamaha	44m 27.033s	23.108s	1m 34.246s	98.2mph	S/S
11	Crutchlow	Ducati	44m 29.705s	25.780s	1m 34.455s	98.2mph	S/S
12	Redding	Honda	44m 43.448s	39.523s	1m 34.886s	97.7mph	S/XS
13	Hernandez	Ducati	44m 46.469s	42.544s	1m 34.949s	97.6mph	S/S
14	Aoyama	Honda	44m 46.661s	42.736s	1m 34.959s	97.6mph	S/XS
15	Abraham	Honda	45m 00.569s	56.644s	1m 35.270s	97.1mph	M/XS
16	Laverty	PBM	45m 18.048s	1m 14.123s	1m 36.087s	96.4mph	S/S
17	Edwards	Yamaha	45m 23.648s	1m 19.723s	1m 35.128s	96.2mph	S/XS
18	Parkes	PBM	45m 34.859s	1m 30.934s	1m 36.272s	95.8mph	S/S
19	Di Meglio	Avintia	45m 38.446s	1m 34.521s	1m 36.759s	95.7mph	S/XS
NF	Iannone	Ducati	1m 41.148s	27 laps	–	92.5mph	S/XS
NF	Barbera	Avintia	1m 46.213s	27 laps	–	88.1mph	S/XS
NF	Hayden	Honda	–	–	–	–	S/XS

CHAMPIONSHIP

	Rider	Nation	Team	Points
1	Marquez	SPA	Repsol Honda Team	125
2	Pedrosa	SPA	Repsol Honda Team	83
3	Rossi	ITA	Movistar Yamaha MotoGP	81
4	Dovizioso	ITA	Ducati Team	53
5	Lorenzo	SPA	Movistar Yamaha MotoGP	45
6	Bradl	GER	LCR Honda MotoGP	39
7	Espargaro P	SPA	Monster Yamaha Tech3	38
8	Espargaro A	SPA	NGM Forward Racing	37
9	Smith	GBR	Monster Yamaha Tech3	34
10	Bautista	SPA	GO&FUN Honda Gresini	26
11	Iannone	ITA	Pramac Racing	25
12	Hayden	USA	Drive M7 Aspar	23
13	Aoyama	JPN	Drive M7 Aspar	21
14	Redding	GBR	GO&FUN Honda Gresini	18
15	Hernandez	COL	Energy T.I. Pramac Racing	16
16	Crutchlow	GBR	Ducati Team	15
17	Abraham	CZE	Cardion AB Motoracing	9
18	Edwards	USA	NGM Forward Racing	7
19	Petrucci	ITA	Ioda Racing Project	2
20	Barbera	SPA	Avintia Racing	2
21	Parkes	AUS	Paul Bird Motorsport	1

12 SCOTT REDDING
Finished second in the Open Class and top Honda RCV1000R, plus he learned a good deal about making the tyres last.

13 YONNY HERNANDEZ
Points again, but frustrated with the way the bike continued to lose grip and understeer after a few laps.

14 HIROSHI AOYAMA
Made up three places in the first two laps, then had a lonely race. Could not match his practice pace, probably, he thought, because of the warmer weather's effect on the soft tyre.

15 KAREL ABRAHAM
Not a good weekend. He ran 16th from the second lap to the last corner, where he passed Edwards – whose motor had cut. 'Beating Colin should be more fun,' was his grim comment.

16 MICHAEL LAVERTY
This was the Ulsterman's fourth 16th place in a row.

17 COLIN EDWARDS
Still struggling to make the bike turn and also had fuelling issues for the third race running. His engine cut out on the run to the flag and he only just got over the line. Colin later tweeted that he had over three litres of fuel left in the tank.

18 BROC PARKES
Had to use his second bike for the race, and struggled with rear grip during the second half.

19 MIKE DI MEGLIO
Used a new, shorter chassis, which seemed to help with the perennial chatter problem. However, three crashes before race day did not help anything. His main problem was rear grip, with stopping the bike a close second. Not a happy home race.

DID NOT FINISH

ANDREA IANNONE
Ran into Hayden at the Dunlop chicane on the first lap. He then crashed on the second lap.

HECTOR BARBERA
Halted by electronics problems; the bike simply stopped on the second lap as he changed up to fifth gear.

NICKY HAYDEN
Failed to score points for the first time this season when he suffered a sideswipe from Iannone.

DID NOT START

DANILO PETRUCCI
Not recovered from his arm injury sustained in warm-up for the Spanish GP. Was supposed to be replaced by Luca Scassa, but Scassa broke a leg in testing.

ITALY
ROUND 6

GRAN PREMIO D'ITALIA TIM
MUGELLO

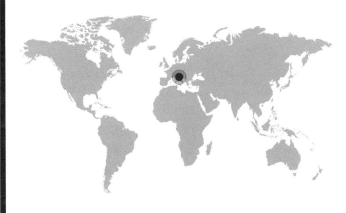

BATTLE STATIONS

Marc Marquez won again from pole but he had a race-long struggle with a resurgent Jorge Lorenzo

Just when you thought it was safe to write off Jorge Lorenzo's season, he reminded us why he is a double MotoGP World Champion. In five races so far this season, he had achieved just one rostrum finish – third in Argentina – and was already the small matter of 80 points behind Marc Marquez's perfect score. There were several reasons: his poor fitness, his dislike of the new tyres and, of course, the resurgence of team-mate Valentino Rossi.

When things do not go well, Jorge tends to take on an air of quiet vulnerability – he does not try to hide the problems. He did not look any happier than usual when he arrived at Mugello, so it was difficult to tell whether the fact that he had won the Italian GP for the past three seasons was helping him or piling on more pressure.

It was easy to forget about Jorge. There was much celebration of the fact that this was Valentino Rossi's 300th Grand Prix; there were memories of Marco Simoncelli, who was inducted as a MotoGP Legend; and there was the sight of another combative young Italian, the increasingly impressive Andrea Iannone, in the middle of the front row.

Marquez again used his second bike as well as his first to take his sixth consecutive pole position. It was not by an enormous margin and it was not really a surprise. The surprise was Iannone's second on the grid on the satellite Pramac Ducati, bettering his previous top qualifying position by the small matter of six places. 'Maniac Joe' got his fast lap behind Rossi, but Valentino made a bad mistake by changing to the soft front tyre for his final run; it did not work and he ended up tenth.

So the question remained: who could give Marquez a race? Maybe the bloke at the other end of the front row – Jorge Lorenzo.

'MY TEAM TOLD ME THAT THE AUDIENCE EXULTED FOR ALL MY OVERTAKING. THIS MAKES ME PROUD'

ANDREA IANNONE

Marquez was not quite his normal chirpy self. He admitted he had been thinking about all the crashing he did at Mugello last year, especially his ultra-high-speed get-off on the front straight – obviously not a happy memory. He would later say that this track was one of the places where his expectations were for a rostrum finish rather than the win. And at last we found out how to turn off that smile and get him to rise to the bait – by mentioning a Spanish media story about him having a special electronics package that has helped him win every race. The reply was snapped back: 'It's always been the same. I had a special engine in Moto2, the same in 125s...' He refused to say any more.

But when victory presented itself, Marquez could not resist risking everything to obtain it. It was racing at its very best. It was sport at its very best.

Lorenzo took the lead on the first lap, shoving Iannone out of the way, looking like his old self only with added aggression. The only question was when Marquez would attack. The answer was seven laps from home, with a classic Mugello slipstreaming move on the front straight. That was it, surely? No, it was not.

There is something life-affirming about a great champion getting off the canvas, rediscovering his will to win and taking the fight to the young gun. Jorge Lorenzo fought tooth and nail to extend his winning run at Mugello but came up short, just, after an epic battle over those final laps. There were repeated slipstreaming battles on the fastest straight on the calendar and repeated outbraking attempts at the end of it. There were passes and repasses in all of the circuit's high-speed S-bends (to call them chicanes is an insult). Every time Marc

OPPOSITE Pol Espargaro and Stefan Bradl both had two big crashes. Pol's were on Friday and Saturday, Stefan's both on Sunday.

LEFT Andrea Iannone followed up his best ever qualifying by leading his home GP.

ABOVE Nicky Hayden's old wrist injury got so bad that he had to miss the race.

ABOVE AND BELOW The fight between Jorge Lorenzo and Marc Marquez was racing at its best, and decided only at the final corner when Lorenzo ran wide.

OPPOSITE Rossi's return to the Mugello podium went down well with the locals.

went past, Jorge hit straight back: he passed the Honda down Casanova Savelli; he passed at the downhill right of Correntaio; he even passed at the end of the straight. There were at least 15 passes – and the very real prospect that Marquez's perfect run might come to an end.

The battle was decided after the slipstreaming move by Marquez that put him in the lead at the start of the final lap. He had enough of a lead to induce a small mistake from Lorenzo on the final corner and he stretched the lead to all of a tenth of a second at the flag. It was so gripping, so close to the edge, that Valentino Rossi's ride from tenth on the grid to third place hardly registered. The Italian crowd even forgot to boo Lorenzo on the rostrum.

What got Jorge back to form? As usual, the answer was the aggregation of small gains: less spinning, a little more wheelie control, a track he and the bike like, better physical condition. There was also the matter of Yamaha's new clutchless downshift system that had arrived in secret at the start of the year. Rossi's side of the garage got it working for them instantly; Jorge's did not. When he finally got it set up to enable him to get into corners properly, he judged the benefit to be at least half a second a lap.

The seamless-shift gearbox that arrived towards the end of 2013 was completely standard on the downshift, requiring use of the clutch. For 2014 the gearbox acquired clutchless operation – not, note, seamless – for downward shifts, making the bike much more stable going into corners.

Marquez's worried look before the start at Mugello was genuine. He knew that Jorge would be fast at the Tuscan circuit – and he also knew that meant Jorge would be fast at the next two circuits on the calendar.

PERFECT PLANNING

At the end of the fourth and final free practice session, Marc Marquez spent several laps shadowing Jorge Lorenzo. The Yamaha rider was putting in his usual long run, reeling off impeccable race-pace laps with Marquez right on his back wheel. There was no attempt to pass, as Marc usually does in that situation and as he had done in identical circumstances in Texas. What was he doing?

The answer became apparent after the race. The Honda team had altered the top-gear ratio after warm-up to enable Marc to take advantage of the Yamaha's slipstream to make a pass at the end of the front straight. In free practice Marquez had been observing the Yamaha, checking its strengths, and he had seen that he no longer had a top-speed advantage. It was another example of brilliant strategic thinking from Marquez and his team.

There was one surprising implication in that decision: the Honda no longer had the ability to motor past the Yamaha on a long straight. That tied in with what we had seen in Qatar. In Argentina, too, Pedrosa had said that his bike finished

several races during 2013 with a tiny amount of fuel left. With a litre less in the tank for 2014, it appeared that the Honda had finally reached the limit of its fuel efficiency – not an issue that has ever troubled HRC in the MotoGP era.

This also illustrated what a good job Yamaha's engineers had done. Rossi was happy to point this out, making specific reference to the drivability of the engine out of slow corners, yet without any compromise in fuel efficiency.

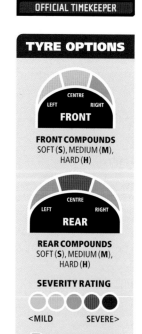

GRAN PREMIO D'ITALIA TIM
MUGELLO
ROUND 6
JUNE 1

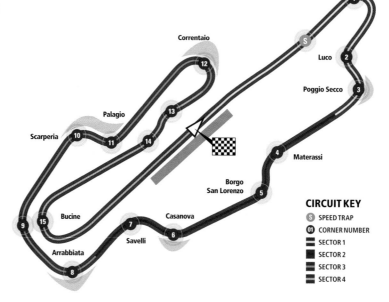

Circuit map with labels: San Donato, Correntaio, Luco, Poggio Secco, Palagio, Scarperia, Materassi, Borgo San Lorenzo, Bucine, Casanova, Savelli, Arrabbiata

CIRCUIT KEY
- (S) SPEED TRAP
- (01) CORNER NUMBER
- SECTOR 1
- SECTOR 2
- SECTOR 3
- SECTOR 4

TYRE OPTIONS

FRONT
CENTRE / LEFT / RIGHT

FRONT COMPOUNDS
SOFT (S), MEDIUM (M), HARD (H)

REAR
CENTRE / LEFT / RIGHT

REAR COMPOUNDS
SOFT (S), MEDIUM (M), HARD (H)

SEVERITY RATING
<MILD   SEVERE>

BRIDGESTONE

RACE RESULTS

CIRCUIT LENGTH 3.259 miles
NO. OF LAPS 23
RACE DISTANCE 74.959 miles
WEATHER Dry, 26°C
TRACK TEMPERATURE 45°C
WINNER Marc Marquez
FASTEST LAP 1m 47.892s, 108.740mph, Marc Marquez
LAP RECORD 1m 47.639s, 108.989mph, Marc Marquez, 2013

QUALIFYING

	Rider	Nation	Motorcycle	Team	Time	Pole +
1	Marquez	SPA	Honda	Repsol Honda Team	1m 47.270s	
2	Iannone	ITA	Ducati	Pramac Racing	1m 47.450s	0.180s
3	Lorenzo	SPA	Yamaha	Movistar Yamaha MotoGP	1m 47.521s	0.251s
4	Pedrosa	SPA	Honda	Repsol Honda Team	1m 47.584s	0.314s
5	Espargaro P	SPA	Yamaha	Monster Yamaha Tech3	1m 47.612s	0.342s
6	Crutchlow	GBR	Ducati	Ducati Team	1m 47.659s	0.389s
7	Smith	GBR	Yamaha	Monster Yamaha Tech3	1m 47.681s	0.411s
8	Dovizioso	ITA	Ducati	Ducati Team	1m 47.754s	0.484s
9	Bradl	GER	Honda	LCR Honda MotoGP	1m 47.765s	0.495s
10	Rossi	ITA	Yamaha	Movistar Yamaha MotoGP	1m 47.791s	0.521s
11	Bautista	SPA	Honda	GO&FUN Honda Gresini	1m 48.132s	0.862s
12	Espargaro A	SPA	Yamaha	NGM Forward Racing	1m 48.218s	0.948s
13	Hernandez	COL	Ducati	Energy T.I. Pramac Racing	1m 48.722s	Q1
14	Redding	GBR	Honda	GO&FUN Honda Gresini	1m 48.754s	Q1
15	Pirro	ITA	Ducati	Ducati Team	1m 48.794s	Q1
16	Abraham	CZE	Honda	Cardion AB Motoracing	1m 48.894s	Q1
17	Aoyama	JPN	Honda	Drive M7 Aspar	1m 49.505s	Q1
18	Edwards	USA	Yamaha	NGM Forward Racing	1m 49.780s	Q1
19	Barbera	SPA	Avintia	Avintia Racing	1m 49.932s	Q1
20	Laverty	GBR	PBM	Paul Bird Motorsport	1m 50.505s	Q1
21	Di Meglio	FRA	Avintia	Avintia Racing	1m 50.515s	Q1
22	Parkes	AUS	PBM	Paul Bird Motorsport	1m 50.875s	Q1
23	Fabrizio	ITA	ART	Octo IodaRacing Team	1m 53.116s	Q1
24	Hayden	USA	Honda	Drive M7 Aspar	1m 55.369s	Q1

1 MARC MARQUEZ
Pole again, keeping his 100 per cent record, but Marc looked less confident than usual. In the race he had to deal with a stunning fight from Lorenzo that saw them swap places a dozen times in the last eight laps. Had trouble with the front tyre but, crucially, had an altered top gear so he could take advantage of the slipstream.

2 JORGE LORENZO
By far his best race of the year. Good qualifying and a magnificent fight for the win with Marquez that went right to the last corner of the last lap.

3 VALENTINO ROSSI
Choosing the wrong front tyre for his final qualifying run put him 10th on the grid but he fought up to fifth by lap two, though by the time he was in third place the front pair had gone. To the joy of his home crowd, Vale stood on the rostrum in his 300th GP.

4 DANI PEDROSA
Still handicapped by the arm-pump operation on his right forearm. Again, Dani did not get going until late in the race, but was never in range of a rostrum finish.

5 POL ESPARGARO
Impressive in qualifying and the race. Redeemed himself after two big crashes in practice and qualifying, and happy to be 'best of the rest' behind four factory bikes. A major dust-up with Iannone meant that he could not get on terms with Pedrosa.

6 ANDREA DOVIZIOSO
Another very clever and courageous ride. The Ducati's straight-line speed and strong braking helped at Turn 1, but the bike's reluctance to turn did not help with Mugello's proliferation of fast changes of direction.

7 ANDREA IANNONE
A brilliant career-best second on the grid, thanks to the softer tyre, put Andrea in the position to fight at the front for the first laps. He then battled with Pedrosa before being caught by Dovi as his tyre faded in the final seven laps.

8 ALVARO BAUTISTA
Struggled with the harder option front tyre – a standard problem. Tried the old fork but to no avail, leaving rider and team puzzled by their inconsistency.

9 ALEIX ESPARGARO
Like his team-mate, struggled the entire meeting with electronics in general and traction control in particular.

10 YONNY HERNANDEZ
His best result for the Pramac team, which he called 'the best possible with this bike' – a 2013 version of the Ducati Desmosedici.

11 MICHELE PIRRO
Rode the 2014 'lab bike' and did what he is employed to do (but did not at Jerez) by bringing the bike home, gathering plenty of data on the way.

LAP CHART

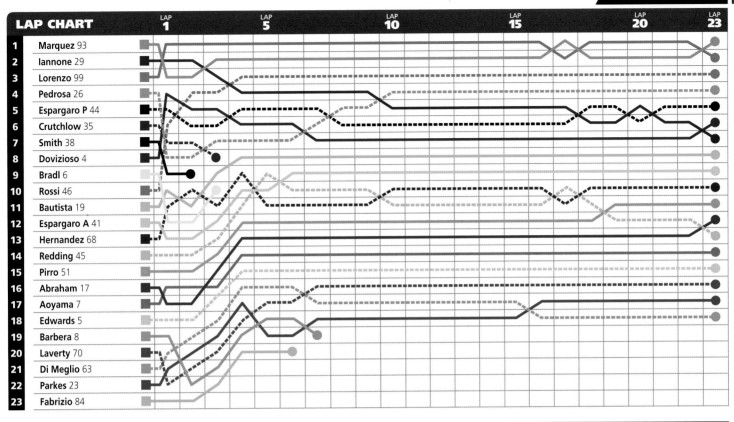

		LAP 1	LAP 5	LAP 10	LAP 15	LAP 20	LAP 23
1	Marquez 93						
2	Iannone 29						
3	Lorenzo 99						
4	Pedrosa 26						
5	Espargaro P 44						
6	Crutchlow 35						
7	Smith 38						
8	Dovizioso 4						
9	Bradl 6						
10	Rossi 46						
11	Bautista 19						
12	Espargaro A 41						
13	Hernandez 68						
14	Redding 45						
15	Pirro 51						
16	Abraham 17						
17	Aoyama 7						
18	Edwards 5						
19	Barbera 8						
20	Laverty 70						
21	Di Meglio 63						
22	Parkes 23						
23	Fabrizio 84						

RACE

	Rider	Motorcycle	Race time	Time +	Fastest lap	Avg. speed	
1	Marquez	Honda	41m 38.254s		1m 47.892s	108.0mph	M/M
2	Lorenzo	Yamaha	41m 38.375s	0.121s	1m 47.984s	108.0mph	M/M
3	Rossi	Yamaha	41m 40.942s	2.688s	1m 48.084s	107.9mph	M/M
4	Pedrosa	Honda	41m 52.300s	14.046s	1m 48.461s	107.4mph	M/M
5	Espargaro P	Yamaha	41m 53.857s	15.603s	1m 48.569s	107.3mph	M/M
6	Dovizioso	Ducati	41m 55.296s	17.042s	1m 48.797s	107.2mph	M/M
7	Iannone	Ducati	41m 55.383s	17.129s	1m 48.407s	107.2mph	M/S
8	Bautista	Honda	42m 05.661s	27.407s	1m 48.846s	106.8mph	M/M
9	Espargaro A	Yamaha	42m 20.140s	41.886s	1m 49.689s	106.2mph	M/M
10	Hernandez	Ducati	42m 23.466s	45.212s	1m 49.126s	106.1mph	M/S
11	Pirro	Ducati	42m 23.687s	45.433s	1m 49.764s	106.1mph	M/S
12	Abraham	Honda	42m 24.085s	45.831s	1m 49.865s	106.1mph	M/S
13	Redding	Honda	42m 24.093s	45.839s	1m 49.642s	106.1mph	M/S
14	Aoyama	Honda	42m 25.088s	46.834s	1m 49.816s	106.0mph	M/S
15	Edwards	Yamaha	42m 47.808s	1m 09.554s	1m 50.586s	105.1mph	M/S
16	Laverty	PBM	42m 56.043s	1m 17.789s	1m 51.019s	104.7mph	M/S
17	Parkes	PBM	43m 13.285s	1m 35.031s	1m 51.702s	104.0mph	M/S
18	Di Meglio	Avintia	43m 15.755s	1m 37.501s	1m 51.064s	104.0mph	M/S
NF	Barbera	Avintia	13m 13.885s	16 laps	1m 51.022s	103.4mph	M/S
NF	Fabrizio	ART	11m 33.997s	17 laps	1m 51.064s	101.4mph	M/S
NF	Crutchlow	Ducati	5m 34.826s	20 laps	1m 49.233s	105.1mph	M/M
NF	Bradl	Honda	5m 35.729s	20 laps	1m 49.208s	104.8mph	M/M
NF	Smith	Yamaha	3m 45.941s	21 laps	1m 49.481s	103.8mph	M/M

CHAMPIONSHIP

	Rider	Nation	Team	Points
1	Marquez	SPA	Repsol Honda Team	150
2	Rossi	ITA	Movistar Yamaha MotoGP	97
3	Pedrosa	SPA	Repsol Honda Team	96
4	Lorenzo	SPA	Movistar Yamaha MotoGP	65
5	Dovizioso	ITA	Ducati Team	63
6	Espargaro P	SPA	Monster Yamaha Tech3	49
7	Espargaro A	SPA	NGM Forward Racing	44
8	Bradl	GER	LCR Honda MotoGP	39
9	Bautista	SPA	GO&FUN Honda Gresini	34
	Smith	GBR	Monster Yamaha Tech3	34
	Iannone	ITA	Pramac Racing	34
12	Hayden	USA	Drive M7 Aspar	23
	Aoyama	JPN	Drive M7 Aspar	23
14	Hernandez	COL	Energy T.I. Pramac Racing	22
15	Redding	GBR	GO&FUN Honda Gresini	21
16	Crutchlow	GBR	Ducati Team	15
17	Abraham	CZE	Cardion AB Motoracing	13
18	Edwards	USA	NGM Forward Racing	8
19	Pirro	ITA	Ducati Team	5
20	Petrucci	ITA	Ioda Racing Project	2
	Barbera	SPA	Avintia Racing	2
22	Parkes	AUS	Paul Bird Motorsport	1

12 KAREL ABRAHAM
Extremely happy with his best race for a couple of years. Happy to be top customer Honda rider.

13 SCOTT REDDING
Started the race well and even overtook Aleix Espargaro, but could not make a break on the Ducatis; he broke his screen trying, so suffered from turbulence and bad aerodynamics.

14 HIROSHI AOYAMA
Raced with a set-up he first tried in warm-up and was caught out by the change in temperature.

15 COLIN EDWARDS
Got a new chassis and relieved to finish the race after recent fuelling problems.

16 MICHAEL LAVERTY
This was the fifth time in six races that he just missed out on opening his points account for the year.

17 BROC PARKES
Missing a whole session thanks to the weather on Friday did not help.

18 MIKE DI MEGLIO
Happier with the bike but still having problems with his fitness.

DID NOT FINISH

HECTOR BARBERA
Found his gearbox contained a variable number of ratios. Only had sixth going into Turn 1 and then got them all back except third, but had to retire.

MICHEL FABRIZIO
Stood in for Petrucci at short notice. Pulled out of the race as he was not back up to speed with carbon brakes.

CAL CRUTCHLOW
Lost the front on lap four and the bike scooped up Bradl.

STEFAN BRADL
Two massive crashes in short order: the first was in warm-up, then he did a 180 when hit by the falling Crutchlow's Ducati.

BRADLEY SMITH
On Bridgestone's advice he had to use the medium front tyre, with which he had only done three laps in practice. Not surprisingly, the result was a crash off the front end early in the race.

DID NOT START

NICKY HAYDEN
Pulled out after the wrist that was operated on over winter became increasingly painful, requiring further surgery.

DANILO PETRUCCI
Failed the medical test on Thursday; his arm injury from Jerez was still in plaster. Replaced, hurriedly, by Michel Fabrizio.

GP MONSTER ENERGY DE CATALUNYA
CIRCUIT DE CATALUNYA

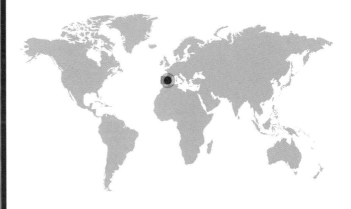

BROTHERS IN ARMS

Marc Marquez's run of pole positions finally came to an end but his winning streak did not

There were signs of hope for the rest. First, Marc Marquez came off his bike for the first time in 2014 and in the process also missed out on pole position for the first time of the year. Then, secondly, in the race, he did not look like the fastest man out there.

That man was Dani Pedrosa, whose chances of victory were ended three corners from the flag when he tagged Marquez's rear tyre with his front and ran wide. That let Valentino Rossi through for second place, which did not seem to bother Pedrosa much. He was just happy to be competitive again after two low-key races following his arm-pump surgery.

After the elegant duel of Mugello, this was a group punch-up featuring both factory Hondas and both factory Yamahas for the entire race. So far in 2014 Marquez had not made a habit of winning races by a distance, his four-second margin in Argentina having been his biggest by far – and here at Catalunya he simply could not get away from his rivals. The record book says the gap was over half a second but that was after the touch with Pedrosa; the quartet ran much closer for most of the race.

As at Mugello, Marc did not seem as confident as usual. Surely the wonder boy was not suffering from home-race nerves? No, it was just his well-founded concern that the sequence of three fast tracks – Mugello, Catalunya, Assen – would be difficult for him. He had not won at any of them in 2013 and they do not play to his strengths, especially now the Honda no longer had a massive speed advantage.

These tracks have few heavy braking areas, something the man himself identifies as a strength. His liking for running his front wheel up the inside kerb of a corner while pushing the front and sliding the rear also does not

ABOVE Jorge Lorenzo maintained the renewed competitiveness he showed in the previous race; his new crash helmet design was for sponsor Alfa Romeo.

RIGHT The race was a case of the factory bikes out in front and Stefan Bradl hanging on to them for as long as he could.

OPPOSITE The injured Danilo Petrucci was replaced by Michel Fabrizio on the Ioda Aprilia.

pay at these tracks. At Catalunya the high kerbs make that technique difficult – there is insufficient room for 'knee, shoulder and everything' – while at Mugello and Assen it is better to take the conventional lines.

So Catalunya is a track where Marc does not necessarily expect to win and is prepared to settle for a rostrum finish. What about the unbeaten run ending? 'It would not be a disaster,' he said before the race. Which is more or less what he said two weeks previously.

'It's impossible to be fastest all the time,' said Marquez after his first fall of the season in final qualifying. He crashed on his last flying lap trying to get back ahead of team-mate Dani Pedrosa, who took his first pole of the season and did not disguise his pleasure at being fastest at home. Jorge Lorenzo was second on the grid and Marc ended up third. He knew he got into the Turn 1 braking zone too hot but stated, 'I say OK, it's the last lap...'

Marquez did not appear bothered in any way by the crash: 'It was my fault, the team did a perfect strategy.' In fact he was much more interested in his little brother Alex's first pole in the Moto3 class: 'I think I'm happier than sometimes when I'm on pole, I'm very proud of him.' This was delivered with the usual boyish charm and was an appealing contrast to the younger sibling's rather gruff persona.

It all felt like a family affair. Dani Pedrosa is from a town just a mile or two down the motorway to Barcelona and happily pointed at his fan club's stickers on his crash helmet; that is about as demonstrative as Dani gets and you get the impression he would be seriously offended if anyone suggested he do something as outlandish as employ a different paint job for his helmet at his home

race. The fastest Open Class man was Aleix Espargaro, who could run back from the track to his parents' house in ten minutes. Moto2 pole man Tito Rabat received the commemorative watch for that feat from his brother Jordi, who runs the family jewellery business in Barcelona.

At first it looked as if Rossi would be the man to end Marc's run of race wins, but he could not extend his lead beyond one second, and his team-mate started to drop off the pace of the other three factory bikes. Of the satellite bike riders, only Stefan Bradl was able to hang on to the works machines for any length of time.

Then the top four were all brought back together by a strange moment at just over two-thirds distance after both Hondas passed Rossi at Turn 1 and then hands went up and Rossi was waved through. At first it looked like the two Honda riders had reverted to the old way of telling race direction that rain was falling. In fact there had been a yellow flag at Turn 1 for Mike di Meglio's crash and Marquez was anxious not to be penalised. In those couple of seconds Lorenzo was able to close up.

Having given away the lead, Marquez immediately retook it and, as Lorenzo faded again, came under attack from his team-mate. The last lap was frantic and the team-mates swapped position four times before their contact. It happened at the first of the three right-handers that conclude the lap. Marquez rode a much tighter, more defensive line than normal and Pedrosa, going for a gap that was not there, did well to only clip Marc's rear tyre as he ran wide. Was it a dirty move? Pedrosa gave no indication that he thought so, saying that it was normal to close the door on the final lap. Marc saw fit to say that Dani was faster than him on the day, while the man himself just looked delighted to be competitive again.

ABOVE Andrea Iannone and the Pramac team look serious on the grid. They knew it was going to be a tough race for the Ducatis.

BELOW This was a race that Dani Pedrosa could have won, but a last-lap tyre kiss with Marquez relegated him to third.

OPPOSITE Stefan Bradl was a fine fifth – a great comeback after his disastrous Mugello.

HONDA CELEBRATES 100 WINS IN MotoGP CLASS

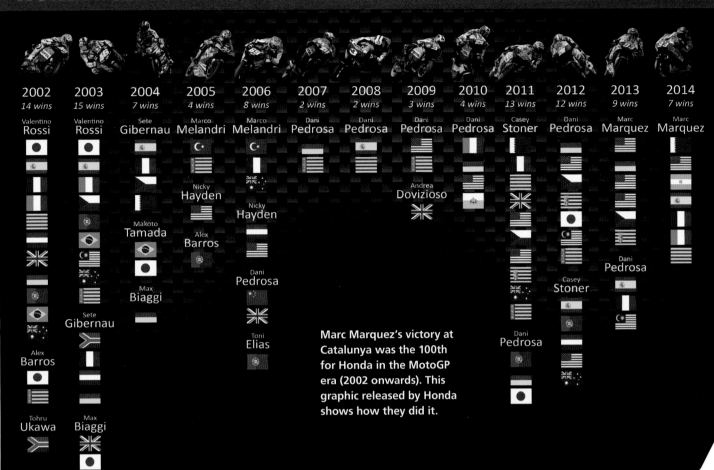

2002	2003	2004	2005	2006	2007	2008	2009	2010	2011	2012	2013	2014
14 wins	15 wins	7 wins	4 wins	8 wins	2 wins	2 wins	3 wins	4 wins	13 wins	12 wins	9 wins	7 wins

| Valentino Rossi | Valentino Rossi | Sete Gibernau | Marco Melandri | Marco Melandri | Dani Pedrosa | Dani Pedrosa | Dani Pedrosa | Dani Pedrosa | Casey Stoner | Dani Pedrosa | Marc Marquez | Marc Marquez |

Nicky Hayden

Makoto Tamada

Nicky Hayden

Andrea Dovizioso

Alex Barros

Max Biaggi

Alex Barros

Casey Stoner

Sete Gibernau

Dani Pedrosa

Dani Pedrosa

Alex Barros

Toni Elias

Dani Pedrosa

Tohru Ukawa

Max Biaggi

Marc Marquez's victory at Catalunya was the 100th for Honda in the MotoGP era (2002 onwards). This graphic released by Honda shows how they did it.

GP MONSTER ENERGY DE CATALUNYA
CIRCUIT DE CATALUNYA
ROUND 7
JUNE 15

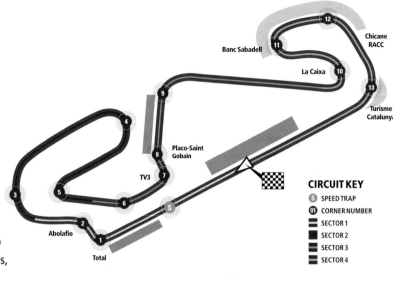

RACE RESULTS

CIRCUIT LENGTH 2.937 miles

NO. OF LAPS 25

RACE DISTANCE 73.431 miles

WEATHER Dry, 22°C

TRACK TEMPERATURE 34°C

WINNER Marc Marquez

FASTEST LAP 1m 42.182s, 103.458mph, Marc Marquez (record)

PREVIOUS LAP RECORD 1m 42.358s, 103.304mph, Dani Pedrosa, 2008

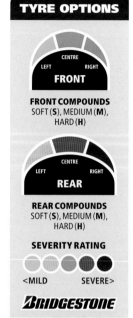

TYRE OPTIONS

FRONT

FRONT COMPOUNDS
SOFT (**S**), MEDIUM (**M**), HARD (**H**)

REAR

REAR COMPOUNDS
SOFT (**S**), MEDIUM (**M**), HARD (**H**)

SEVERITY RATING

<MILD   SEVERE>

BRIDGESTONE

CIRCUIT KEY

- **S** SPEED TRAP
- **01** CORNER NUMBER
- SECTOR 1
- SECTOR 2
- SECTOR 3
- SECTOR 4

QUALIFYING

	Rider	Nation	Motorcycle	Team	Time	Pole +
1	Pedrosa	SPA	Honda	Repsol Honda Team	1m 40.985s	
2	Lorenzo	SPA	Yamaha	Movistar Yamaha MotoGP	1m 41.100s	0.115s
3	Marquez	SPA	Honda	Repsol Honda Team	1m 41.135s	0.150s
4	Bradl	GER	Honda	LCR Honda MotoGP	1m 41.220s	0.235s
5	Rossi	ITA	Yamaha	Movistar Yamaha MotoGP	1m 41.290s	0.305s
6	Espargaro A	SPA	Yamaha	NGM Forward Racing	1m 41.308s	0.323s
7	Dovizioso	ITA	Ducati	Ducati Team	1m 41.337s	0.352s
8	Smith	GBR	Yamaha	Monster Yamaha Tech3	1m 41.491s	0.506s
9	Hernandez	COL	Ducati	Energy T.I. Pramac Racing	1m 41.671s	0.686s
10	Espargaro P	SPA	Yamaha	Monster Yamaha Tech3	1m 41.677s	0.692s
11	Iannone	ITA	Ducati	Pramac Racing	1m 41.751s	0.766s
12	Bautista	SPA	Honda	GO&FUN Honda Gresini	1m 42.024s	1.039s
13	Crutchlow	GBR	Ducati	Ducati Team	1m 42.578s	Q1
14	Redding	GBR	Honda	GO&FUN Honda Gresini	1m 42.730s	Q1
15	Pirro	ITA	Ducati	Ducati Team	1m 42.955s	Q1
16	Hayden	USA	Honda	Drive M7 Aspar	1m 43.043s	Q1
17	Edwards	USA	Yamaha	NGM Forward Racing	1m 43.226s	Q1
18	Abraham	CZE	Honda	Cardion AB Motoracing	1m 43.360s	Q1
19	Parkes	AUS	PBM	Paul Bird Motorsport	1m 43.530s	Q1
20	Aoyama	JPN	Honda	Drive M7 Aspar	1m 43.564s	Q1
21	Laverty	GBR	PBM	Paul Bird Motorsport	1m 43.737s	Q1
22	Barbera	SPA	Avintia	Avintia Racing	1m 44.115s	Q1
23	Di Meglio	FRA	Avintia	Avintia Racing	1m 45.012s	Q1
24	Fabrizio	ITA	ART	Octo IodaRacing Team	1m 46.214s	Q1

1 MARC MARQUEZ
Missed out on pole and had his first crash of the season yet still managed to fight off his team-mate and the factory Yamahas in one of the best races seen for years. It was also Honda's 100th MotoGP win, and little brother Alex won the Moto3 race. Not a bad home event.

2 VALENTINO ROSSI
Very happy that he led for much of the race but the novelty of simply being competitive is wearing off. Unusually for Valentino, he was outperformed on used tyres at the end of the race.

3 DANI PEDROSA
Did not seem too upset with third despite looking to be the fastest man out there; Dani's chance to win went on the last lap when he touched Marquez's rear tyre with his front and ran wide. Wanted to run up front again and did so in qualifying and the race.

4 JORGE LORENZO
Not the follow-up to the heroics of Mugello everyone was expecting. Happy to have cured most of his problems on the brakes but frustrated to have lost the advantage he had in corner speed in the vital last two corners.

5 STEFAN BRADL
A great comeback after the horror show of Mugello. Very fast all weekend and very consistent in the race for a great result, despite being the only rider to use the hard front tyre.

6 ALEIX ESPARGARO
Very happy with what he called his best race of the year, finishing only 14 seconds behind the leader and lapping at the same pace as Bradl; the only disappointment was his start.

7 POL ESPARGARO
Not as stellar a display at his home round as in the previous two races. Lack of rear grip was the problem, especially in the fast corners of the final sector. Did well to fight off Dovizioso.

8 ANDREA DOVIZIOSO
This event was a microcosm of his season so far; Dovi's finishing position looks unimpressive but the gap to the leader was halved.

9 ANDREA IANONNE
Like the other Ducati riders, he did not have an easy weekend. Always looking for grip, used the soft tyre and ran closer than expected to Dovi and Espargaro.

10 BRADLEY SMITH
A great weekend up to qualifying. Found the feel of the bike changed totally on race day, got a bad start and although lapping well at the end was too far back to make progress. Not happy.

11 YONNY HERNANDEZ
Did some clever following in practice and qualifying but struggled with the different conditions on race day.

LAP CHART

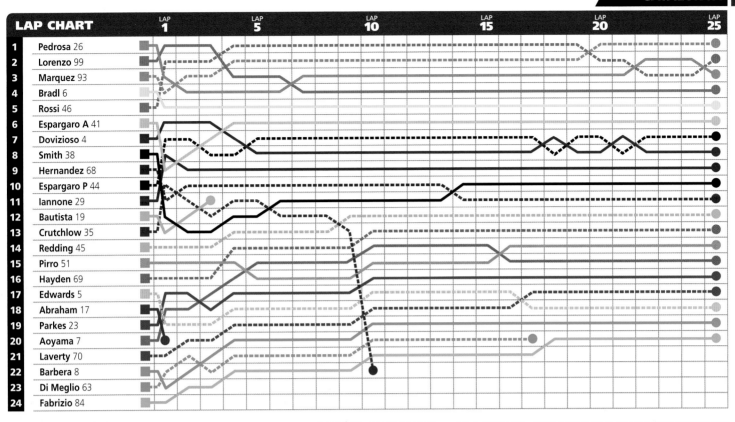

		LAP 1	LAP 5	LAP 10	LAP 15	LAP 20	LAP 25
1	Pedrosa 26						
2	Lorenzo 99						
3	Marquez 93						
4	Bradl 6						
5	Rossi 46						
6	Espargaro A 41						
7	Dovizioso 4						
8	Smith 38						
9	Hernandez 68						
10	Espargaro P 44						
11	Iannone 29						
12	Bautista 19						
13	Crutchlow 35						
14	Redding 45						
15	Pirro 51						
16	Hayden 69						
17	Edwards 5						
18	Abraham 17						
19	Parkes 23						
20	Aoyama 7						
21	Laverty 70						
22	Barbera 8						
23	Di Meglio 63						
24	Fabrizio 84						

RACE

	Rider	Motorcycle	Race time	Time +	Fastest lap	Avg. speed	
1	Marquez	Honda	42m 56.914s		1m 42.182s	102.5mph	M/M
2	Rossi	Yamaha	42m 57.426s	0.512s	1m 42.408s	102.5mph	M/M
3	Pedrosa	Honda	42m 58.748s	1.834s	1m 42.364s	102.5mph	M/M
4	Lorenzo	Yamaha	43m 01.454s	4.540s	1m 42.387s	102.4mph	M/M
5	Bradl	Honda	43m 08.062s	11.148s	1m 42.434s	102.1mph	H/M
6	Espargaro A	Yamaha	43m 11.127s	14.213s	1m 42.775s	102.0mph	M/M
7	Espargaro P	Yamaha	43m 13.041s	16.127s	1m 42.975s	101.9mph	M/M
8	Dovizioso	Ducati	43m 13.089s	16.175s	1m 43.002s	101.9mph	M/M
9	Iannone	Ducati	43m 14.954s	18.040s	1m 42.873s	101.8mph	M/S
10	Smith	Yamaha	43m 21.695s	24.781s	1m 43.416s	101.6mph	M/M
11	Hernandez	Ducati	43m 34.067s	37.153s	1m 42.942s	101.1mph	M/S
12	Hayden	Honda	43m 40.213s	43.299s	1m 44.003s	100.8mph	M/S
13	Redding	Honda	43m 40.321s	43.407s	1m 43.779s	100.8mph	M/S
14	Pirro	Ducati	43m 52.071s	55.157s	1m 44.504s	100.4mph	M/S
15	Aoyama	Honda	43m 56.105s	59.191s	1m 44.289s	100.2mph	M/S
16	Parkes	PBM	43m 57.820s	1m 00.906s	1m 44.435s	100.2mph	M/S
17	Laverty	PBM	43m 58.198s	1m 01.284s	1m 44.861s	100.2mph	M/S
18	Edwards	Yamaha	44m 03.035s	1m 06.121s	1m 44.721s	100.0mph	M/M
19	Barbera	Avintia	44m 22.109s	1m 25.195s	1m 44.850s	99.3mph	M/S
20	Fabrizio	ART	44m 37.579s	1m 40.665s	1m 46.439s	98.7mph	M/S
NF	Di Meglio	Avintia	30m 17.319s	8 laps	1m 45.163s	98.9mph	M/S
NF	Crutchlow	Ducati	18m 11.451s	15 laps	1m 43.840s	96.9mph	M/M
NF	Bautista	Honda	5m 16.507s	22 laps	1m 43.216s	100.2mph	M/M
NF	Abraham	Honda	1m 51.504s	24 laps		94.8mph	M/S

CHAMPIONSHIP

	Rider	Nation	Team	Points
1	Marquez	SPA	Repsol Honda Team	175
2	Rossi	ITA	Movistar Yamaha MotoGP	117
3	Pedrosa	SPA	Repsol Honda Team	112
4	Lorenzo	SPA	Movistar Yamaha MotoGP	78
5	Dovizioso	ITA	Ducati Team	71
6	Espargaro P	SPA	Monster Yamaha Tech3	58
7	Espargaro A	SPA	NGM Forward Racing	54
8	Bradl	GER	LCR Honda MotoGP	50
9	Iannone	ITA	Pramac Racing	41
10	Smith	GBR	Monster Yamaha Tech3	40
11	Bautista	SPA	GO&FUN Honda Gresini	34
12	Hayden	USA	Drive M7 Aspar	27
	Hernandez	COL	Energy T.I. Pramac Racing	27
14	Redding	GBR	GO&FUN Honda Gresini	24
	Aoyama	JPN	Drive M7 Aspar	24
16	Crutchlow	GBR	Ducati Team	15
17	Abraham	CZE	Cardion AB Motoracing	13
18	Edwards	USA	NGM Forward Racing	8
19	Pirro	ITA	Ducati Team	7
20	Petrucci	ITA	Ioda Racing Project	2
	Barbera	SPA	Avintia Racing	2
22	Parkes	AUS	Paul Bird Motorsport	1

12 NICKY HAYDEN
Not sure if he could race with his recently repaired wrist so qualified downfield but raced well with lots of confidence in the front.

13 SCOTT REDDING
Crossed the line as top customer Honda but relegated one place after the event for taking the short cut at Turn 1.

14 MICHELE PIRRO
Wild-card entry on the Ducati 'lab bike'. Raced with experimental electronics that gave problems from the start, but persevered to gather valuable data.

15 HIROSHI AOYAMA
Started well but lost ground late on. Kept up his record of scoring points at every round.

16 BROC PARKES
Best qualifying of the year and second-best result. A little peeved that the team again missed out on a point.

17 MICHAEL LAVERTY
Happy with the gap to the leader although the cooler temperatures on race day did not suit the bike as well as the heat of Friday and Saturday.

18 COLIN EDWARDS
Made a big change after warm-up but did not get the results he expected. Lots of wheelspin and difficulty in turning.

19 HECTOR BARBERA
Getting depressed about a bike on which reaching the flag represents the best he can do. The problem was again the rear, both going into and coming out of corners.

20 MICHEL FABRIZIO
Replaced Petrucci for the second time and managed to finish a MotoGP race for the first time since 2004.

DID NOT FINISH

MIKE DI MEGLIO
Stopped because the traction control was cutting in on every corner, perhaps because of a wiring fault.

CAL CRUTCHLOW
Like his team-mate, Cal's race was a microcosm of his season so far: problems from the start followed by a bunch of warning lights on the dash and an early retirement.

ALVARO BAUTISTA
Badly beaten up in a qualifying crash; he had to use the same tyres in the first and second sessions. On race day, the bike cut out on the third lap.

KAREL ABRAHAM
Made a mess of the start and then highsided on the first lap trying to make up for it.

GENERALI GENERALI GENERAL

IVECO TT ASSEN
TT CIRCUIT ASSEN

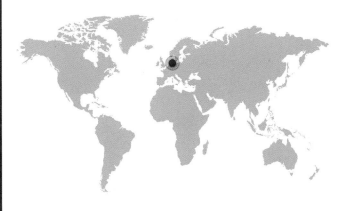

DUTCH COURAGE

Marc Marquez dealt with another new challenge – and won comfortably with Andrea Dovizioso next best

About the only type of race that Marc Marquez had yet to win was a true flag-to-flag event involving changing from wet to dry bikes (or vice versa). Australia the previous season was a 'bike-swap' race but only for safety reasons, and did not involve racing on different types of rubber. True to form, the weather at Assen conspired to try to catch out the riders, first in qualifying and then in the race. Rain in qualifying brought a little bit of history (see panel on page 105), while in the race it simply reaffirmed what we already knew – that Marquez's air of invincibility was rapidly solidifying into hard fact.

Marquez did miss out on pole position again, for he was caught out – like most of the field – by a shower just as the second and final qualifying session started. In the race the only time he looked like losing was after swapping from his wet-tyred bike to the slick-shod one. On his out-lap he had a massive moment, losing the front at the end of the back straight, running off-track and handing Andrea Dovizioso a four-second lead. This was on the seventh lap of 24, so no-one, especially Dovizioso, thought it would last. It did not. Marquez took the lead on lap 16 and pulled away, crossing the line lying flat on the tank of his Honda doing an imitation of the breaststroke.

Flag-to-flag races always throw up a strange result or two, and Dovi's second place, his best on the Ducati, probably counts as one. He had been only third-fastest Ducati rider in qualifying but managed to, in his own words, 'interpret the track quicker than the others' and, with Marquez, opened up a gap very rapidly. This was more evidence of the intelligence and precision Dovi brings to his job.

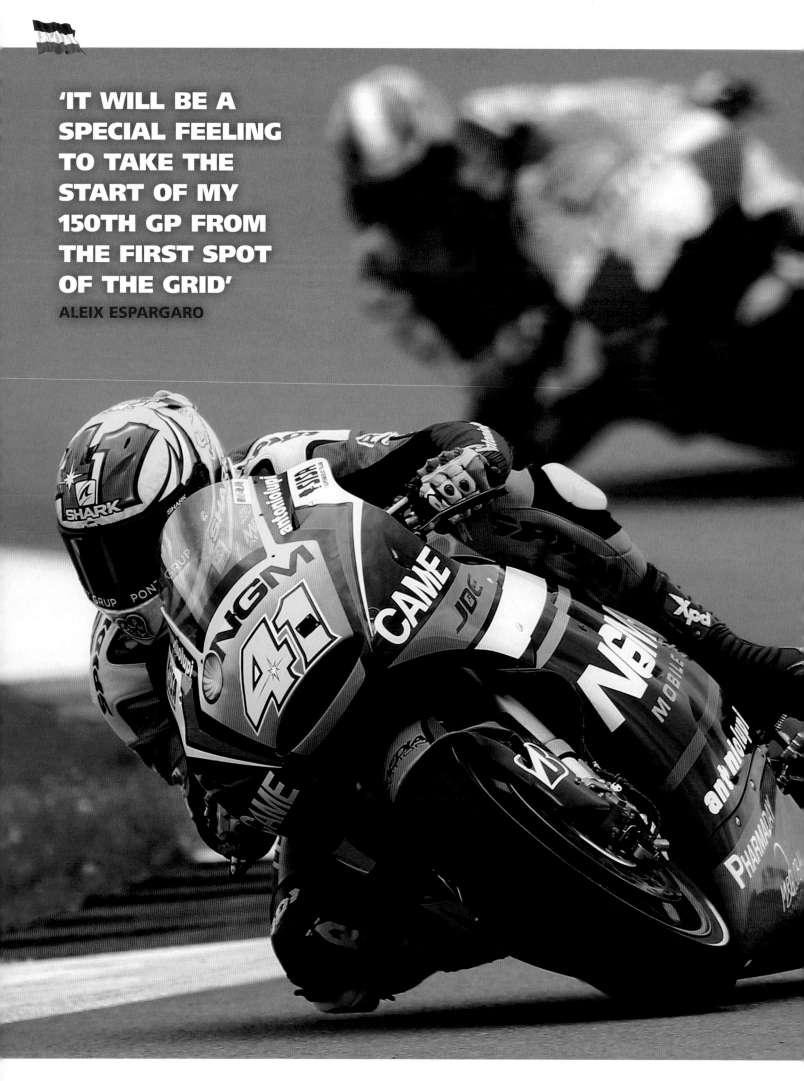

'IT WILL BE A SPECIAL FEELING TO TAKE THE START OF MY 150TH GP FROM THE FIRST SPOT OF THE GRID'

ALEIX ESPARGARO

There was a good fight for third between pole man Aleix Espargaro and Dani Pedrosa. The Forward Yamaha rider used the softer tyre to good effect but eventually Pedrosa exerted his authority to secure the position, trailing in ten seconds behind the leader.

It was a very bad weekend for the factory Yamahas. Both riders made a mess of qualifying, with Lorenzo ninth and Rossi 12th. For the race Valentino gambled on going to the grid on slicks, but on the warm-up lap he realised this was a serious error and returned for his wet-tyred bike, thus electing to start from pit lane. When the track dried quickly, requiring another bike change, his race was ruined. As for Jorge, he was haunted by memories of the previous year, when he crashed in wet conditions and broke his collarbone. He was honest and brave enough to admit that seeing rain on his visor part way through the race spooked him.

Cal Crutchlow's ninth place was down to a massively brave lap in the first qualifying session after he had endured a truly awful FP4. It did not look as if he could progress, but one truly gutsy lap put him through to Q2, where he was prepared to push harder than a lot of people and secured a second-row start. As his lap times hitherto over the weekend were starting to draw unfavourable comparisons with those in World Superbike and British Superbike, bringing mutterings of 'Melandri Syndrome' from parts of the Italian press, this was a very timely achievement. Yes, it may have been fortuitous and bore no resemblance to his potential

LEFT After starting from pole – a first for an Open Class bike – Aleix Espargaro fought Dani Pedrosa for third, and finished fourth.

ABOVE Pol Espargaro did not enjoy his first wet-weather ride on the Yamaha M1 and was the race's only retirement.

ABOVE Jorge Lorenzo met his ghosts from the 2013 Assen race and they relegated him to 13th.

BELOW Marc Marquez and Andrea Dovizioso enter pitlane to change to their dry bikes.

OPPOSITE Broc Parkes had to start on slicks, so did not have to pit and scored a career-best finish.

race pace, as Cal himself pointed out, but the qualifying lap was clever and the one that got him into Q2 was a reminder of what a tough competitor he is. It was worth recalling that Cal was on pole here the previous year.

The other somewhat unexpected success belonged to Broc Parkes of the PBM team. He had the misfortune to be knocked off his wet bike on the sighting lap and therefore started the race from pitlane on slicks, thus losing nearly a minute to the leader in four laps. He thought about pulling in but persevered and as the track dried found himself as high as sixth and involved in a high-quality midfield dice. It was not until lap 12 that Valentino Rossi got past. There was a classic moment on the front straight as the Aussie glanced to his right at the bike coming alongside, realised who it was and did a massive double-take.

For Valentino it was another of those races where he rued what might have been. He had the pace for a rostrum finish at least but two weather-related mistakes denied him the chance. On the other side of the pit, Jorge Lorenzo found another way to transport himself to racing purgatory. Dani Pedrosa again put a brave face on things but was again handily beaten by his team-mate.

As Dovizioso observed, the problem is that Marquez does not have a weakness, so there is nothing to attack. He also pointed out that not long ago we were all saying the same thing about Jorge Lorenzo. If you are trying to beat someone every weekend, you need a thread of hope to cling to.

OPEN SEASON

We had been wondering about a question posed by the new rules. Was there any track at which an Open Class bike could use its softer tyre to beat the Factory bikes to pole position and/or the win? Now we knew the answer – at least to the first part of the question.

The answer was 'yes': pole position was possible at Assen provided circumstances conspired just a little with a clever rider. That man was Aleix Espargaro, who used a soft tyre on a tricky surface to get in a quick lap before the rain came down.

Conditions were so obviously going to get worse when the lights went green for the final qualifying session that nearly all of the 12 men in Q2 left in a group, with Marc Marquez arriving late and trying to find a way to the front. He could not do so, or rather he could not do so until they came to the right/left chicane at the end of the back straight. There he pushed his way first under Pedrosa, then past Pol Espargaro – who had him boxed in against the kerb – and finally round the outside of Lorenzo. It was a piece of riding straight from his first lap off the back of the Moto2 grid at Valencia –

astonishing, audacious and, to ordinary mortals, downright dangerous. It got him on the front row.

Aleix Espargaro had been brave enough to let the pack go, giving him a useful target as he made good use of the soft tyre available to Open Class

entries. On that second flying lap he took 1.5sec out of the group and secured his first pole position in any class. His and the Forward team's only regret was that on race day the chaos on the grid did not allow them time to enjoy the experience.

OFFICIAL TIMEKEEPER

IVECO TT ASSEN
TT CIRCUIT ASSEN
ROUND 8
JUNE 28

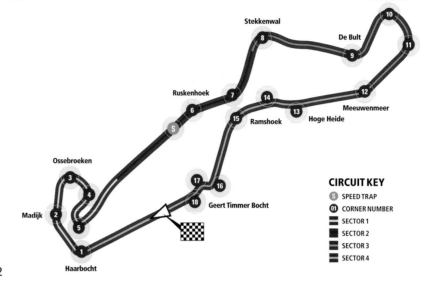

RACE RESULTS

CIRCUIT LENGTH 2.822 miles
NO. OF LAPS 26
RACE DISTANCE 73.379 miles
WEATHER Wet, 19°C
TRACK TEMPERATURE 25°C
WINNER Marc Marquez
FASTEST LAP 1m 34.575s,
107.373mph, Marc Marquez
LAP RECORD 1m 34.548s,
107.460mph, Dani Pedrosa, 2012

CIRCUIT KEY

- **S** SPEED TRAP
- **01** CORNER NUMBER
- ▬ SECTOR 1
- ▬ SECTOR 2
- ▬ SECTOR 3
- ▬ SECTOR 4

TYRE OPTIONS

FRONT

FRONT COMPOUNDS
EXTRA (**XS**), SOFT (**S**), MEDIUM (**M**)
WET SOFT (**WS**), WET HARD (**WH**)

REAR

REAR COMPOUNDS
SOFT (**S**), MEDIUM (**M**), HARD (**H**)
WET SOFT (**WS**), WET HARD (**WH**)

SEVERITY RATING
<MILD   SEVERE>

BRIDGESTONE

QUALIFYING

	Rider	Nation	Motorcycle	Team	Time	Pole +
1	Espargaro A	SPA	Yamaha	NGM Forward Racing	1m 38.789s	
2	Marquez	SPA	Honda	Repsol Honda Team	1m 40.194s	1.405s
3	Pedrosa	SPA	Honda	Repsol Honda Team	1m 40.732s	1.943s
4	Iannone	ITA	Ducati	Pramac Racing	1m 40.786s	1.997s
5	Crutchlow	GBR	Ducati	Ducati Team	1m 40.796s	2.007s
6	Smith	GBR	Yamaha	Monster Yamaha Tech3	1m 40.818s	2.029s
7	Dovizioso	ITA	Ducati	Ducati Team	1m 41.140s	2.351s
8	Bradl	GER	Honda	LCR Honda MotoGP	1m 41.982s	3.193s
9	Lorenzo	SPA	Yamaha	Movistar Yamaha MotoGP	1m 42.259s	3.470s
10	Bautista	SPA	Honda	GO&FUN Honda Gresini	1m 42.884s	4.095s
11	Espargaro P	SPA	Yamaha	Monster Yamaha Tech3	1m 43.085s	4.296s
12	Rossi	ITA	Yamaha	Movistar Yamaha MotoGP	1m 43.625s	4.836s
13	Abraham	CZE	Honda	Cardion AB Motoracing	1m 34.907s	Q1
14	Aoyama	JPN	Honda	Drive M7 Aspar	1m 34.930s	Q1
15	Hernandez	COL	Ducati	Energy T.I. Pramac Racing	1m 35.056s	Q1
16	Redding	GBR	Honda	GO&FUN Honda Gresini	1m 35.059s	Q1
17	Petrucci	ITA	ART	Octo IodaRacing Team	1m 35.346s	Q1
18	Edwards	USA	Yamaha	NGM Forward Racing	1m 35.484s	Q1
19	Parkes	AUS	PBM	Paul Bird Motorsport	1m 35.513s	Q1
20	Barbera	SPA	Avintia	Avintia Racing	1m 35.631s	Q1
21	Laverty	GBR	PBM	Paul Bird Motorsport	1m 35.731s	Q1
22	Hayden	USA	Honda	Drive M7 Aspar	1m 35.792s	Q1
23	Di Meglio	FRA	Avintia	Avintia Racing	1m 35.980s	Q1

1 MARC MARQUEZ
This was Marc's first wet-and-dry race and he won it. As at Catalunya, he missed out on pole position and had a crash. But in the race he was impeccable. His only serious moment came on the out-lap after changing bikes, when he temporarily handed the lead to Dovizioso.

2 ANDREA DOVIZIOSO
Used the soft tyre in qualifying to get a front-row start, then rode cleverly and with no mistakes. Led for eight laps after Marquez's moment, but the result was never in doubt. This was Dovi's best result of the season so far.

3 DANI PEDROSA
Did not push too hard early on as he thought the rain would come again and wanted to conserve his tyres. Once on to dry tyres, he spent most of the race in a battle with Aleix Espargaro.

4 ALEIX ESPARGARO
Achieved an historic pole position on an Open Class machine, followed by a great race. Ran in third on the wet bike despite being 'cautious' about the conditions, changed bike at the right time and then enjoyed a terrific battle with Pedrosa for the final rostrum position.

5 VALENTINO ROSSI
Another race that could have been so much better. Qualified at the back of Q2 then got tyre choice wrong and had to start from pit lane. The race showed he could and should have been fighting for a rostrum finish at least.

6 ANDREA IANONNE
Another stellar qualifying performance followed by a gritty effort in the type of conditions that have always made him uncomfortable. Went with the majority in changing bikes on lap six and equalled his best finish of the season.

7 ALVARO BAUTISTA
One of many riders happier in the wet than the dry, as he struggled to get heat in his slicks. Had to work hard to hold off Smith in the final laps.

8 BRADLEY SMITH
Not quick in the wet, and made a mistake in staying out for an extra lap, losing ten seconds. Blazingly quick in the dry but could not quite catch Bautista – which he described as 'irritating'.

9 CAL CRUTCHLOW
The crucial lap of his weekend was the last one in first qualifying that put him

into the second session. He then took advantage of a damp track to secure a second-row start.

10 STEFAN BRADL
Crashed on the sighting lap, ran back to start on his second bike, but never felt right with either bike.

11 BROC PARKES
Crashed on the warm-up lap and started from pit lane on his dry bike, so did not have to pit again. Thought about pulling in before the rain stopped, but took full advantage as the track dried and was involved in a high-quality midfield dice.

LAP CHART

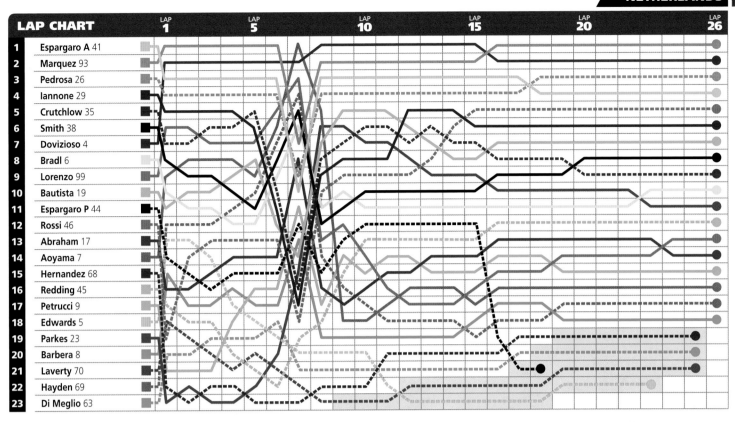

	LAP 1	LAP 5	LAP 10	LAP 15	LAP 20	LAP 26
1	Espargaro A 41					
2	Marquez 93					
3	Pedrosa 26					
4	Iannone 29					
5	Crutchlow 35					
6	Smith 38					
7	Dovizioso 4					
8	Bradl 6					
9	Lorenzo 99					
10	Bautista 19					
11	Espargaro P 44					
12	Rossi 46					
13	Abraham 17					
14	Aoyama 7					
15	Hernandez 68					
16	Redding 45					
17	Petrucci 9					
18	Edwards 5					
19	Parkes 23					
20	Barbera 8					
21	Laverty 70					
22	Hayden 69					
23	Di Meglio 63					

RACE

	Rider	Motorcycle	Race time	Time +	Fastest lap	Avg. speed	
1	Marquez	Honda	43m 29.954s		1m 34.575s	101.2mph	WS/WS
2	Dovizioso	Ducati	43m 36.668s	6.714s	1m 35.047s	100.9mph	WS/WS
3	Pedrosa	Honda	43m 40.745s	10.791s	1m 34.692s	100.8mph	WS/WS
4	Espargaro A	Yamaha	43m 49.153s	19.199s	1m 35.513s	100.4mph	WS/WS
5	Rossi	Yamaha	43m 55.767s	25.813s	1m 35.001s	100.2mph	WS/WS
6	Iannone	Ducati	43m 58.957s	29.003s	1m 35.349s	100.0mph	WS/WS
7	Bautista	Honda	44m 00.836s	30.882s	1m 35.379s	100.0mph	WS/WS
8	Smith	Yamaha	44m 00.939s	30.985s	1m 34.870s	100.0mph	WS/WS
9	Crutchlow	Ducati	44m 13.985s	44.031s	1m 36.291s	99.5mph	WS/WS
10	Bradl	Honda	44m 18.616s	48.662s	1m 35.971s	99.4mph	WS/WS
11	Parkes	PBM	44m 21.817s	51.863s	1m 36.955s	99.2mph	SS/SS
12	Redding	Honda	44m 30.283s	1m 00.329s	1m 36.589s	98.9mph	WS/WS
13	Lorenzo	Yamaha	44m 34.595s	1m 04.641s	1m 35.288s	98.7mph	WS/WS
14	Abraham	Honda	44m 35.934s	1m 05.980s	1m 36.364s	98.7mph	WS/WS
15	Petrucci	ART	44m 47.565s	1m 17.611s	1m 37.390s	98.2mph	WS/WS
16	Aoyama	Honda	44m 49.707s	1m 19.753s	1m 36.847s	98.2mph	WS/WS
17	Hayden	Honda	44m 57.584s	1m 27.630s	1m 37.400s	97.9mph	WS/WS
18	Barbera	Avintia	44m 58.096s	1m 28.142s	1m 36.896s	97.9mph	WS/WS
19	Hernandez	Ducati	43m 41.754s	1 lap	1m 36.617s	96.9mph	SS/SS
20	Di Meglio	Avintia	43m 58.159s	1 lap	1m 37.505s	96.3mph	WS/WS
21	Laverty	PBM	44m 49.966s	1 lap	1m 36.716s	94.4mph	WS/WS
22	Edwards	Yamaha	43m 33.704s	3 laps	1m 38.534s	89.4mph	WS/WS
NF	Espargaro P	Yamaha	33m 22.034s	8 laps	1m 36.611s	91.3mph	WS/WS

CHAMPIONSHIP

	Rider	Nation	Team	Points
1	Marquez	SPA	Repsol Honda Team	200
2	Rossi	ITA	Movistar Yamaha MotoGP	128
3	Pedrosa	SPA	Repsol Honda Team	128
4	Dovizioso	ITA	Ducati Team	91
5	Lorenzo	SPA	Movistar Yamaha MotoGP	81
6	Espargaro A	SPA	NGM Forward Racing	67
7	Espargaro P	SPA	Monster Yamaha Tech3	58
8	Bradl	GER	LCR Honda MotoGP	56
9	Iannone	ITA	Pramac Racing	51
10	Smith	GBR	Monster Yamaha Tech3	48
11	Bautista	SPA	GO&FUN Honda Gresini	43
12	Redding	GBR	GO&FUN Honda Gresini	28
13	Hayden	USA	Drive M7 Aspar	27
	Hernandez	COL	Energy T.I. Pramac Racing	27
15	Aoyama	JPN	Drive M7 Aspar	24
16	Crutchlow	GBR	Ducati Team	22
17	Abraham	CZE	Cardion AB Motoracing	15
18	Edwards	USA	NGM Forward Racing	8
19	Pirro	ITA	Ducati Team	7
20	Parkes	AUS	Paul Bird Motorsport	6
21	Petrucci	ITA	Octo IodaRacing Team	3
22	Barbera	SPA	Avintia Racing	2

12 SCOTT REDDING
Started from the back of the grid after a late tyre change for his first taste of a MotoGP bike in the wet. It took a few laps to gain any confidence but in the dry he was fast, finishing as the top RCV1000R rider – and becoming the top Open Class Honda rider in the points table.

13 JORGE LORENZO
'Definitely my worst ever race.' The reason? Memories of the previous season, when he broke his collarbone crashing in the wet. He had no problems in the dry, but when it was spitting it was a different story. Apologised to his fans and team.

14 KAREL ABRAHAM
One of the minority who did not come in to change bikes at the end of lap six. Once on the dry bike, he rode away from the group in which he had been dicing.

15 DANILO PETRUCCI
Back after missing three races through injury. Stalled at the start, losing 20 seconds, because his hand was numbed with painkillers. Rode superbly on the drying track and held on for the last point.

16 HIROSHI AOYAMA
Fast in the wet but not so happy in the dry. Used a new front fork.

17 NICKY HAYDEN
Like his team-mate, much happier in the wet than the dry. Lost a lot of time in the two laps after the bike change with front-end and acceleration problems.

18 HECTOR BARBERA
Still at sea with the electronics despite a test after Barcelona. Pleasantly surprised by the bike in the wet and by his dice with Hayden in the dry.

19 YONNY HERNANDEZ
Started on slicks so had to change bikes twice, a decision that ended Yonny's run of scoring points in every race this year.

20 MIKE DI MEGLIO
Used the bike he had ridden all through practice in the wet, and one he had not touched in the dry. Neither worked well.

21 MICHAEL LAVERTY
In total contrast to the other side of the garage, Michael was left ruing what could have been. Pitted early only to find his second bike was not ready, so had to go out and return to change bikes, losing any chance of points.

22 COLIN EDWARDS
Pitted three times. A horrible last race at Assen.

DID NOT FINISH

POL ESPARGARO
The start of the race was his first time on the Yamaha M1 in the wet. A last-minute tyre change saw him start from pitlane. Not surprisingly, lost ground and then crashed trying to make up for it on his dry bike. Swapped bikes a second time but it was on wet tyres, so retired.

GERMANY
ROUND 9

eni MOTORRAD GRAND PRIX DEUTSCHLAND
SACHSENRING CIRCUIT

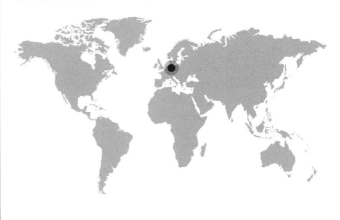

RAIN DANCE

Marc Marquez won again, this time from pitlane, but only after one of the strangest starts ever seen

As the lights went out at the start of the Sachsenring race, only the man in third place on the grid and the eight forming the final three rows were in their correct places. The other 14 were in a hectic scrum at the pitlane exit, waiting for the field to pass so they could join the race.

It had rained – heavily – before the riders went to the grid and then stopped. Their sighting lap revealed a circuit that was soaking wet on each and every corner. Not surprisingly, the front men, from pole to 15th, were on wets. Of those factory and satellite riders, only Stefan Bradl's crew attempted to change his bike over from full wet to dry settings before the start of the race, and they nearly made it. Meanwhile, the men with nothing to lose, the eight at the back, had lined up on slicks. Had there been another minute or two before the lights went out, Stefan Bradl would have won his home race – but it was not to be.

The warm-up lap, which as usual started precisely 18 minutes after the sighting lap, revealed a totally different racing surface. There was now only one corner that could properly be described as wet, but the trouble was that it was the left-hander at the bottom of the hill after the long, fast downhill straight – the most important overtaking place on the track. Nevertheless, 14 riders dived into pitlane at the end of the sighting lap to change their bikes and subsequently form up at the pitlane exit. As usual, Marc Marquez got everything right, including his flying change from saddle to saddle without touching the ground, and arrived at the end of pitlane to claim the equivalent of pole position on the left of the front row of the packed 'minigrid'.

Bradl duly led off the field in what looked like three

'I AM
SPEECHLESS
RIGHT NOW
BECAUSE THIS IS
THE WORST WAY TO
END MY HOME RACE'
STEFAN BRADL

waves: the solitary German at the front, the privateers led by Laverty and Petrucci, and finally the slipping, sliding, elbowing mob that emerged from pitlane. Later both Marquez and Aleix Espargaro said they enjoyed the start because it reminded them of their motocross days, although in the cold light of day most riders conceded that it had been more than a little dangerous. Jorge Lorenzo cut across the lines that mark the exit to avoid a collision when he found his brakes were not up to working temperature; he had the presence of mind to put his hand up and let two bikes back past. Jorge's team-mate, Valentino Rossi, looked to have made best use of his elbows until he too discovered that his brakes did not want to work and ran wide.

Bradl, meanwhile, never got his lead much above two and a half seconds over the quickest of the Open Class bikes and at the end of the first lap Marquez was less than eight seconds behind him. By lap four Marquez was in second place, and two laps later he was in front. The German was soon dropping through he field, usually being passed on the brakes at the bottom of that hill. What happened to Bradl, or rather to his bike?

Had his team managed to completely change the set-up on the grid, Stefan would have started the race with an effective advantage of well over ten seconds. His team did indeed change the rear suspension, the wheels and the brakes, but they could not complete their work on the front forks. So Stefan rode a 'dry' bike with soft, wet-weather front fork springs and damping, and there was no way he could brake hard without bottoming out his front suspension.

For the last 20 laps of the 30-lap race, Marquez did

OPPOSITE Stefan Bradl started from the grid on slicks but his crew could not change all suspension settings to 'dry' in time.

ABOVE The Open Class bikes chase Bradl off the start; the factory men have yet to emerge from pitlane.

BELOW Rossi's Yamaha is changed from wet to dry set-up in pitlane after the warm-up lap.

every lap in the 1min 22sec bracket. Bradl was in the 1min 24sec bracket for all but two of those laps, when he dropped into the 25s. Just to put the tin hat on it, he lost out on the last point when Danilo Petrucci passed him with four laps to go.

It did not take long for the race to resolve into what looked like a normal GP. Second-placed Dani Pedrosa pressed but every time he got within range his team-mate opened up the gap again. Jorge Lorenzo rode a great race to third, without any of the angst of Assen, passing Valentino Rossi along the way. Behind the factory riders, the satellite men also formed up in what reads like a resumé of the season so far: Andrea Ianonne was fifth – and again best Ducati by a distance – in front of the Espargaro brothers.

And so the magical young man made it nine in a row. Apart from the frantic start, Marquez did not look to make a mistake or have a problem, even in the tricky conditions in which he cut his way through the field.

There was one moment on Friday morning, though, when it did look as if Marc might be in serious trouble. He highsided as he pulled the bike over to the right for Turn 3, having inadvertently touched the gear lever and selected third; John Hopkins had an identical crash in 2005 that was caught on camera, unlike Marc's. It was not fast but it was nasty. Marc came down on his head, giving his neck a vicious tweak, and spent a lot time rotating his arms and holding his chest after he had taken quite a while to get up. It looked bad, but of course he was fast in the afternoon session.

The gods keep conspiring to find ways of stopping him, but Marc Marquez keeps finding ways of winning.

ABOVE Pol Espargaro closes on the factory Ducatis; after a very steady start he scored good points.

BELOW Still in pain from his Jerez injury, Danilo Petrucci was happy to score a point.

OPPOSITE Marc Marquez demonstrates his tactic of using the inside kerb on his way to win number nine.

THE FAST LANE

The traffic jam in pitlane at the start of the Sachsenring race caused a few palpitations but, thankfully, no accidents. That was more by luck than judgement, a view echoed even by those riders who said they enjoyed reliving their motocross days at the start.

Subsequently Race Direction started looking into the situation to ensure that it would not arise again. The first decision was to instigate a first-come, first-served queue at the end of pitlane rather than the five-abreast shoving match – reminiscent of a 1980s club-racing grid – that ensued in Germany. In future, the second man to the end of pitlane will form up behind the guy who got there first, and so on. It could be said that this will shift the problem elsewhere, because the warm-up lap will become a race on the wrong tyres for the conditions, but there is no alternative if the principle of a flag-to-flag race is to be retained.

Following some near misses in pitlane during bike swaps, Race Direction decided later in the season to regulate the procedure for such changeovers. The incoming bike must now pull behind the outgoing bike and stop between it and the pit garage. The outgoing bike must be aligned almost parallel to the direction of travel along pitlane to avoid the possibility of a rider pulling out across and in front of moving bikes. Priority must now be given to moving bikes, and teams will now be required to ensure safe release of their man.

Penalties will be applied if these new rules are broken.

Similarly, TV crews and other media have been warned to stay out of the three-metre corridor defined for the changeovers and must remain on the pit wall or in garages. They too will be fined for any transgressions.

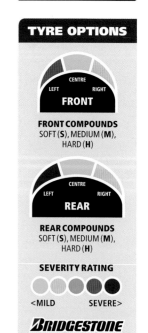

eni MOTORRAD GRAND PRIX DEUTSCHLAND
SACHSENRING CIRCUIT
ROUND 9
JULY 13

RACE RESULTS

CIRCUIT LENGTH 2.281 miles

NO. OF LAPS 30

RACE DISTANCE 68.432 miles

WEATHER Wet/dry, 21°C

TRACK TEMPERATURE 27°C

WINNER Marc Marquez

FASTEST LAP 1m 22.037s, 100.041mph, Marc Marquez

LAP RECORD 1m 21.846s, 100.351mph, Dani Pedrosa, 2011

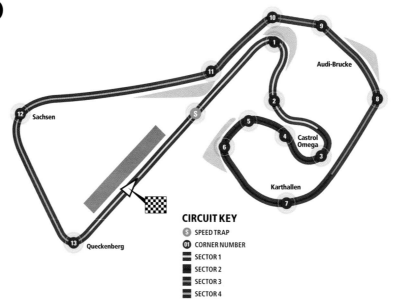

TYRE OPTIONS

FRONT

FRONT COMPOUNDS
SOFT (**S**), MEDIUM (**M**), HARD (**H**)

REAR

REAR COMPOUNDS
SOFT (**S**), MEDIUM (**M**), HARD (**H**)

SEVERITY RATING

<MILD   SEVERE>

BRIDGESTONE

CIRCUIT KEY
- **S** SPEED TRAP
- **01** CORNER NUMBER
- SECTOR 1
- SECTOR 2
- SECTOR 3
- SECTOR 4

QUALIFYING

	Rider	Nation	Motorcycle	Team	Time	Pole +
1	Marquez	SPA	Honda	Repsol Honda Team	1m 20.937s	
2	Pedrosa	SPA	Honda	Repsol Honda Team	1m 21.233s	0.296s
3	Bradl	GER	Honda	LCR Honda MotoGP	1m 21.340s	0.403s
4	Espargaro A	SPA	Yamaha	NGM Forward Racing	1m 21.376s	0.439s
5	Lorenzo	SPA	Yamaha	Movistar Yamaha MotoGP	1m 21.508s	0.571s
6	Rossi	ITA	Yamaha	Movistar Yamaha MotoGP	1m 21.651s	0.714s
7	Iannone	ITA	Ducati	Pramac Racing	1m 21.679s	0.742s
8	Espargaro P	SPA	Yamaha	Monster Yamaha Tech3	1m 21.771s	0.834s
9	Smith	GBR	Yamaha	Monster Yamaha Tech3	1m 21.794s	0.857s
10	Bautista	SPA	Honda	GO&FUN Honda Gresini	1m 21.906s	0.969s
11	Dovizioso	ITA	Ducati	Ducati Team	1m 22.120s	1.183s
12	Hayden	USA	Honda	Drive M7 Aspar	1m 22.647s	1.710s
13	Hernandez	COL	Ducati	Energy T.I. Pramac Racing	1m 22.411s	Q1
14	Redding	GBR	Honda	GO&FUN Honda Gresini	1m 22.436s	Q1
15	Crutchlow	GBR	Ducati	Ducati Team	1m 22.529s	Q1
16	Aoyama	JPN	Honda	Drive M7 Aspar	1m 22.659s	Q1
17	Abraham	CZE	Honda	Cardion AB Motoracing	1m 22.778s	Q1
18	Laverty	GBR	PBM	Paul Bird Motorsport	1m 22.845s	Q1
19	Edwards	USA	Yamaha	NGM Forward Racing	1m 22.888s	Q1
20	Barbera	SPA	Avintia	Avintia Racing	1m 23.029s	Q1
21	Di Meglio	FRA	Avintia	Avintia Racing	1m 23.423s	Q1
22	Parkes	AUS	PBM	Paul Bird Motorsport	1m 23.428s	Q1
23	Petrucci	ITA	ART	Octo IodaRacing Team	1m 23.484s	Q1

1 MARC MARQUEZ
Had his biggest crash of the year on Friday afternoon but came back to take pole in record time. Copied the strategy of the works Yamahas at the start to limit the chances of losing points, then rode the perfect race – again.

2 DANI PEDROSA
Did everything right but just when you thought he was closing in on his team-mate, the gap widened. Looked happy enough but knew that if he could not beat Marquez on this track his chances of doing so anywhere must be very small.

3 JORGE LORENZO
Had to take avoiding action coming out of pitlane at the start and crossed the pitlane exit, so gave back some places immediately – then he got to work and more than made up for the disappointments of Assen and Catalunya.

4 VALENTINO ROSSI
A little underwhelmed with his performance. Made all the right noises about a good first half of the season but obviously was not happy with being beaten by his team-mate – or the gap to the winner.

5 ANDREA IANNONE
Underlined his brilliant first half of the season with a career-best result under the most trying of conditions. Gritted his teeth and pushed hard in the early laps to keep the Yamahas in sight and reaped the rewards.

6 ALEIX ESPARGARO
Enjoyed the 'motocross-style' start from the pits but was wrong to chose the soft front tyre, which did not last long – front-tyre performance is extremely temperature-sensitive at Sachsenring. Thought he could have been with the factory Yamahas.

7 POL ESPARGARO
Got boxed in behind Dovizioso in the pitlane crowd, then was further held up when Dovi left his pitlane speed limiter switched on. Very cautious because of lack of experience in mixed conditions, he did not reach a points-scoring position until lap 11, but then rode past seven bikes for a brilliant result.

8 ANDREA DOVIZIOSO
Should have exploited the conditions but left his pitlane speed limiter switched on at the start, ran wide at Turn 11 and got held up dicing with Aleix Espargaro. Never had the pace expected.

9 ALVARO BAUTISTA
Followed the factory bikes into pitlane and ended up on the second row of the impromptu grid for the start. That compromised his whole race but he picked up a couple of valuable places in the final laps.

10 CAL CRUTCHLOW
A much better result than anyone expected after practice and qualifying. Lost three places in the last four laps but was happy that he had extracted the maximum possible from the Ducati.

LAP CHART

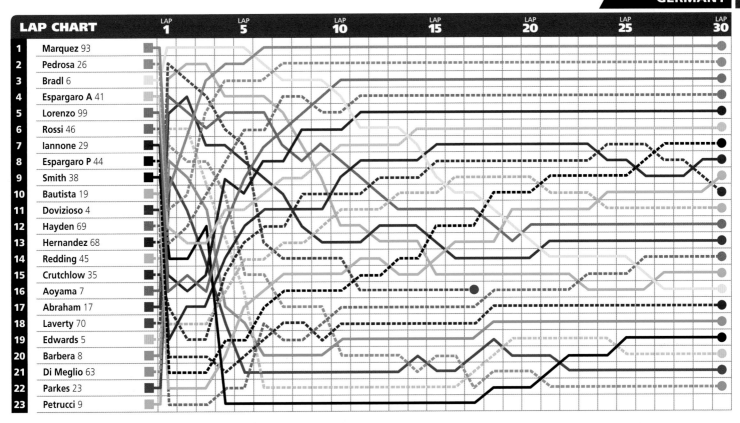

		LAP 1	LAP 5	LAP 10	LAP 15	LAP 20	LAP 25	LAP 30
1	Marquez 93							
2	Pedrosa 26							
3	Bradl 6							
4	Espargaro A 41							
5	Lorenzo 99							
6	Rossi 46							
7	Iannone 29							
8	Espargaro P 44							
9	Smith 38							
10	Bautista 19							
11	Dovizioso 4							
12	Hayden 69							
13	Hernandez 68							
14	Redding 45							
15	Crutchlow 35							
16	Aoyama 7							
17	Abraham 17							
18	Laverty 70							
19	Edwards 5							
20	Barbera 8							
21	Di Meglio 63							
22	Parkes 23							
23	Petrucci 9							

RACE

	Rider	Motorcycle	Race time	Time +	Fastest lap	Avg. speed	
1	Marquez	Honda	41m 47.664s		1m 22.037s	98.2mph	M/M
2	Pedrosa	Honda	41m 49.130s	1.466s	1m 22.162s	98.2mph	M/M
3	Lorenzo	Yamaha	41m 57.981s	10.317s	1m 22.284s	97.8mph	M/M
4	Rossi	Yamaha	42m 06.858s	19.194s	1m 22.513s	97.5mph	M/M
5	Iannone	Ducati	42m 11.173s	23.509s	1m 22.718s	97.3mph	S/S
6	Espargaro A	Yamaha	42m 15.473s	27.809s	1m 22.688s	97.1mph	S/S
7	Espargaro P	Yamaha	42m 20.917s	33.253s	1m 22.670s	96.9mph	M/M
8	Dovizioso	Ducati	42m 21.532s	33.868s	1m 23.070s	96.9mph	S/S
9	Bautista	Honda	42m 21.895s	34.231s	1m 22.869s	96.9mph	M/M
10	Crutchlow	Ducati	42m 22.340s	34.676s	1m 23.038s	96.9mph	S/S
11	Redding	Honda	42m 25.408s	37.744s	1m 23.153s	96.7mph	H/S
12	Aoyama	Honda	42m 32.682s	45.018s	1m 23.665s	96.5mph	S/S
13	Abraham	Honda	42m 32.841s	45.177s	1m 23.446s	96.5mph	S/S
14	Hayden	Honda	42m 34.340s	46.676s	1m 23.335s	96.4mph	S/S
15	Petrucci	ART	42m 40.433s	52.769s	1m 24.012s	96.2mph	M/S
16	Bradl	Honda	42m 41.553s	53.889s	1m 24.318s	96.1mph	S/M
17	Hernandez	Ducati	42m 42.140s	54.476s	1m 23.683s	96.1mph	S/S
18	Barbera	Avintia	42m 43.879s	56.215s	1m 23.659s	96.1mph	S/S
19	Smith	Yamaha	42m 43.957s	56.293s	1m 22.803s	96.1mph	M/M
20	Edwards	Yamaha	42m 51.747s	1m 04.083s	1m 23.538s	95.8mph	S/S
21	Parkes	PBM	42m 58.592s	1m 10.928s	1m 24.243s	95.5mph	M/S
22	Di Meglio	Avintia	43m 07.639s	1m 19.975s	1m 24.731s	95.2mph	S/S
NF	Laverty	PBM	24m 24.698s	13 laps	1m 23.347s	95.3mph	M/S

CHAMPIONSHIP

	Rider	Nation	Team	Points
1	Marquez	SPA	Repsol Honda Team	225
2	Pedrosa	SPA	Repsol Honda Team	148
3	Rossi	ITA	Movistar Yamaha MotoGP	141
4	Dovizioso	ITA	Ducati Team	99
5	Lorenzo	SPA	Movistar Yamaha MotoGP	97
6	Espargaro A	SPA	NGM Forward Racing	77
7	Espargaro P	SPA	Monster Yamaha Tech3	67
8	Iannone	ITA	Pramac Racing	62
9	Bradl	GER	LCR Honda MotoGP	56
10	Bautista	SPA	GO&FUN Honda Gresini	50
11	Smith	GBR	Monster Yamaha Tech3	48
12	Redding	GBR	GO&FUN Honda Gresini	33
13	Hayden	USA	Drive M7 Aspar	29
14	Crutchlow	GBR	Ducati Team	28
15	Aoyama	JPN	Drive M7 Aspar	28
16	Hernandez	COL	Energy T.I. Pramac Racing	27
17	Abraham	CZE	Cardion AB Motoracing	18
18	Edwards	USA	NGM Forward Racing	8
19	Pirro	ITA	Ducati Team	7
20	Parkes	AUS	Paul Bird Motorsport	6
21	Petrucci	ITA	Octo IodaRacing Team	4
22	Barbera	SPA	Avintia Racing	2

11 SCOTT REDDING
Top customer Honda again despite. Took risks on the wet track and did not suffer too much when the soft tyre dropped off. Only caught by his team-mate and Pol Espargaro in the final stages.

12 HIROSHI AOYAMA
Comfortable in the wet conditions at the start and in the dry conditions at the end, but not through the middle of the race.

13 KAREL ABRAHAM
Started on slicks, followed Aoyama, then passed him but got repassed again. Happy to beat Hayden and Bradl.

14 NICKY HAYDEN
Annoyed with himself for being a little over-cautious at the start. Much faster in the final 15 laps.

15 DANILO PETRUCCI
Suffered from chatter that aggravated his wrist and was not cured by a new engine map. Happy to get the point.

16 STEFAN BRADL
Nearly completed changing the bike from wet to dry on the grid, but his crew ran out of time to alter the fork settings. He led easily for five laps but became helpless when the track dried.

17 YONNY HERNANDEZ
Crashed in warm-up, so the conditions, not surprisingly, put him in completely the wrong frame of mind for the race.

18 HECTOR BARBERA
Making up for lack of acceleration off the brakes and in corners, he could not have tried harder.

19 BRADLEY SMITH
Practice saw two major crashes plus a more gentle slide-off, and then he had another slide-off in warm-up. Had his fifth crash of the weekend during the race but got back on and at least finished.

20 COLIN EDWARDS
Started on slicks but had no confidence in the bike and was too far back to make up ground when the track dried.

21 BROC PARKES
Had to race his second bike after a Turn 11 crash on Saturday; started on slicks with full dry set-up. Denied a chance of points by problems with his transponder.

22 MIKE DI MEGLIO
Much happier than at Assen and looked as if he might get in the points before an electrical problem forced him into short-shifting everywhere.

DID NOT FINISH

MICHAEL LAVERTY
Started on slicks, enjoyed running as high as second in the opening laps, and looked set for good points – but then he crashed.

RED BULL
INDIANAPOLIS GRAND PRIX
INDIANAPOLIS MOTOR SPEEDWAY

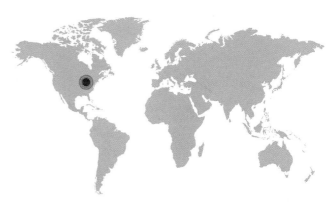

DOUBLE FIGURES

Ten in a row for Marquez, but only after a ferocious struggle in the early laps

It took a while, but finally MotoGP and the Indianapolis Motor Speedway feel like they belong together. Until 2014 the lap record had been the slowest of the season at 95mph, but some subtle track modifications and complete resurfacing of the infield section, which eliminated a lot of bumps, helped to increase the record to over 103mph.

While no-one was claiming to be madly in love with the track, nearly everyone was impressed – and the exceptions were generally riding Hondas. The elimination of first-gear corners, especially the one before the start/finish straight, removed a major advantage that Honda riders had used to good effect in previous years. The changes at corners two to four, four to seven and fourteen to sixteen all opened up what had been horribly slow, tricky sections, although looking at the first sequence of corners, especially in the opening laps of the race, it was difficult to imagine it had been even tighter.

The other big change was the atmosphere. A year ago the future of the event was distinctly precarious but the combination of investment by the Indianapolis Motor Speedway (IMS) and an enthusiastic crowd bodes well. By tradition, the IMS does not release crowd figures, but this was the first time a MotoGP crowd at the Brickyard has been heard above the noise of the bikes. It happened when Rossi took the lead – when else?

The atmosphere spread to downtown Indianapolis. Hundreds of bikes crowded the area around the Monument on Meridian Avenue, closed to cars on Friday and Saturday nights. It was a crash course in American biking sub-cultures: Harleys of every type, a good scattering of Ducatis and plenty of the local speciality – a Hayabusa or ZX10 with a stretched swinging arm ready

ABOVE Colin Edwards finished 13th in his last race, wearing camouflage leathers.

RIGHT Turn 1, Lap 1: Valentino Rossi and Andrea Dovizioso lead the field towards the oval circuit.

OPPOSITE Alvaro Bautista's race did not get past Turn 4, where he crashed with Hernandez.

for the drag strip. But the stretched Kawasaki with a live scorpion in a cage mounted in front of the rear wheel was a little over the top.

While middle America was busy embracing MotoGP, the sport was contemplating a lack of American riders at the top level. Nicky Hayden was forced to miss his home race after having a big wrist operation to finally try to sort out the problems he has been experiencing for years. His team announced that he would miss two races, with Leon Camier coming in to replace him. In reality, however, it was obvious that Nicky would miss more, with those close to his family talking about him missing the rest of the European season.

MotoGP's other American, Colin Edwards, had already announced that he would retire at the end of the season (see page 57) but it now emerged that Indianapolis would be his last race, as the Forward Racing Team would put Alex de Angelis on the bike for the rest of the year. No-one was saying why, not even Colin, who wore camouflage riding kit in a tribute to his friends in the armed services. American Yamaha had the foresight to organise a farewell party for fans on the Saturday to say goodbye to Colin on the assumption that this would be his last GP on American soil, and everyone from old team managers to Valentino Rossi turned up to say goodbye to him. Edwards' son Hayes uttered the best quote when asked what it was like having Colin as a dad: 'Kinda sketchy.'

Interestingly, Wayne Rainey was at the track, mostly in high-level meetings with Dorna management. There were rumours of plans for Rainey to mentor local talent but no official statement was forthcoming.

'I CANNOT EXPLAIN, BUT EVERY RACE I FEEL SO STRONG'
MARC MARQUEZ

ABOVE Andrea Dovizioso collects some rubber on his leathers during early skirmishes for the lead.

BELOW Scott Redding got through to Qualifying 2 for the first time, then finished top Open Class bike for the first time.

Back on track not only did the Yamaha riders suddenly find that they liked Indy but so did the Ducati men. Andrea Dovizioso started from the front row thanks to clever use of the soft tyre in qualifying and tagging on to Marc Marquez. He then made good use of a new, more powerful engine to stay with the factory Hondas and Yamahas and even lead for a while. Dovi ended up with a lot of rubber on his leathers when Valentino Rossi pushed past, anxious to try to make a break while Marquez was embroiled a few yards further back. That plan was scuppered when Marc went from third to first in one corner, passing both the Yamahas in one go. It was the move that decided the race, but it took ten laps for Marc to decide it was safe to push. He had had a few tyre worries, mainly because the track temperature on race day was ten degrees higher than on previous days.

The factory Yamahas gave chase but Marc never gave them hope. Although Rossi had made the early pace and was by far the more aggressive, it was Jorge Lorenzo who pulled away. It felt very like normal service being resumed, with Dani Pedrosa a rather distant fourth, having been unable to find grip all weekend.

The only minor shock was that Aleix Espargaro was not top Open Class finisher; he was tailgated by Stefan Bradl. That meant that the seriously impressive Scott Redding took Open honours after a race-long duel with Cal Crutchlow's factory Ducati. Scott had been top customer Honda rider before, but never top Open. He said that he had decided to be a little more aggressive in the second half of the season and was having real trouble pretending that being so far from the rostrum was fun. Previously he had managed to toe the party line about a learning year and being happy to be top RCV1000R rider, but now he did not bother to disguise his frustration.

Marquez's tenth consecutive victory broke a few more records and made him the youngest to achieve that feat. The others who have won ten in a row? Mick Doohan, Giacomo Agostini, Mike Hailwood and John Surtees. Not bad company. And what was Marc's first thought when he turned up after the summer break? To wonder if he would still be as fast after the lull. He was.

BURGESS AT THE BRICKYARD

Jerry Burgess was a welcome, if low-profile, visitor to the MotoGP paddock for the first time since Valentino Rossi dispensed with his services at the end of the previous season.

Just to make sure no-one misunderstood, he wore a number 46 baseball cap. Rossi tweeted a picture of the two of them with their arms round each other, describing Burgess as 'my racing father'.

It seems that everyone but Jerry himself was to a greater or lesser extent outraged by the manner of the parting. The man himself is very clear. Top-level sportsmen can allow no self-doubt to creep in. Valentino was in a situation where he needed to change things, so that was what happened. In fact Jerry had started making preparations for his departure from the paddock when Rossi showed serious interest in Formula 1 a good few years ago.

As one would expect, Burgess has interesting views on racing but admits he is still constrained by the fact that he remains a Yamaha employee. He thinks Marc Marquez is good, very good in fact, but not as good as the competition is making him look. He is particularly interested in the way Marc seems to move himself forwards and backwards on the bike while at full lean, but not interested enough to consider a return to the paddock.

Jerry is restoring a couple of classic British sports cars and is more than a little surprised at the interest he has developed in golf – he plays two rounds a week. And he does not miss the stress – not one little bit.

RIGHT Leon Camier replaced Nicky Hayden on Aspar's customer Honda and impressed.

RED BULL
INDIANAPOLIS GRAND PRIX
INDIANAPOLIS MOTOR SPEEDWAY

ROUND 10
AUGUST 10

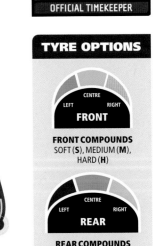

OFFICIAL TIMEKEEPER

RACE RESULTS

CIRCUIT LENGTH 2.591 miles

NO. OF LAPS 27

RACE DISTANCE 69.957 miles

WEATHER Dry, 29°C

TRACK TEMPERATURE 46°C

WINNER Marc Marquez

FASTEST LAP 1m 32.831s, 100.476 mph, Marc Marquez (record)

PREVIOUS LAP RECORD 1m 39.044s, 95.194mph, Marc Marquez, 2012

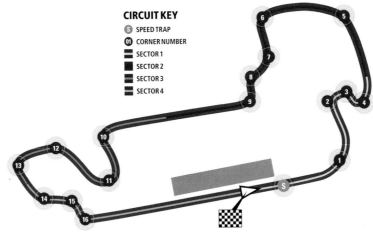

CIRCUIT KEY
- S SPEED TRAP
- 01 CORNER NUMBER
- SECTOR 1
- SECTOR 2
- SECTOR 3
- SECTOR 4

TYRE OPTIONS

FRONT

FRONT COMPOUNDS
SOFT (**S**), MEDIUM (**M**), HARD (**H**)

REAR

REAR COMPOUNDS
SOFT (**S**), MEDIUM (**M**), HARD (**H**)

SEVERITY RATING

<MILD   SEVERE>

BRIDGESTONE

QUALIFYING

	Rider	Nation	Motorcycle	Team	Time	Pole +
1	Marquez	SPA	Honda	Repsol Honda Team	1m 31.619s	
2	Dovizioso	ITA	Ducati	Ducati Team	1m 31.844s	0.225s
3	Lorenzo	SPA	Yamaha	Movistar Yamaha MotoGP	1m 31.869s	0.250s
4	Espargaro A	SPA	Yamaha	NGM Forward Racing	1m 32.113s	0.494s
5	Rossi	ITA	Yamaha	Movistar Yamaha MotoGP	1m 32.160s	0.541s
6	Espargaro P	SPA	Yamaha	Monster Yamaha Tech3	1m 32.243s	0.624s
7	Iannone	ITA	Ducati	Pramac Racing	1m 32.254s	0.635s
8	Pedrosa	SPA	Honda	Repsol Honda Team	1m 32.331s	0.712s
9	Smith	GBR	Yamaha	Monster Yamaha Tech3	1m 32.343s	0.724s
10	Bradl	GER	Honda	LCR Honda MotoGP	1m 32.514s	0.895s
11	Redding	GBR	Honda	GO&FUN Honda Gresini	1m 32.714s	1.095s
12	Crutchlow	GBR	Ducati	Ducati Team	1m 32.794s	1.175s
13	Hernandez	COL	Ducati	Energy T.I. Pramac Racing	1m 33.166s	Q1
14	Bautista	SPA	Honda	GO&FUN Honda Gresini	1m 33.294s	Q1
15	Edwards	USA	Yamaha	NGM Forward Racing	1m 33.625s	Q1
16	Camier	GBR	Honda	Drive M7 Aspar	1m 33.747s	Q1
17	Petrucci	ITA	ART	Octo IodaRacing Team	1m 33.837s	Q1
18	Aoyama	JPN	Honda	Drive M7 Aspar	1m 33.948s	Q1
19	Di Meglio	FRA	Avintia	Avintia Racing	1m 34.244s	Q1
20	Barbera	SPA	Avintia	Avintia Racing	1m 34.332s	Q1
21	Abraham	CZE	Honda	Cardion AB Motoracing	1m 34.369s	Q1
22	Parkes	AUS	PBM	Paul Bird Motorsport	1m 34.764s	Q1
23	Laverty	GBR	PBM	Paul Bird Motorsport	1m 34.814s	Q1

1 MARC MARQUEZ
Ten wins in a row, and he had to fight for this one after a bad start. Marc had to deal with the Ducatis of Iannone and Dovizioso before chasing down Rossi. Track temperature also meant that Marc had to be patient before he regained his 'good feeling' and pushed hard.

2 JORGE LORENZO
After the wobbles of the first half of the season, this looked more like the real Jorge. He got the better of his team-mate despite a bad start, but by the time he had secured second place Marquez was too far in front.

3 VALENTINO ROSSI
This was his first rostrum at Indy since winning here on the début visit in 2008. Vale led the race from the second corner and opened a small gap; after Marquez and Lorenzo got past Dovi on lap 6 there was a frenzied dice before the leading pair's break left Rossi third.

4 DANI PEDROSA
Dani was never happy with the revised track and unable to find grip at any time during the weekend. He was only eighth in qualifying, and although he made up places in the race, he was never in contention for a podium finish.

5 POL ESPARGARO
Tried but failed to hang on to Pedrosa off the start, and thereafter had a lonely race chasing down the Ducatis of Iannone and Dovizioso.

6 BRADLEY SMITH
Another crash further damaged his already mangled little finger, but Bradley looked his old self in the race. Preserved the rear tyre and was closing on his team-mate at the end of the race.

7 ANDREA DOVIZIOSO
Dovizioso followed Marquez's 'crazy lines' for second on the grid, then spent the first laps of the race fighting for the lead – which involved collecting rubber from Rossi's front tyre on his leathers. Inevitably his medium tyre dropped off and the satellite Yamahas got him.

8 CAL CRUTCHLOW
Looked to be well off the pace of his team-mate during practice and qualifying but finished only one place behind him, although Cal was displeased with the size of the gap. The after-effects of his arm operation did not help, especially in the first ten laps, but he was consistently fast in the second half.

9 SCOTT REDDING
His best weekend in MotoGP. Got through to Qualifying 2 for the first time, then in the race was top-placed Open Class bike for the first time, well ahead of the rest of the customer Hondas. Scott spent much of the race in a fierce battle with Crutchlow.

10 HIROSHI AOYAMA
Had a lot of problems with the new surface, and was unsure of his tyre choice right up to the race. Chose hard, felt comfortable for the first time and got his second top-ten finish of the year.

LAP CHART

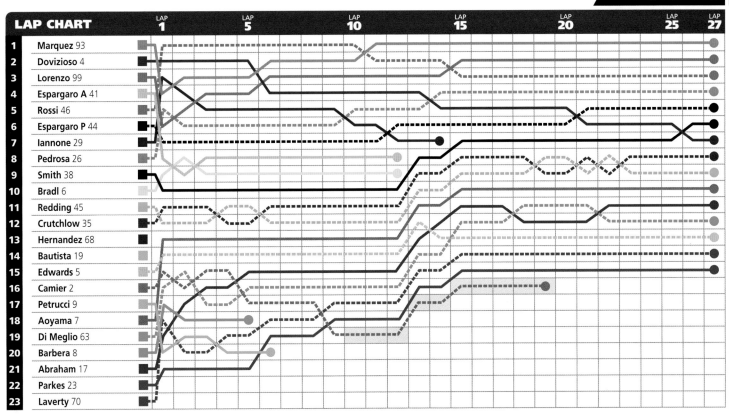

		LAP 1	LAP 5	LAP 10	LAP 15	LAP 20	LAP 25	LAP 27
1	Marquez 93							
2	Dovizioso 4							
3	Lorenzo 99							
4	Espargaro A 41							
5	Rossi 46							
6	Espargaro P 44							
7	Iannone 29							
8	Pedrosa 26							
9	Smith 38							
10	Bradl 6							
11	Redding 45							
12	Crutchlow 35							
13	Hernandez 68							
14	Bautista 19							
15	Edwards 5							
16	Camier 2							
17	Petrucci 9							
18	Aoyama 7							
19	Di Meglio 63							
20	Barbera 8							
21	Abraham 17							
22	Parkes 23							
23	Laverty 70							

RACE

	Rider	Motorcycle	Race time	Time +	Fastest lap	Avg. speed	🅱
1	Marquez	Honda	42m 07.041s		1m 32.831s	99.6mph	M/H
2	Lorenzo	Yamaha	42m 08.844s	1.803s	1m 32.939s	99.5mph	M/H
3	Rossi	Yamaha	42m 13.599s	6.558s	1m 33.191s	99.4mph	M/H
4	Pedrosa	Honda	42m 17.057s	10.016s	1m 33.456s	99.2mph	H/H
5	Espargaro P	Yamaha	42m 24.848s	17.807s	1m 33.666s	98.9mph	M/H
6	Smith	Yamaha	42m 26.645s	19.604s	1m 33.581s	98.9mph	M/H
7	Dovizioso	Ducati	42m 27.800s	20.759s	1m 33.376s	98.8mph	M/M
8	Crutchlow	Ducati	42m 46.837s	39.796s	1m 34.165s	98.1mph	M/M
9	Redding	Honda	42m 47.548s	40.507s	1m 34.099s	98.1mph	M/M
10	Aoyama	Honda	43m 02.801s	55.760s	1m 34.536s	97.5mph	M/M
11	Abraham	Honda	43m 12.171s	1m 05.130s	1m 34.956s	97.1mph	M/M
12	Di Meglio	Avintia	43m 12.387s	1m 05.346s	1m 35.257s	97.1mph	M/M
13	Edwards	Yamaha	43m 15.960s	1m 08.919s	1m 34.971s	97.0mph	M/M
14	Laverty	PBM	43m 16.244s	1m 09.203s	1m 35.402s	97.0mph	M/M
15	Parkes	PBM	43m 37.654s	1m 30.613s	1m 35.891s	96.2mph	M/M
NF	Camier	Honda	33m 00.397s	8 laps	1m 35.238s	89.5mph	M/M
NF	Iannone	Ducati	22m 04.599s	13 laps	1m 33.631s	98.5mph	M/M
NF	Espargaro A	Yamaha	18m 56.502s	15 laps	1m 33.878s	98.5mph	M/M
NF	Bradl	Honda	18m 56.531s	15 laps	1m 33.886s	98.5mph	M/H
NF	Petrucci	ART	10m 11.520s	21 laps	1m 36.105s	91.5mph	H/M
NF	Barbera	Avintia	8m 07.660s	22 laps	1m 35.647s	95.6mph	M/M
NF	Hernandez	Ducati	–	–	–	–	M/M
NF	Bautista	Honda	–	–	–	–	M/M

CHAMPIONSHIP

	Rider	Nation	Team	Points
1	Marquez	SPA	Repsol Honda Team	250
2	Pedrosa	SPA	Repsol Honda Team	161
3	Rossi	ITA	Movistar Yamaha MotoGP	157
4	Lorenzo	SPA	Movistar Yamaha MotoGP	117
5	Dovizioso	ITA	Ducati Team	108
6	Espargaro P	SPA	Monster Yamaha Tech3	78
7	Espargaro A	SPA	NGM Forward Racing	77
8	Iannone	ITA	Pramac Racing	62
9	Smith	GBR	Monster Yamaha Tech3	58
10	Bradl	GER	LCR Honda MotoGP	56
11	Bautista	SPA	GO&FUN Honda Gresini	50
12	Redding	GBR	GO&FUN Honda Gresini	40
13	Crutchlow	GBR	Ducati Team	36
14	Aoyama	JPN	Drive M7 Aspar	34
15	Hayden	USA	Drive M7 Aspar	29
16	Hernandez	COL	Energy T.I. Pramac Racing	27
17	Abraham	CZE	Cardion AB Motoracing	23
18	Edwards	USA	NGM Forward Racing	11
19	Pirro	ITA	Ducati Team	7
	Parkes	AUS	Paul Bird Motorsport	7
21	Di Meglio	FRA	Avintia Racing	4
	Petrucci	ITA	Octo IodaRacing Team	4
23	Laverty	GBR	Paul Bird Motorsport	2
	Barbera	SPA	Avintia Racing	2

11 KAREL ABRAHAM
His best finish this season, obtained by a pragmatic approach to the race after passing Edwards. Karel waited for the following group to close before passing di Meglio and opening up a safe gap.

12 MIKE DI MEGLIO
Mike scored his first MotoGP points despite problems with the full tank that had him dragging the engine cases in left-handers.

13 COLIN EDWARDS
Colin always knew this would be his last race in the USA, but it turned out to be his last race ever – for reasons as yet unexplained. He had a good start and managed the race nicely.

14 MICHAEL LAVERTY
Scored his first points of the year, and it could have been even better had Michael found a way past Edwards' Yamaha, which was fast on the straights.

15 BROC PARKES
Had trouble with corner entry and was a little detuned after a qualifying crash, but made sure both PBM machines finished with points for the first time in the team's history.

DID NOT FINISH

LEON CAMIER
An impressive replacement for Hayden, Qualified 16th for his first MotoGP but a misfire caused his early retirement.

ANDREA IANONNE
Very impressive in practice, but in the race knew something was wrong with the bike: the new-spec engine lost power and he had to stop on lap 14.

ALEIX ESPARGARO
Unlucky to be rammed from behind by Bradl while in eighth place.

STEFAN BRADL
Started from the front row but tailgated Aleix Espargaro just before half distance.

DANILO PETRUCCI
Suffered from instability on the brakes, then noticed some droplets appearing on the inside of his screen and assumed the front brake's hydraulics were leaking. The team found nothing wrong.

ALVARO BAUTISTA
Lucky to escape uninjured from a massive highside on Saturday, and unlucky to get tangled up with Hernandez on the first lap of the race.

YONNY HERNANDEZ
Came together with Bautista at Turn 4 on the first lap, having been seriously impressive throughout practice and qualifying.

HECTOR BARBERA
Electronics problems – probably a failed sensor – made the bike impossible to ride and he retired on lap 2.

CZECH REPUBLIC
ROUND 11

bwin GRAND PRIX
CESKÉ REPUBLIKY
AUTODROM BRNO

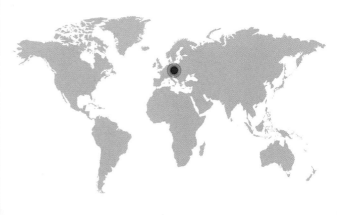

THE END
OF THE LINE

Marc Marquez's winning streak
came to halt not with a roar
but with a whisper

We knew it had to happen some time and Marc knew it had to happen some time – and he was philosophical about the prospect. At all the recent races he had been asked about the winning streak and every time he had produced the same answer. The only pressure on him, he said, was from the media constantly going on about it. When the time came, he would be quite happy to think about the championship and settle for good points.

At Brno the winning streak did come to an end for Marc but not for the Repsol Honda team, as Dani Pedrosa picked up the baton with his first win in nearly a year.

Winning the opening ten races of a season is an unprecedented feat in the MotoGP era, but watching the sequence end turned out to be a deflating experience. Perhaps that was because Marquez was never really in contention for the win. The streak ended not with a fight but with a rather underwhelming fourth place – not even a rostrum.

What happened? Good question. In true Honda tradition, very little in the way of information escaped from the team. The sight of Marc missing apexes and looking pretty uncomfortable on the bike at Brno – a track he said he did not really like – was not confined to race day. Although he did find a blindingly fast lap for pole thanks to new tyres, he did not dominate practice in his usual fashion. On used rubber, he said after the race, he was losing out to his team-mate every time he opened the throttle. There was also the matter of the relatively low track temperature on race day: the received wisdom is that a Honda needs heat in the track to find grip whereas a Yamaha's vital edge grip is enhanced on cooler tarmac.

ABOVE Alex de Angelis returned to the MotoGP class as replacement for the retired Colin Edwards.

RIGHT The Ducatis of the two Andreas, Iannone and Dovizioso, started from the front row and then led the race.

OPPOSITE Valentino Rossi crashed heavily on Saturday, damaging a finger.

Add up that collection of small problems and it is easy to explain why Marc did not have a particularly good time come race day. He did not get a good start and had trouble with the Ducatis, particularly that of Andrea Iannone, who was quite willing to trade places – and paint – in an early skirmish.

What Marquez's difficulties do not explain is Dani Pedrosa's performance. Marquez gave it his best but was dispatched by both factory Yamahas with relative ease. When Rossi took third off him, he did not try too hard to get the place back. Valentino was pleasantly surprised to be on the podium after a tough weekend. He had a big crash on Saturday and made a mess of the little finger on his left hand, and was narrowly missed by Alvaro Bautista's Honda when the Spaniard had an identical crash a few seconds later.

The mangled digit meant that Valentino could not be as precise with the clutch as he wanted off the start and he did not get away well. The finger was definitely a problem through the race, and afterwards he said that his left leg had troubled him too; ever since he fractured his right leg in 2010, he has had problems with the other one. And now, aged 35, and equalling Alex Barros's record number of 245 Grand Prix starts, his body is starting to complain. However, he was able to up the pace and for him to finish in front of Marquez was, he admitted, 'a great pleasure'.

The most surprising sight of the weekend was that of two Ducatis on the front row and then leading from the start. Andrea Iannone got the holeshot followed by Andrea Dovizioso, and the two of them were involved in fights with all of the leaders. It only

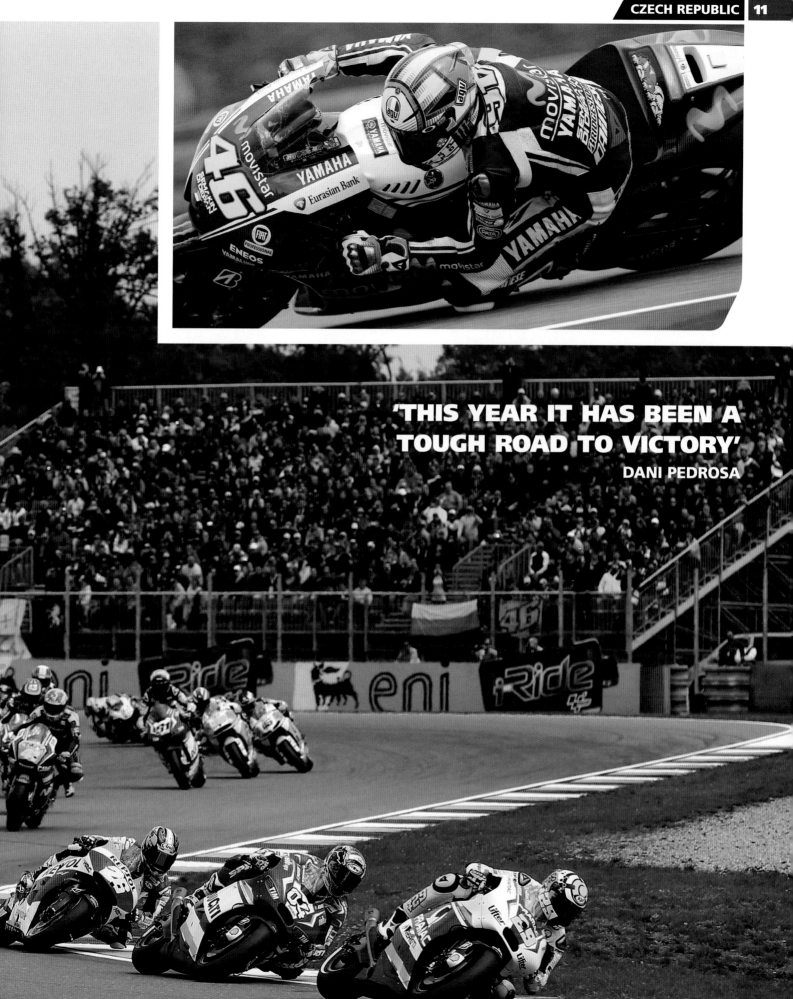

'THIS YEAR IT HAS BEEN A TOUGH ROAD TO VICTORY'
DANI PEDROSA

took Jorge Lorenzo a lap to find a way past both of them, but it took Marquez five, by which time he was 1.5sec behind the leader. Pedrosa had been more efficient and by this time was right on Lorenzo's back wheel, moving past on the next lap and pulling out a lead of 0.5sec in just two laps.

After that it was a classic Dani performance. This should not have felt like a surprise, but such has been Marquez's dominance that it did. Pedrosa's lead never got above 1.8sec and it shrunk alarmingly in the final few laps, leaving Lorenzo frustrated and wishing he had had one more lap. Despite the situation closely resembling a fuel shortage, the team maintained that Dani had controlled the race perfectly, the only problem the rider admitting to being a minor front-tyre glitch that provoked some chatter.

As for Marc, he was also adamant that neither he nor his team had made a mistake. It was, he said, one of those weekends when they did not find the feeling he needed. There were mutterings about the rear tyre, especially after the Monday test when the problems seemed to disappear, but Marc refused to discuss the subject on the grounds that people might think he was making excuses, and Bridgestone were dismissive. If there was a single, significant reason for Marc not finishing on the rostrum, it was brilliantly covered up.

If he was anything more than mildly irked by the end of his record run of victories, Marc did not show it. After all, he still had the prospect of retaining his title at home in Aragón three races later and, for extra motivation, the target of beating Mick Doohan's record of 12 wins in a season.

ABOVE Karel Abraham finished in the points in his home race – a welcome improvement on recent form.

BELOW Ducati's test rider Michele Pirro returned for another wild-card ride on the 'laboratory bike'.

BELOW Finally, the other side of the garage got to celebrate.

HISTORY MEN

Marc Marquez's ten wins in a row is a record for the MotoGP era and equals Mick Doohan's run in the 1997 season. Doohan's sequence was also ended by a team-mate, Tady Okada, leading to muttering from Mick about being sick of acting as a tow truck. However, neither of the Repsol Honda men is anywhere near the record for consecutive wins.

John Surtees won every 500cc race – and every 350cc race too – for two seasons running in 1958 and 1959, and then the first two 500cc races of 1960 before he crashed at Assen while making up time after three pit stops to cure a misfire.

Mike Hailwood won 12 in a row, comprising the last six races of 1963 and the first six of 1964; his run finished when he crashed a 250 MZ while dicing with Phil Read for the lead of the East German GP and his injuries caused him to miss the next race.

And so to Giacomo Agostini's record run of 20 wins. It started with the small matter of winning all ten races in the 1968 season before going on to take the first ten the following year; the MV Agusta team did not bother to contest

the final two races. It was the same again for the 1970 season: ten wins followed by not turning up for the remaining races. Then in 1971 Ago won the first eight races and of the remaining three rounds only contested Monza, where the unthinkable happened – he stopped with mechanical problems.

Ago may have had little opposition, but race and lap records were lowered most years. As anyone who worked with him will tell you, the man did not do complacency.

So, over four seasons Ago won 38 races of the 39 he contested and he won them consecutively. That's more than two seasons' worth of races by today's standards of an 18-race year.

bwin GRAND PRIX ČESKÉ REPUBLIKY
AUTODROM BRNO
ROUND 11
AUGUST 17

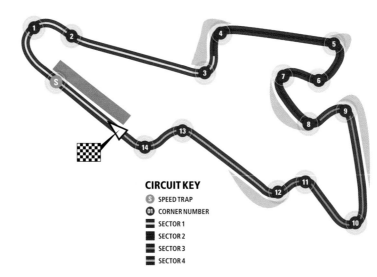

RACE RESULTS

CIRCUIT LENGTH 3.357 miles

NO. OF LAPS 22

RACE DISTANCE 73.860 miles

WEATHER Dry, 17°C

TRACK TEMPERATURE 23°C

WINNER Dani Pedrosa

FASTEST LAP 1m 56.027s, 104.142 mph, Dani Pedrosa

PREVIOUS LAP RECORD 1m 56.135s, 104.018mph, Marc Marquez, 2013

CIRCUIT KEY
- ⓢ SPEED TRAP
- ⓪① CORNER NUMBER
- SECTOR 1
- SECTOR 2
- SECTOR 3
- SECTOR 4

TYRE OPTIONS

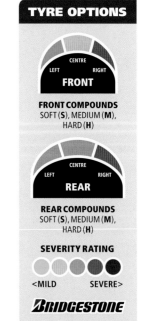

FRONT

FRONT COMPOUNDS SOFT (**S**), MEDIUM (**M**), HARD (**H**)

REAR

REAR COMPOUNDS SOFT (**S**), MEDIUM (**M**), HARD (**H**)

SEVERITY RATING

<MILD   SEVERE>

BRIDGESTONE

QUALIFYING

	Rider	Nation	Motorcycle	Team	Time	Pole +
1	Marquez	SPA	Honda	Repsol Honda Team	1m 55.585s	
2	Dovizioso	ITA	Ducati	Ducati Team	1m 55.714s	0.129s
3	Iannone	ITA	Ducati	Pramac Racing	1m 55.726s	0.141s
4	Smith	GBR	Yamaha	Monster Yamaha Tech3	1m 55.730s	0.145s
5	Pedrosa	SPA	Honda	Repsol Honda Team	1m 55.812s	0.227s
6	Lorenzo	SPA	Yamaha	Movistar Yamaha MotoGP	1m 55.871s	0.230s
7	Rossi	ITA	Yamaha	Movistar Yamaha MotoGP	1m 55.821s	0.236s
8	Bradl	GER	Honda	LCR Honda MotoGP	1m 55.871s	0.286s
9	Espargaro P	SPA	Yamaha	Monster Yamaha Tech3	1m 55.899s	0.314s
10	Espargaro A	SPA	Yamaha	NGM Forward Racing	1m 56.090s	0.505s
11	Crutchlow	GBR	Ducati	Ducati Team	1m 56.129s	0.544s
12	Hernandez	COL	Ducati	Energy T.I. Pramac Racing	1m 56.622s	1.037s
13	Pirro	ITA	Ducati	Ducati Team	1m 57.093s	Q1
14	Bautista	SPA	Honda	GO&FUN Honda Gresini	1m 57.428s	Q1
15	Redding	GBR	Honda	GO&FUN Honda Gresini	1m 57.557s	Q1
16	Aoyama	JPN	Honda	Drive M7 Aspar	1m 57.984s	Q1
17	Abraham	CZE	Honda	Cardion AB Motoracing	1m 58.100s	Q1
18	Camier	GBR	Honda	Drive M7 Aspar	1m 58.635s	Q1
19	Petrucci	ITA	ART	Octo IodaRacing Team	1m 58.863s	Q1
20	De Angelis	RSM	Yamaha	NGM Forward Racing	1m 58.948s	Q1
21	Barbera	SPA	Avintia	Avintia Racing	1m 58.968s	Q1
22	Laverty	GBR	PBM	Paul Bird Motorsport	1m 58.968s	Q1
23	Parkes	AUS	PBM	Paul Bird Motorsport	1m 59.581s	Q1
24	Di Meglio	FRA	Avintia	Avintia Racing	2m 00.117s	Q1

1 DANI PEDROSA
Close to the front all through practice and qualifying, then inch-perfect in the race, setting the fastest lap – Dani won a MotoGP race for the first time in nearly a year. Fittingly, it was the 26th win of his career in the top class, matching his race number.

2 JORGE LORENZO
Not particularly happy with failing to win after dominating warm-up and the early laps. Jorge closed down Dani in the final laps and was left lamenting his lack of aggression after Dani had passed him.

3 VALENTINO ROSSI
A big crash on Saturday left Vale with a mangled little finger, which really bothered him in warm-up. He did not have so much pain in the race but was a little cautious in the opening laps. Found his rhythm and was able to pass Marquez for his third successive third place.

4 MARC MARQUEZ
The end of the run, thanks to a bike that did not want to go where it was pointed. Although the paddock felt deflated, the disappointment did not appear to bother Marc much.

5 ANDREA IANNONE
Andrea's most impressive GP so far. Qualified on the front row, led the race for a lap, and bashed fairings with Marquez. Ran in fifth for most of the race then fought off a late charge from his fellow Ducati rider Dovizioso.

6 ANDREA DOVIZIOSO
A typically clever race from Dovi. Used the softer tyre to good effect in qualifying but had to be gentle with it in the race. His engine, new for the previous race, started losing power towards the end so Andrea could not stay in his team-mate's slipstream.

7 STEFAN BRADL
Did not start well and could not catch the Ducatis, then struggled with his front tyre as soon as the rear's performance started to drop.

8 ALEIX ESPARGARO
Satisfied with the placing and finishing as top Open Class bike after a difficult weekend. Had front-end woes, as at Indianapolis, and his engine's lack of grunt did not help.

9 BRADLEY SMITH
Qualified a superb fourth but then in the race found himself with significantly less rear grip, losing time coming out of corners as his traction control worked overtime.

10 ALVARO BAUTISTA
Another difficult weekend. Struggled with rear grip problems, specifically the inability to feel what was going on with the rear tyre. Lost places early on going into corners but fought back well.

11 SCOTT REDDING
Top customer Honda rider again despite lacking confidence on the cold track after a morning warm-up crash. Could not find a way past Pirro for much of the

LAP CHART

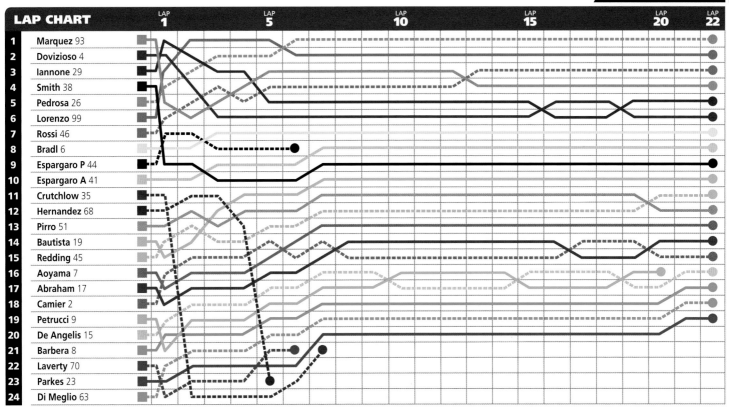

		LAP 1	LAP 5	LAP 10	LAP 15	LAP 20	LAP 22
1	Marquez 93						
2	Dovizioso 4						
3	Iannone 29						
4	Smith 38						
5	Pedrosa 26						
6	Lorenzo 99						
7	Rossi 46						
8	Bradl 6						
9	Espargaro P 44						
10	Espargaro A 41						
11	Crutchlow 35						
12	Hernandez 68						
13	Pirro 51						
14	Bautista 19						
15	Redding 45						
16	Aoyama 7						
17	Abraham 17						
18	Camier 2						
19	Petrucci 9						
20	De Angelis 15						
21	Barbera 8						
22	Laverty 70						
23	Parkes 23						
24	Di Meglio 63						

RACE

	Rider	Motorcycle	Race time	Time +	Fastest lap	Avg. speed	
1	Pedrosa	Honda	42m 47.800s		1m 56.027s	103.5mph	M/M
2	Lorenzo	Yamaha	42m 48.210s	0.410s	1m 56.066s	103.5mph	S/M
3	Rossi	Yamaha	42m 53.059s	5.259s	1m 56.280s	103.3mph	M/M
4	Marquez	Honda	42m 58.254s	10.454s	1m 56.163s	103.1mph	M/M
5	Iannone	Ducati	43m 05.439s	17.639s	1m 56.396s	102.8mph	M/S
6	Dovizioso	Ducati	43m 05.634s	17.834s	1m 56.684s	102.8mph	M/S
7	Bradl	Honda	43m 11.619s	23.819s	1m 56.910s	102.6mph	M/M
8	Espargaro A	Yamaha	43m 17.421s	29.621s	1m 57.319s	102.4mph	M/S
9	Smith	Yamaha	43m 18.164s	30.364s	1m 57.267s	102.3mph	S/M
10	Bautista	Honda	43m 25.439s	37.639s	1m 57.711s	102.0mph	M/M
11	Redding	Honda	43m 43.404s	55.604s	1m 58.305s	101.3mph	M/S
12	Pirro	Ducati	43m 44.527s	56.727s	1m 58.452s	101.3mph	M/S
13	Aoyama	Honda	43m 44.708s	56.908s	1m 58.449s	101.3mph	M/S
14	Abraham	Honda	43m 51.935s	1m 04.135s	1m 58.796s	101.0mph	M/S
15	Camier	Honda	43m 52.708s	1m 04.902s	1m 58.576s	101.0mph	M/S
16	De Angelis	Yamaha	44m 08.466s	1m 20.666s	1m 59.103s	100.4mph	S/S
17	Barbera	Avintia	44m 12.082s	1m 24.282s	1m 59.517s	100.2mph	M/S
18	Di Meglio	Avintia	44m 15.236s	1m 27.436s	1m 59.553s	100.1mph	M/S
19	Parkes	PBM	44m 26.667s	1m 38.867s	1m 59.945s	99.7mph	S/M
NF	Petrucci	ART	40m 08.079s	2 laps	1m 59.437s	100.4mph	M/S
NF	Crutchlow	Ducati	15m 19.341s	15 laps	1m 58.123s	92.0mph	M/S
NF	Espargaro P	Yamaha	11m 50.445s	16 laps	1m 57.239s	102.0mph	M/M
NF	Laverty	PBM	12m 07.340s	16 laps	1m 59.487s	99.7mph	S/S
NF	Hernandez	Ducati	10m 17.409s	17 laps	1m 58.096s	97.9mph	M/S

CHAMPIONSHIP

	Rider	Nation	Team	Points
1	Marquez	SPA	Repsol Honda Team	263
2	Pedrosa	SPA	Repsol Honda Team	186
3	Rossi	ITA	Movistar Yamaha MotoGP	173
4	Lorenzo	SPA	Movistar Yamaha MotoGP	137
5	Dovizioso	ITA	Ducati Team	118
6	Espargaro A	SPA	NGM Forward Racing	85
7	Espargaro P	SPA	Monster Yamaha Tech3	78
8	Iannone	ITA	Pramac Racing	73
9	Bradl	GER	LCR Honda MotoGP	65
9	Smith	GBR	Monster Yamaha Tech3	65
11	Bautista	SPA	GO&FUN Honda Gresini	56
12	Redding	GBR	GO&FUN Honda Gresini	45
13	Aoyama	JPN	Drive M7 Aspar	37
14	Crutchlow	GBR	Ducati Team	36
15	Hayden	USA	Drive M7 Aspar	29
16	Hernandez	COL	Energy T.I. Pramac Racing	27
17	Abraham	CZE	Cardion AB Motoracing	25
18	Edwards	USA	NGM Forward Racing	11
18	Pirro	ITA	Ducati Team	11
20	Parkes	AUS	Paul Bird Motorsport	7
21	Di Meglio	FRA	Avintia Racing	4
21	Petrucci	ITA	Octo IodaRacing Team	4
23	Laverty	GBR	Paul Bird Motorsport	2
23	Barbera	SPA	Avintia Racing	2
25	Camier	GBR	Drive M7 Aspar	1

race despite having a few tenths in hand but managed to make a move when Aoyama closed in late on.

12 MICHELE PIRRO
Found himself short of race fitness as he had not been on track for nearly two months.

13 HIROSHI AOYAMA
Improved on his qualifying position despite a bad start and was right with the Redding/Pirro dice at the flag.

14 KAREL ABRAHAM
Always feels the pressure at his home

race so happy to get away with some points –and happy with the good news that the event would continue.

15 LEON CAMIER
A point-scoring ride in only his second MotoGP start. Impressed from the start and fought nearly all the race with Aoyama and Abraham.

16 ALEX DE ANGELIS
Replacing Colin Edwards for the rest of the season, Alex found it hard to readjust after more than half a season in Moto2 but was generally satisfied with his progress over the weekend.

17 HECTOR BARBERA
Happy with the consistency of his race after a difficult start to the weekend.

18 MIKE DI MEGLIO
Broke his new chassis on Saturday so had to race the original model. Stayed with his team-mate for 15 laps but was less comfortable when the fuel load went down.

19 BROC PARKES
Another race with front-end problems. The only time he had a set-up that pleased him was in Sunday morning warm-up.

DID NOT FINISH

DANILO PETRUCCI
Passed both Avintia bikes and had sized up de Angelis when the engine shut down. The problem was a battery lead that vibrated out of its holder and then chafed against bodywork until it caused a short circuit.

CAL CRUTCHLOW
Ran off-track at Turn 3 on the second lap and wrenched his shoulder wrestling the Ducati through the gravel trap; retired to save himself for his home GP a fortnight later.

POL ESPARGARO
Lost ground to the leading group when he ran on thanks to a nervous front end. Recovered but pushed too hard when Bradl came past.

MICHAEL LAVERTY
Had a launch-control problem off the start. When he pushed the front the forks bottomed and he fell.

YONNY HERNANDEZ
Forced to retire early on when his front tyre started to lose pressure.

HERTZ BRITISH
GRAND PRIX
SILVERSTONE

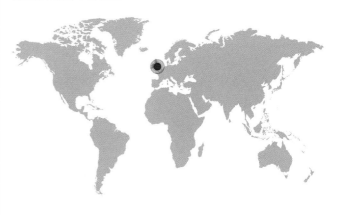

BATTLE OF BRITAIN

Marquez takes revenge for the previous race as well as for the previous year's British Grand Prix

For the second year running, British fans basked in late summer sunshine and saw Marc Marquez and Jorge Lorenzo fight to the flag. It took a typically audacious move by Marquez two laps from home to settle the issue, and, yes, he was thinking about the defeat of the previous year. Given the move he made, he was thinking about it a lot. It never looked like Marc had suffered any permanent damage from losing the Czech race, but he did describe himself as being 'a little angry' about not standing on the rostrum there. As he said that, he was grinning like a Cheshire Cat and holding a thumb and forefinger about a centimetre apart.

Both factory Yamahas had to improve massively over the weekend to give Marc a race. Valentino Rossi was third, albeit seven seconds behind his team-mate. It felt a bit like normal service being resumed, the pattern from last season re-established. That means Lorenzo riding at 100 per cent from lights-out with his astonishing, metronomic precision, trying to build up a lead he can defend in the closing stages but just failing to beat Marquez's late charge. Last year, Pedrosa would have been third with Rossi a little way back, just ahead of the satellite bikes and the occasional Ducati. This year, Vale's second back on the Yamaha, he was bringing to bear all his experience – at Silverstone he set a new record of 246 Grand Prix starts – and rattling up the rostrum placings, often without getting in range of Marquez.

As 2014 progressed Pedrosa seemed to rediscover inconsistency while Jorge somehow managed to get over his nightmare start to the season. While his championship chances were long gone by this stage of the season, Jorge was still willing to put it all on the line for the chance of a win.

'FINISHING AS TOP BRIT AT
THE BRITISH GRAND PRIX
IS ALWAYS GOOD'
SCOTT REDDING

The real change from 2013 was the performance of the Ducatis, not just in their finishing positions but also the gap to the winner. Last year at Silverstone Andrea Dovizioso crashed – a rare event – and the first Ducati home was Nicky Hayden's, 36 seconds behind Lorenzo. This year Dovi was under ten seconds behind Marc. That is progress.

As was Scott Redding's tenth place in front of two Ducatis. Last year Scott won the Moto2 race, and this year he was under nearly as much pressure from the financial and political issues surrounding his future. His Gresini team looked to be switching to Aprilia for 2015, meaning Scott would go to whichever team had the satellite Honda that would be available. Despite feeling distinctly unsettled, Scott again fed on the home-race pressure and put in a stellar performance throughout the three days. For the fifth race running, he finished as top customer Honda rider.

The race at the front was always between Lorenzo and Marquez, the pair helped by Rossi, Dovizioso and Aleix Espargaro fighting among themselves for long enough to allow the leaders to escape. In another echo of the previous year's race, Dani Pedrosa started badly and crossed a gap to the group ahead, but could not make any further progress.

Lorenzo made the running from the start, riding, as he later said, 'like an animal'. Jorge forced a lead of nearly half a second before Marquez started his implacable progress. When Marc went to the front just before three-quarters distance, the crowd assumed that the race was over. It most assuredly was not. As he had done at Mugello, Lorenzo took two laps to gather his

LEFT Scott Redding continued his run of form with tenth at his home race, and top customer Honda for the fifth race running.

ABOVE Yet again there was a Ducati on the front row and it finished within ten seconds of the winner – a massive improvement compared with the previous year.

forces and then pushed back to the front and stayed there for a couple of laps.

Marquez's final attack came two laps from the flag, starting, but not finishing, at the fast left of Farm. Lorenzo pushed back in front at the slower right-hander that followed, Village, and headed for the apex of the next corner, a slow left, no doubt thinking that he had the corner as he was right over the paint. Not so. Marquez was under him, forcing Jorge to lift. It was the decisive move, but was it entirely fair? The consensus was 'yes', just, as it was right on the limit of the acceptable.

The fight for third also held the attention of the crowd, mainly because it included Valentino Rossi. Vale had to work for his rostrum, fending off the impressive Dovizioso for most of the race and having to retake third from Pedrosa towards the end.

Marquez admitted post-race that he had indeed been thinking not just of his defeat last time out but of the way Lorenzo had beaten him at Silverstone 12 months previously: 'I had a score to settle.' That race, too, had been decided at the last corner.

When he had calmed down a little, Marc admitted that he was somewhat surprised by Lorenzo's pace at the start and had to balance the contradictory demands of nursing his tyres while not allowing Jorge to open a significant gap. As usual, when the tyres started to go off, it was the Honda that coped better. Or rather it was Marquez who coped better with worn tyres – one of his strengths.

And talking of coping, Lorenzo made a good effort at that in considering Marquez's tough move. He muttered about it not being his job to decide what was fair and what was not. Yes, it felt just like old times.

ABOVE Bradley Smith had a nightmare home race thanks to a cracked wheel rim.

BELOW Valentino Rossi leads the fight for third place.

OPPOSITE Yonny Hernandez on his way to 11th place.

GREEN, GREEN GRASS

The British Grand Prix took place amid much speculation about its future.

Rumours, confirmed soon after race weekend, were that the Circuit of Wales, or rather the Heads of the Valleys Development Company that is due to build the new circuit near Ebbw Vale, would get the race. And as they offered more money than Silverstone, they did – despite the fact that there is no chance of the track being completed for a 2015 race.

This situation is not unique: circuits that have yet to be built have been awarded GPs previously. Despite not possessing a track, the Circuit of Wales organisation has a five-year contract for the British Grand Prix, so they had to find a venue for 2015. That meant one of the two circuits in the UK with international homologation: Silverstone – obviously – and Donington Park. The deal had to be done quickly as Dorna intended to publish the 2015 calendar around the time of the Aragón race, less than a month away.

The decision did indeed come quickly, and it was in favour of Donington Park. The track is currently homologated for World Superbikes, but not for MotoGP, although the required modifications are not major.

Donington Park is no stranger to MotoGP, having hosted the British Grand Prix from 1987 to 2009. Riders have always liked the track, at least from the first corner, Redgate, round to Fogarty's Esses. The Melbourne Loop that concludes the lap, however, is another matter.

Valentino Rossi, who had not been averse to a return to the sweeps of Donington, did not seem quite so sure after getting his first rostrum at Silverstone. 'Maybe Silverstone is not so bad after you have some years to learn it…'

HERTZ BRITISH GRAND PRIX
SILVERSTONE
ROUND 12
AUGUST 31

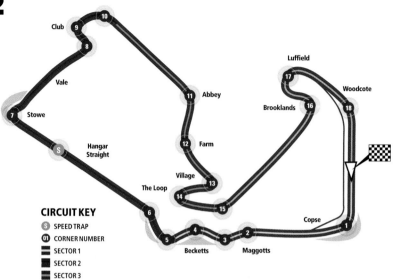

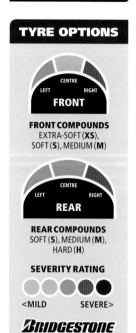

TYRE OPTIONS

CENTRE
LEFT · RIGHT
FRONT

FRONT COMPOUNDS
EXTRA-SOFT (**XS**),
SOFT (**S**), MEDIUM (**M**)

CENTRE
LEFT · RIGHT
REAR

REAR COMPOUNDS
SOFT (**S**), MEDIUM (**M**),
HARD (**H**)

SEVERITY RATING

<MILD   SEVERE>

BRIDGESTONE

RACE RESULTS

CIRCUIT LENGTH 3.666 miles
NO. OF LAPS 20
RACE DISTANCE 73.322 miles
WEATHER Dry, 18°C
TRACK TEMPERATURE 29°C
WINNER Marc Marquez
FASTEST LAP 2m 01.980s,
108.181mph, Marc Marquez
LAP RECORD 2m 01.941s,
108.181mph, Dani Pedrosa, 2013

CIRCUIT KEY
- Ⓢ SPEED TRAP
- ⑪ CORNER NUMBER
- ▬ SECTOR 1
- ▬ SECTOR 2
- ▬ SECTOR 3
- ▬ SECTOR 4

QUALIFYING

	Rider	Nation	Motorcycle	Team	Time	Pole +
1	Marquez	SPA	Honda	Repsol Honda Team	2m 00.829s	
2	Dovizioso	ITA	Ducati	Ducati Team	2m 01.140s	0.311s
3	Lorenzo	SPA	Yamaha	Movistar Yamaha MotoGP	2m 01.175s	0.346s
4	Espargaro A	SPA	Yamaha	NGM Forward Racing	2m 01.448s	0.619s
5	Pedrosa	SPA	Honda	Repsol Honda Team	2m 01.464s	0.635s
6	Rossi	ITA	Yamaha	Movistar Yamaha MotoGP	2m 01.550s	0.721s
7	Smith	GBR	Yamaha	Monster Yamaha Tech3	2m 01.593s	0.764s
8	Espargaro P	SPA	Yamaha	Monster Yamaha Tech3	2m 01.747s	0.918s
9	Bradl	GER	Honda	LCR Honda MotoGP	2m 01.973s	1.144s
10	Iannone	ITA	Ducati	Pramac Racing	2m 02.064s	1.235s
11	Redding	GBR	Honda	GO&FUN Honda Gresini	2m 02.116s	1.287s
12	Bautista	SPA	Honda	GO&FUN Honda Gresini	2m 03.618s	2.789s
13	Hernandez	COL	Ducati	Energy T.I. Pramac Racing	2m 03.046s	Q1
14	Abraham	CZE	Honda	Cardion AB Motoracing	2m 03.206s	Q1
15	Crutchlow	GBR	Ducati	Ducati Team	2m 03.407s	Q1
16	Aoyama	JPN	Honda	Drive M7 Aspar	2m 03.563s	Q1
17	De Angelis	RSM	Yamaha	NGM Forward Racing	2m 03.686s	Q1
18	Camier	GBR	Honda	Drive M7 Aspar	2m 03.696s	Q1
19	Petrucci	ITA	ART	Octo IodaRacing Team	2m 04.755s	Q1
20	Laverty	GBR	PBM	Paul Bird Motorsport	2m 04.836s	Q1
21	Barbera	SPA	Avintia	Avintia Racing	2m 04.957s	Q1
22	Di Meglio	FRA	Avintia	Avintia Racing	2m 05.451s	Q1
23	Parkes	AUS	PBM	Paul Bird Motorsport	2m 06.106s	Q1

1 MARC MARQUEZ
Revenge for the previous race and revenge for the previous year. Surprised by the improvement in pace the Yamahas found and again started badly, but prepared to bang fairings to get the win.

2 JORGE LORENZO
A remarkable race given how far back both factory Yamahas were on Friday. Delighted and proud of the work done by his team and of his own performance, but could not hide a touch of displeasure over Marquez's riding.

3 VALENTINO ROSSI
Like his team-mate, made a massive recovery from a dreadful first day to get his first podium at Silverstone. Second-row qualifying meant he had to deal with a spirited Pol Espargaro before crossing the gap to Dovizioso, then he tried to cross to the leaders but was reeled back in.

4 DANI PEDROSA
One of those weekends when he was largely invisible. Spun up off the start and never really got with the leaders. Spent most of the race in close company with Dovizioso and Rossi.

5 ANDREA DOVIZIOSO
Probably the best ride of the weekend. Second on the grid followed by fifth in the race. Crucially, loss of grip affected Dovi badly in three or four corners and meant he could not fight for third place. That he was actually disappointed about that is a measure of the progress made.

6 POL ESPARGARO
Gambled on the hard front tyre, which he had not tried until race day. Understandably cautious early on, but got quicker. Happy with his finishing position but not the gap to the leaders.

7 STEFAN BRADL
After two big crashes, not a bad result. Started well but dropped back to 13th after a major mistake, then fought back despite rear grip issues.

8 ANDREA IANNONE
Rear tyre grip dropped off very quickly and gave him big problems both going into and out of corners.

9 ALEIX ESPARGARO
Fast and combative in the early laps when he fought for fourth place. Frustrated to lose out on Silverstone's straights but was top Open Class bike.

10 SCOTT REDDING
Seriously quick in practice and by far the best customer Honda rider in the race as well as top Brit. Put a tough pass on Hernandez three laps from the flag to secure a top-ten finish in front of two Ducatis.

11 YONNY HERNANDEZ
Like his team-mate, lost rear grip but not as quickly. He was in the group fighting for sixth to eleventh places for most of the race but had no defence against Redding's attack late on. Happy to finish in the points after a run of bad luck.

LAP CHART

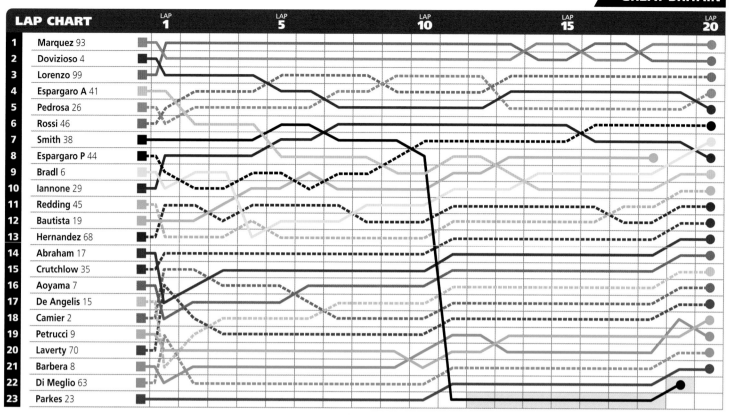

	Rider	LAP 1	LAP 5	LAP 10	LAP 15	LAP 20
1	Marquez 93					
2	Dovizioso 4					
3	Lorenzo 99					
4	Espargaro A 41					
5	Pedrosa 26					
6	Rossi 46					
7	Smith 38					
8	Espargaro P 44					
9	Bradl 6					
10	Iannone 29					
11	Redding 45					
12	Bautista 19					
13	Hernandez 68					
14	Abraham 17					
15	Crutchlow 35					
16	Aoyama 7					
17	De Angelis 15					
18	Camier 2					
19	Petrucci 9					
20	Laverty 70					
21	Barbera 8					
22	Di Meglio 63					
23	Parkes 23					

RACE

	Rider	Motorcycle	Race time	Time +	Fastest lap	Avg. speed	🏁
1	Marquez	Honda	40m 51.835s		2m 01.980s	107.6mph	M/M
2	Lorenzo	Yamaha	40m 52.567s	0.732s	2m 02.066s	107.6mph	M/M
3	Rossi	Yamaha	41m 00.354s	8.519s	2m 02.043s	107.2mph	M/M
4	Pedrosa	Honda	41m 00.529s	8.694s	2m 02.013s	107.2mph	M/M
5	Dovizioso	Ducati	41m 01.073s	9.238s	2m 02.006s	107.2mph	M/M
6	Espargaro P	Yamaha	41m 16.581s	24.746s	2m 03.209s	106.6mph	M/M
7	Bradl	Honda	41m 18.552s	26.717s	2m 02.916s	106.4mph	M/M
8	Iannone	Ducati	41m 18.745s	26.910s	2m 02.947s	106.4mph	S/M
9	Espargaro A	Yamaha	41m 25.290s	33.455s	2m 03.037s	106.2mph	M/S
10	Redding	Honda	41m 30.929s	39.094s	2m 03.273s	105.9mph	S/S
11	Hernandez	Ducati	41m 32.090s	40.255s	2m 03.409s	105.9mph	S/S
12	Crutchlow	Ducati	41m 34.862s	43.027s	2m 03.708s	105.8mph	M/M
13	Abraham	Honda	41m 44.080s	52.245s	2m 04.169s	105.4mph	S/S
14	Aoyama	Honda	41m 50.816s	58.981s	2m 04.655s	105.1mph	S/S
15	De Angelis	Yamaha	41m 50.999s	59.164s	2m 04.641s	105.1mph	S/M
16	Camier	Honda	41m 57.515s	1m 05.680s	2m 04.793s	104.8mph	S/S
17	Laverty	PBM	42m 02.774s	1m 10.939s	2m 05.417s	104.6mph	S/S
18	Petrucci	ART	42m 08.669s	1m 16.834s	2m 05.697s	104.3mph	S/S
19	Barbera	Avintia	42m 08.739s	1m 16.904s	2m 05.495s	104.3mph	S/S
20	Di Meglio	Avintia	42m 26.774s	1m 34.939s	2m 05.974s	103.6mph	S/S
21	Parkes	PBM	42m 30.277s	1m 38.442s	2m 06.119s	103.5mph	S/S
22	Smith	Yamaha	42m 39.042s	1 lap	2m 02.935s	97.9mph	S/M
NF	Bautista	Honda	37m 09.736s	2 laps	2m 03.146s	106.5mph	M/M

CHAMPIONSHIP

	Rider	Nation	Team	Points
1	Marquez	SPA	Repsol Honda Team	288
2	Pedrosa	SPA	Repsol Honda Team	199
3	Rossi	ITA	Movistar Yamaha MotoGP	189
4	Lorenzo	SPA	Movistar Yamaha MotoGP	157
5	Dovizioso	ITA	Ducati Team	129
6	Espargaro A	SPA	NGM Forward Racing	92
7	Espargaro P	SPA	Monster Yamaha Tech3	88
8	Iannone	ITA	Pramac Racing	81
9	Bradl	GER	LCR Honda MotoGP	74
10	Smith	GBR	Monster Yamaha Tech3	65
11	Bautista	SPA	GO&FUN Honda Gresini	56
12	Redding	GBR	GO&FUN Honda Gresini	51
13	Crutchlow	GBR	Ducati Team	40
14	Aoyama	JPN	Drive M7 Aspar	39
15	Hernandez	COL	Energy T.I. Pramac Racing	32
16	Hayden	USA	Drive M7 Aspar	29
17	Abraham	CZE	Cardion AB Motoracing	28
18	Edwards	USA	NGM Forward Racing	11
	Pirro	ITA	Ducati Team	11
20	Parkes	AUS	Paul Bird Motorsport	7
21	Di Meglio	FRA	Avintia Racing	4
	Petrucci	ITA	Octo IodaRacing Team	4
23	Laverty	GBR	Paul Bird Motorsport	2
	Barbera	SPA	Avintia Racing	2
25	De Angelis	RSM	NGM Forward Racing	1
	Camier	GBR	Drive M7 Aspar	1

12 CAL CRUTCHLOW
An unhappy home race, not helped by the shoulder injury Cal picked up at Brno. After his history of injuries at Silverstone, he was happy – or should that be relieved? – just to finish.

13 KAREL ABRAHAM
Really good pace in the middle of the race but too slow in the first three laps and then hit rear grip issues late on.

14 HIROSHI AOYAMA
Lost the feeling he had during warm-up, resulting in loss of rear grip and a couple of mistakes.

15 ALEX DE ANGELIS
Two crashes in warm-up left Alex with a very sore right wrist, but he still scored his first point.

16 LEON CAMIER
Just missed a point due to a problem with the brakes that nearly resulted in a crash on the warm-up lap.

17 MICHAEL LAVERTY
Major improvements on the previous year's race time. Worked well through the weekend and raced with three other British riders early on before grip deteriorated.

18 DANILO PETRUCCI
Depressed by the fact that whatever the team did to the ART bike, it seemed to have no effect. The only good thing, Danilo said, was that he overtook Barbera on the last lap.

19 HECTOR BARBERA
Again had electronics problems, this time with the gear sensor failing, meaning that the engine software did not know which gear the bike was in. That was the cap on a weekend when the Avintia's deficiencies were amplified by the circuit.

20 MIKE DI MEGLIO
Problems, but different ones from his team-mate: in the race Mike's Avintia simply had no grip at the rear compared with practice and qualifying.

21 BROC PARKES
Broc turned the PBM bike inside-out trying to find a setting that worked for him. Hoped the hotter conditions of race day would help, but it was not to be.

22 BRADLEY SMITH
Pitted and found the rear wheel rim was cracked; went back out again and got a great reception from the fans.

DID NOT FINISH

ALVARO BAUTISTA
Another blow to Alvaro's morale: he was in a safe seventh, a big improvement on practice, when he crashed two laps from the flag. Said he knew he could not catch Pol Espargaro so he was not pushing.

GP TIM DI SAN MARINO
E DELLA RIVIERA DI RIMINI
MISANO WORLD CIRCUIT MARCO SIMONCELLI

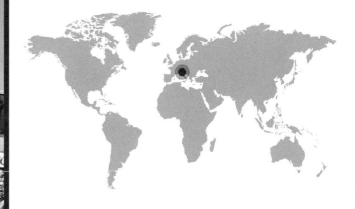

TIME
TRAVELLER

**Valentino Rossi won at home
for the first time in five years
while Marc Marquez fell**

It was, said the man himself, a better win than Assen last year. That was Valentino Rossi's first victory after his return to Yamaha following two fallow years at Ducati. Rossi's second win could not have been better. None of his rivals was injured and any mechanical or tyre woes they may have had were self-inflicted.

This was a classic Rossi win – and Vale even had the sort of clever helmet design that was once obligatory for a home race. He started with a crash on a thoroughly damp and dismal Friday, then progressed through his first front-row start of the season to a dominant race win, bringing him to a record career points tally of over 5,000. Who, you might ask, writes his scripts?

By the end of Saturday it was clear to Rossi that for once his Yamaha had an advantage over the Honda. Marc Marquez was looking and sounding like the Marquez of Brno, not the Marquez who won ten in a row. Jorge Lorenzo secured Yamaha's first pole of the year with Rossi in third, sandwiching the Ducati of Andrea Iannone, who was impressive once again. Both factory Hondas were on the second row, the first time this year for Marquez; the gaps were not big but they were significant.

Race day was appreciably warmer than the rest of the weekend and led to Lorenzo choosing to race, uniquely and untypically, with the hard front tyre. He knew almost immediately that it was a mistake and ended up slower than he had been the previous year and even when he had been on the 800cc Yamaha. Nevertheless, he was quick enough to finish a comfortable second and honest enough to admit that he thought the result would have been the same had he used the same front tyre as the rest of the field.

ABOVE Fifth-placed Andrea Iannone qualified his Ducati on the front row and held off Dani Pedrosa in the race until the inevitable tyre drop-off.

RIGHT Leon Camier and Alvaro Bautista fight for position as Danilo Petrucci spins out behind them.

OPPOSITE Jorge Lorenzo started from pole position but could not match his team-mate's race pace.

As usual, Jorge managed to start well but was quickly relegated to third by Rossi and Marquez in what has become the now-standard early skirmishing. This time the action included one pass by Rossi on Marquez at Curvone, the fearsome right-hander at the end of the straight that may very well be the fastest corner of the year. That move was another indication of the difficulties Marc was having.

Marquez hung on to Rossi until the tenth lap, when he ran his front wheel up the inside kerb going into Turn 4, a slow right-hander, and slipped off. It was his bad luck that the bike stopped and he needed a push from a bunch of marshals to restart. He tweeted his thanks to them after the race. The crash put him so far back that it was all he could do to recover to 15th place at the flag for one championship point. That ruined his chances of retaining his title on home soil at Aragón next time out – which was the reason he had been pushing so hard.

After the incident Marc lapped at much the same pace as team-mate Dani Pedrosa, who was now in third but over five seconds adrift of Rossi. Before the crash, however, Marc had been between 0.2sec and 0.6sec a lap quicker than Pedrosa – an indication of just how hard he was pushing and of how many liberties he was taking as he tried to keep tabs on the Yamahas. Like Lorenzo, Marquez said that the crash did not alter the result, as he felt that he would not have beaten Rossi in any case.

So, should Marc have settled for points rather than risking all for the win? Given his massive lead in the championship – still 74 points after this race – that seems a silly question. However, at this exact point last season he first mentioned riding for the title rather than wins, so

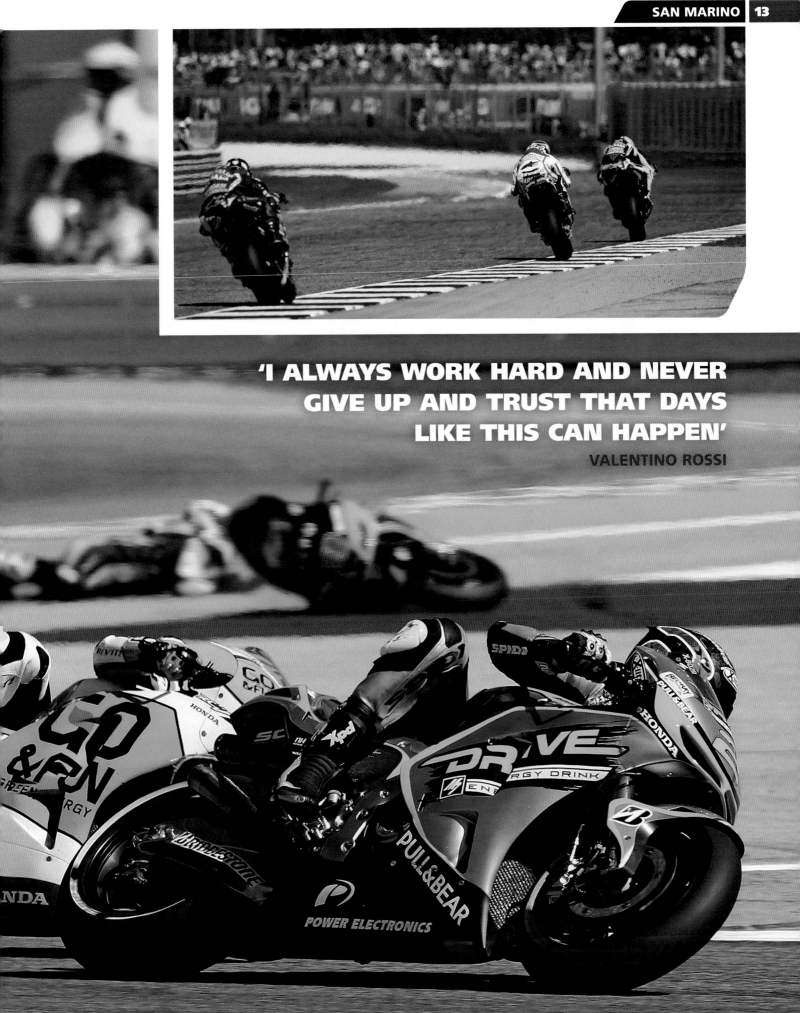

'I ALWAYS WORK HARD AND NEVER GIVE UP AND TRUST THAT DAYS LIKE THIS CAN HAPPEN'

VALENTINO ROSSI

the question is valid. Aside from the argument that he risked injury by pressing when he knew the chances of a win were very small, the result ensured that Marc could not now retain his title until Japan, which would at least make Honda happy.

All of which cleared the stage for Valentino Rossi to roll back the years in front of nearly 60,000 delirious (mainly) Italian fans. He did not put a foot wrong, maintaining concentration and pace for the whole race, never dropping out of the 1min 34sec bracket on a flying lap. For a man of 35, that is an impressive feat. Hell, it would have been impressive for a 25-year-old.

It was notable that Valentino took his crew chief Silvano Galbusera up to the rostrum not just to accept the constructors' trophy but also to stand on the winner's box with him. It was another reminder to the world at large and the media in particular that he had made the correct decision in parting from Jerry Burgess. There was probably also a tinge of relief as Galbusera has never in his career gone through a season without a victory.

Where does Vale continue to get his motivation? Before the race he said his main objective for the year was to win a race again. Then there were the longer-term objectives of fighting Dani Pedrosa for second in the championship as well as re-asserting authority over his team-mate. He was getting very close to achieving all three.

ABOVE Karel Abraham finally got a break and finished top of the Open Class.

BELOW Bradley Smith's seventh place was a welcome return to something like true form.

OPPOSITE All four Ducatis finished in the top ten, with Dovi best of them in fourth.

AMERICAN IDLE

The continuing absence of Nicky Hayden from the MotoGP grid and the sacking of Josh Herrin by the Caterham Moto2 team meant that there was no American on the grid in any class of a Grand Prix for the first time since the German GP of 2002 – when Kenny Roberts Jnr was recovering from an operation and John Hopkins was hurt in practice.

To find a GP without an American entered in the top class, you have to go back to Venezuela in 1979, when Kenny Roberts Snr was recovering from a winter testing crash. And to find a GP with no American entered in any of the classes, you have to go back to the last race of 1975 at Brno, in what was then Czechoslovakia.

Through all the years in between Americans have won 15 500cc or MotoGP world titles, from Roberts Snr in 1978 to Hayden in 2006. But the supply of fast racers from the United States has dried up. In recent years, the takeover of domestic racing by the Daytona

Motorsports Group in 2009 has led to teams and manufacturers leaving the championship in droves, and the loss of TV coverage.

From the 2015 season, the American championship, known as MotoAmerica, will be under the control of the KRAVE Group, fronted by triple 500cc World Champion Wayne Rainey. It is difficult to think of a man more respected within the industry, not just in the US but

worldwide. The task is to rebuild what used to be the most important domestic championship in the world and re-establish a route for American talent to reach GP racing. Currently, it is nigh-on impossible to see where the next American GP racer is going to come from, let alone the next American World Champion.

It is going to be a tough job, but Rainey has done tougher.

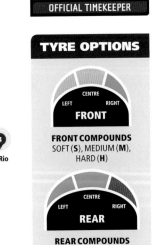

GP TIM DI SAN MARINO E DELLA RIVIERA DI RIMINI

MISANO WORLD CIRCUIT MARCO SIMONCELLI

ROUND 13

SEPTEMBER 14

RACE RESULTS

CIRCUIT LENGTH 2.626 miles

NO. OF LAPS 28

RACE DISTANCE 73.528 miles

WEATHER Dry, 25°C

TRACK TEMPERATURE 37°C

WINNER Valentino Rossi

FASTEST LAP 1m 34.108s, 100.414mph, Marc Marquez

LAP RECORD 1m 33.906s, 100.662mph, Jorge Lorenzo, 2011

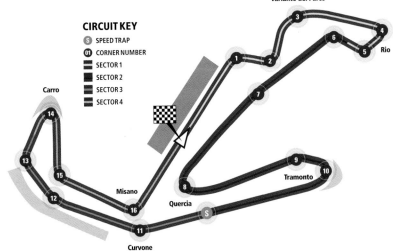

CIRCUIT KEY
- **S** SPEED TRAP
- **01** CORNER NUMBER
- SECTOR 1
- SECTOR 2
- SECTOR 3
- SECTOR 4

Variante del Parco · Rio · Tramonto · Quercia · Misano · Curvone · Carro

TYRE OPTIONS

FRONT
CENTRE · LEFT · RIGHT

FRONT COMPOUNDS
SOFT (**S**), MEDIUM (**M**), HARD (**H**)

REAR
CENTRE · LEFT · RIGHT

REAR COMPOUNDS
SOFT (**S**), MEDIUM (**M**), HARD (**H**)

SEVERITY RATING

<MILD ● ● ● ● ● SEVERE>

BRIDGESTONE

MotoGP · TISSOT OFFICIAL TIMEKEEPER

QUALIFYING

	Rider	Nation	Motorcycle	Team	Time	Pole +
1	Lorenzo	SPA	Yamaha	Movistar Yamaha MotoGP	1m 33.238s	
2	Iannone	ITA	Ducati	Pramac Racing	1m 33.289s	0.051s
3	Rossi	ITA	Yamaha	Movistar Yamaha MotoGP	1m 33.302s	0.064s
4	Marquez	SPA	Honda	Repsol Honda Team	1m 33.360s	0.122s
5	Pedrosa	SPA	Honda	Repsol Honda Team	1m 33.418s	0.180s
6	Dovizioso	ITA	Ducati	Ducati Team	1m 33.439s	0.201s
7	Espargaro P	SPA	Yamaha	Monster Yamaha Tech3	1m 33.557s	0.319s
8	Espargaro A	SPA	Yamaha	NGM Forward Racing	1m 33.713s	0.475s
9	Smith	GBR	Yamaha	Monster Yamaha Tech3	1m 33.761s	0.523s
10	Bradl	GER	Honda	LCR Honda MotoGP	1m 33.995s	0.757s
11	Hernandez	COL	Ducati	Energy T.I. Pramac Racing	1m 34.283s	1.045s
12	Bautista	SPA	Honda	GO&FUN Honda Gresini	1m 34.640s	1.402s
13	Crutchlow	GBR	Ducati	Ducati Team	1m 34.495s	Q1
14	Redding	GBR	Honda	GO&FUN Honda Gresini	1m 34.919s	Q1
15	Aoyama	JPN	Honda	Drive M7 Aspar	1m 34.966s	Q1
16	Camier	GBR	Honda	Drive M7 Aspar	1m 35.275s	Q1
17	Abraham	CZE	Honda	Cardion AB Motoracing	1m 35.292s	Q1
18	Laverty	GBR	PBM	Paul Bird Motorsport	1m 35.589s	Q1
19	De Angelis	RSM	Yamaha	NGM Forward Racing	1m 35.679s	Q1
20	Parkes	AUS	PBM	Paul Bird Motorsport	1m 36.317s	Q1
21	Barbera	SPA	Avintia	Avintia Racing	1m 36.689s	Q1
22	Di Meglio	FRA	Avintia	Avintia Racing	1m 42.497s	Q1
23	Petrucci	ITA	ART	Octo IodaRacing Team	1m 37.417s	Q1

1 VALENTINO ROSSI
The most popular of home wins brought a record career points haul of over 5,000. No luck involved: Rossi just used the Yamaha's strengths, passing Marquez on the fastest corner of the year, and riding like he was 20 years old again. With the bonus of his best helmet design for years.

2 JORGE LORENZO
Chose the hard front tyre, departing not only from his usual practice but also the rest of the field's choice. Did it lose him the race? Probably not. The tyre did not work to his advantage as it had in Brno.

3 DANI PEDROSA
Average qualifying followed by a bad start and a race-long fight for position, mainly with Dovizioso. Reported grip problems front and rear and only near the end of the race was he lapping at the same pace as the Yamahas.

4 ANDREA DOVIZIOSO
Another stunning ride, finishing just five seconds behind the winner and right on the tail of third-place man Pedrosa on a track that is supposed to be difficult for the Ducati. Team and rider delighted.

5 ANDREA IANNONE
Equalled his best finish of the year and was closer to the winner than he has ever been, despite being slightly down on power. Had trouble with a full tank problem but still diced with the Monster Yamahas – and Pedrosa had to force his way past. Another impressive ride.

6 POL ESPARGARO
Used the softer tyres, which with hindsight he thought could have been a mistake. Rather confused by the lack of dry track time and the rise in temperatures, so happy to get sixth and overtake his brother in the standings.

7 BRADLEY SMITH
A great improvement on the last two races. Ran off-track at Turn 7 on the second lap, which cost two places.

8 ALVARO BAUTISTA
Suffered his usual problems with stopping the bike. Lost eighth place when he had a problem with his visor, only to regain the position on the last lap when Aleix Espargaro crashed.

9 CAL CRUTCHLOW
As is now usual, Cal had trouble stopping the bike with a full tank but picked up the pace before hitting tyre trouble.

10 YONNY HERNANDEZ
Lit up the soaking wet first day with some stunning riding then had a good race to a top-ten finish.

11 KAREL ABRAHAM
Top customer Honda and top Open Class bike. Improved his lap times through the race, after radically changing front-fork settings in the search for grip.

12 HIROSHI AOYAMA
Much happier than at Silverstone but hit grip problems with his front tyre and lost top customer Honda slot when he could not fend off Abraham.

LAP CHART

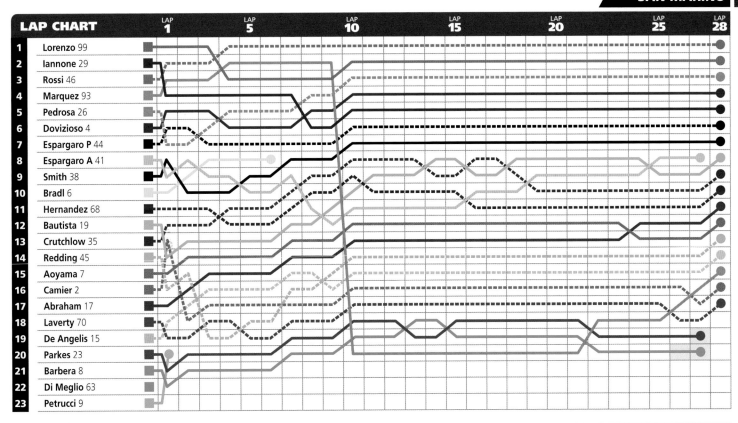

	Rider	LAP 1	LAP 5	LAP 10	LAP 15	LAP 20	LAP 25	LAP 28
1	Lorenzo 99							
2	Iannone 29							
3	Rossi 46							
4	Marquez 93							
5	Pedrosa 26							
6	Dovizioso 4							
7	Espargaro P 44							
8	Espargaro A 41							
9	Smith 38							
10	Bradl 6							
11	Hernandez 68							
12	Bautista 19							
13	Crutchlow 35							
14	Redding 45							
15	Aoyama 7							
16	Camier 2							
17	Abraham 17							
18	Laverty 70							
19	De Angelis 15							
20	Parkes 23							
21	Barbera 8							
22	Di Meglio 63							
23	Petrucci 9							

RACE

	Rider	Motorcycle	Race time	Time +	Fastest lap	Avg. speed	
1	Rossi	Yamaha	44m 14.586s		1m 34.165s	99.7mph	M/M
2	Lorenzo	Yamaha	44m 16.164s	1.578s	1m 34.295s	99.6mph	H/M
3	Pedrosa	Honda	44m 18.862s	4.276s	1m 34.320s	99.5mph	M/M
4	Dovizioso	Ducati	44m 20.096s	5.510s	1m 34.330s	99.5mph	M/M
5	Iannone	Ducati	44m 26.357s	11.771s	1m 34.751s	99.2mph	M/M
6	Espargaro P	Yamaha	44m 33.585s	18.999s	1m 34.888s	99.0mph	M/M
7	Smith	Yamaha	44m 37.686s	23.100s	1m 34.981s	98.8mph	M/M
8	Bautista	Honda	44m 51.044s	36.458s	1m 35.293s	98.3mph	M/M
9	Crutchlow	Ducati	44m 53.066s	38.480s	1m 35.390s	98.2mph	M/M
10	Hernandez	Ducati	45m 00.464s	45.878s	1m 35.279s	98.0mph	M/S
11	Abraham	Honda	45m 09.351s	54.765s	1m 35.826s	97.7mph	M/S
12	Aoyama	Honda	45m 11.361s	56.775s	1m 35.954s	97.6mph	M/S
13	Redding	Honda	45m 17.320s	1m 02.734s	1m 36.040s	97.4mph	M/S
14	De Angelis	Yamaha	45m 28.132s	1m 13.546s	1m 36.478s	97.0mph	M/S
15	Marquez	Honda	45m 30.534s	1m 15.948s	1m 34.108s	96.9mph	M/M
16	Camier	Honda	45m 35.346s	1m 20.760s	1m 37.012s	96.7mph	M/S
17	Laverty	PBM	45m 41.008s	1m 26.422s	1m 36.996s	96.6mph	M/S
18	Parkes	PBM	44m 17.702s	1 lap	1m 37.314s	96.0mph	M/S
19	Barbera	Avintia	44m 17.921s	1 lap	1m 37.314s	96.0mph	M/S
NF	Espargaro A	Yamaha	43m 14.298s	1 lap	1m 35.108s	98.4mph	M/M
NF	Bradl	Honda	9m 36.915s	22 laps	1m 34.591s	98.3mph	M/M
NF	Petrucci	ART	1m 45.903s	27 laps	–	89.2mph	M/S
NF	Di Meglio	Avintia	–	–	–	–	M/S

CHAMPIONSHIP

	Rider	Nation	Team	Points
1	Marquez	SPA	Repsol Honda Team	289
2	Pedrosa	SPA	Repsol Honda Team	215
3	Rossi	ITA	Movistar Yamaha MotoGP	214
4	Lorenzo	SPA	Movistar Yamaha MotoGP	177
5	Dovizioso	ITA	Ducati Team	142
6	Espargaro P	SPA	Monster Yamaha Tech3	98
7	Espargaro A	SPA	NGM Forward Racing	92
8	Iannone	ITA	Pramac Racing	92
9	Bradl	GER	LCR Honda MotoGP	74
10	Smith	GBR	Monster Yamaha Tech3	74
11	Bautista	SPA	GO&FUN Honda Gresini	64
12	Redding	GBR	GO&FUN Honda Gresini	54
13	Crutchlow	GBR	Ducati Team	47
14	Aoyama	JPN	Drive M7 Aspar	43
15	Hernandez	COL	Energy T.I. Pramac Racing	38
16	Abraham	CZE	Cardion AB Motoracing	33
17	Hayden	USA	Drive M7 Aspar	29
18	Edwards	USA	NGM Forward Racing	11
	Pirro	ITA	Ducati Team	11
20	Parkes	AUS	Paul Bird Motorsport	7
21	Di Meglio	FRA	Avintia Racing	4
	Petrucci	ITA	Octo IodaRacing Team	4
23	De Angelis	RSM	NGM Forward Racing	3
24	Laverty	GBR	Paul Bird Motorsport	2
	Barbera	SPA	Avintia Racing	2
26	Camier	GBR	Drive M7 Aspar	1

---

13 SCOTT REDDING
Called the weekend a disaster. With three crashes and then a seized rear brake in the race, you can see his point. Considered pulling in but worked his way up three places after running off-track on the third lap. The first time in six races he had not been top customer Honda.

14 ALEX DE ANGELIS
In pain from his wrist – it turned out to be a broken scaphoid. Scoring points under those circumstances is pretty impressive.

15 MARC MARQUEZ
Finally, a mistake! Tipped off in a slow corner when forcing the Honda to go as fast as the Yamahas. When he got going again, he settled back to lap at the same speed as Pedrosa.

16 LEON CAMIER
Had a great start but was tucking the front at every corner. The combination of higher track temperatures and a full tank got the blame.

17 MICHAEL LAVERTY
Had problems stopping the bike, resulting in the rear brake overheating.

Michael did not think that altered his result by more than one place but not happy because he did not get the best out of the bike.

18 BROC PARKES
Nearly taken out by both di Meglio's and Petrucci's crashes, and avoiding action meant he lost touch with the group. Second half of his race again compromised by lack of rear grip.

19 HECTOR BARBERA
Lots of chatter on a low-grip circuit plus a distinct top-speed deficit meant another tough weekend.

DID NOT FINISH

ALEIX ESPARGARO
Knew from the start that he had less rear grip than in warm-up, and it finally caught him out on the last lap.

STEFAN BRADL
Crashed unhurt on lap 7 when he lost the front in Turn 13.

DANILO PETRUCCI
A horrible weekend despite the presence of two factory Aprilia engineers. Kept out of qualifying by technical problems, then lost the front in the race.

MIKE DI MEGLIO
Crashed out at the second corner of the first lap and broke two bones in his left hand. Operated on in Barcelona on the Monday after the race.

ARAGÓN
ROUND 14

GRAN PREMIO IVECO
DE ARAGÓN
MOTORLAND ARAGÓN

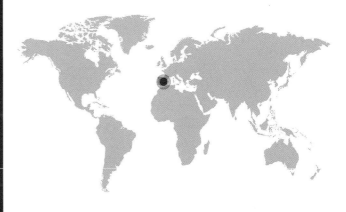

DOUBLE TROUBLE

Lorenzo wins as the Hondas push their luck too far, while an Open Class bike and a Ducati complete the rostrum

Anybody familiar with the workings of bookmakers would not have troubled themselves to place a bet on this race. Of all the tracks MotoGP visits, Aragón is the one where a Honda win is a nailed-on certainty. In fact, anything other than a Repsol Honda one-two would count as a shock. So, what to make of a podium that did not even include a Honda rider and a race that was won by Jorge Lorenzo on a Yamaha despite the fact that neither rider nor bike had triumphed there in the past.

The race hinged on Marc Marquez coming across a set of circumstances he had not previously encountered and, for once, making an incorrect decision. With his Misano mistake having ensured that he could not retain the title on home soil, Marc had let it be known that he would start thinking about the championship in Japan. He was here in Aragón, his favourite track, to win what he regards as his true home race.

True to form, after the first day of practice the factory Yamahas were an embarrassingly long way behind not just the Hondas but the private Yamahas and a couple of Ducatis. A day later things were no better: they were facing the prospect of lining up for the race having failed to get within a second of Marquez's pole time, which almost inevitably tore the circuit lap record to pieces.

Yet again, for the fifth race in a row, there was a Ducati on the front row, and this time it was a new one – well, new-ish. The GP14.2 had a narrower tank that made it easier for the rider to move around on the bike, but according to riders the modifications did not address the basic problem of understeer. However, with rain forecast for Sunday there was a feeling in the

ABOVE Scott Redding had a difficult weekend but a strong race. Danilo Petrucci finished top Italian after Andrea Iannone, Valentino Rossi and Andrea Dovizioso fell.

RIGHT Aleix Espargaro gambled and was the first to swap bikes. He was rewarded with a podium finish.

OPPOSITE Avintia's Hector Barbera got a Ducati to replace the team's ex-CRT Kawasaki, but had a bit of trouble.

Bologna camp that Andrea Dovizioso could be on for a rostrum finish at least.

Sure enough, it rained on Sunday but not quite when it was expected. The race started with everyone on slicks but expecting a bike change as the lightest of rain fell. Dani Pedrosa had stormed the wet morning warm-up using the harder option rain tyre, so that was the tyre on the spare bikes being warmed up in case they were needed.

Under leaden skies, Lorenzo grabbed the advantage with what he called the best start of his career. Even though Marquez was able to pass him, Jorge was able to get back in front. This was the Lorenzo of 12 months earlier, combative and a genuine threat to the Hondas. It was also a remarkable improvement on his form of Friday and Saturday. Valentino Rossi also looked like he had found something but ran off track avoiding the back of Pedrosa's bike and crashed on wet Astroturf, briefly losing consciousness but avoiding serious injury.

The rain gradually got heavier as the Hondas and Lorenzo pulled away from the dogged Dovizioso, and by lap 16 of 23 it became obvious that it was going to be impossible to get to the flag on slicks. Pit crews had already been whipping tyre warmers off and on for a few laps and now they looked anxiously for their riders. On lap 17 Aleix Espargaro was the first man in as the leaders kept looking at each other, followed a lap later by most of the midfield runners, including Bradley Smith, Stefan Bradl and Cal Crutchlow, these three going on to dispute the final two spaces on the podium.

Another lap later and Dovizioso became the first of the front men to ask too much of his slicks. Lorenzo

'I'M GOING TO PARTY
UNTIL JAPAN!'

ALEIX ESPARGARO

ABOVE Jorge Lorenzo stayed out longer than most but, crucially, came in before the Hondas.

BELOW Cal Crutchlow and Aleix Espargaro race over the line after bashing fairings.

was now dropping back as the Hondas pressed on, and on lap 20 he decided to pit. As Jorge went up pitlane, Pedrosa locked the front going into the first corner and fell. Still Marquez pressed on, no doubt calculating that he was now past the point where he would be able to regain the time lost in changing bikes. Next time round, he too was on the floor.

Hindsight is always 20/20, but it was obvious that the conditions would cool tyres well below the temperature where they generate useable grip. It was also obvious that Marquez and Pedrosa were caught in the trap of not daring to make a move until the other one did.

Aleix Espargaro got his reward for changing early while his younger brother Pol – so impressive in practice, qualifying and the drier part of the race – assumed that the more experienced riders in front of him were doing the right thing and stayed out too long. When the timing screens settled down, they showed Aleix in second with Crutchlow, Bradl and Smith all in with a chance of third. Bradley, on the harder wets, could not get the tyres working and lost touch as Cal and Stefan closed down the older Espargaro.

Cal was on Aleix coming out of the final corner but spun the rear on the white line and suffered a wheelie when the tyre hit tarmac again, sending him across the track to bang fairings and elbows with Espargaro – and causing Cal to just lose out on second place. Not that Crutchlow was complaining about a thoroughly unexpected podium, his first on a Ducati. He put it down to luck, but everyone else put it down to the stunning lap in qualifying that took him from a depressing position to the second row. Aleix Espargaro was equally delighted with his list of firsts: his and the Forward Racing Team's first podium in MotoGP and the first ever by an Open Class bike.

Lorenzo's win was not just unexpected but also put him in serious contention with Rossi and Pedrosa for second place in the championship. Given the disastrous start to Jorge's season, that was a remarkable place to be with four races to go.

SUZUKI TO RETURN

Immediately after the Aragón race, Suzuki confirmed that it would return to MotoGP in 2015 with a new GSX-RR and that its riders would be Spanish duo Aleix Espargaro and Maverick Viñales. The Italian Davide Brivio, a long-time Yamaha man and manager of Valentino Rossi, would be team manager.

The new Suzuki was tested during 2014 at Malaysia, Circuit of the Americas and Argentina – as well as in Europe – by Randy de Puniet, Nobuatsu Aoki and Takuya Tsuda. It showed steady improvement without looking like a game-changer.

The factory's 1993 World Champion,

Kevin Schwantz, joined the Texas test. Schwantz also gave the bike its public début at the Japanese round at Twin-Ring Motegi, riding alongside 1982 World Champion Franco Uncini on the GSV–R, the last MotoGP machine fielded by Suzuki back in 2011. Uncini, now MotoGP's Safety Officer, won his world title on a Suzuki.

Suzuki also confirmed that de Puniet would début the bike as a wild card in the last race of 2014 – Valencia – and then move on to the factory's World Superbike Championship team for 2015.

The GSX-RR bears little resemblance to Suzuki's last MotoGP machine in that it is an in-line four rather than a V4. The factory, therefore, is following the practice of the other Japanese factories in mirroring the basic layout and nomenclature of its flagship street bike range in its MotoGP design.

As a newcomer, Suzuki will benefit from the same concessions as Ducati while being able to use its own electronics package. The team will fill the grid slots vacated by Paul Bird Motorsport, which will not return to MotoGP in 2015.

BELOW Andrea Dovizioso crashed out of fourth place just before the leaders swapped bikes – a lost opportunity.

GRAN PREMIO IVECO DE ARAGÓN
MOTORLAND ARAGÓN
ROUND **14**
SEPTEMBER 28

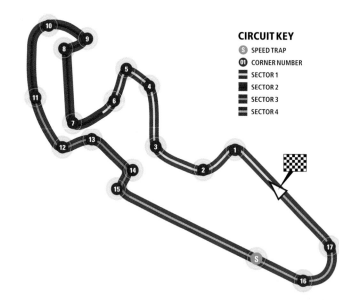

CIRCUIT KEY
- **S** SPEED TRAP
- **01** CORNER NUMBER
- SECTOR 1
- SECTOR 2
- SECTOR 3
- SECTOR 4

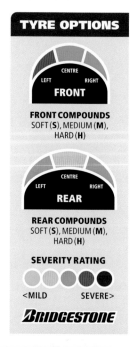

TYRE OPTIONS

FRONT
LEFT · CENTRE · RIGHT

FRONT COMPOUNDS
SOFT (**S**), MEDIUM (**M**), HARD (**H**)

REAR
LEFT · CENTRE · RIGHT

REAR COMPOUNDS
SOFT (**S**), MEDIUM (**M**), HARD (**H**)

SEVERITY RATING
<MILD   SEVERE>

BRIDGESTONE

RACE RESULTS

CIRCUIT LENGTH 3.155 miles
NO. OF LAPS 23
RACE DISTANCE 72.572 miles
WEATHER Dry, 18°C
TRACK TEMPERATURE 20°C
WINNER Jorge Lorenzo
FASTEST LAP 1m 49.107s, 104.080mph, Jorge Lorenzo
LAP RECORD 1m 48.565s, 104.577mph, Dani Pedrosa, 2013

QUALIFYING

	Rider	Nation	Motorcycle	Team	Time	Pole +
1	Marquez	SPA	Honda	Repsol Honda Team	1m 47.187s	
2	Pedrosa	SPA	Honda	Repsol Honda Team	1m 47.549s	0.362s
3	Iannone	ITA	Ducati	Pramac Racing	1m 47.685s	0.498s
4	Espargaro P	SPA	Yamaha	Monster Yamaha Tech3	1m 47.865s	0.678s
5	Crutchlow	GBR	Ducati	Ducati Team	1m 47.897s	0.710s
6	Rossi	ITA	Yamaha	Movistar Yamaha MotoGP	1m 48.226s	1.039s
7	Lorenzo	SPA	Yamaha	Movistar Yamaha MotoGP	1m 48.246s	1.059s
8	Bradl	GER	Honda	LCR Honda MotoGP	1m 48.368s	1.181s
9	Dovizioso	ITA	Ducati	Ducati Team	1m 48.542s	1.355s
10	Espargaro A	SPA	Yamaha	NGM Forward Racing	1m 48.568s	1.381s
11	Smith	GBR	Yamaha	Monster Yamaha Tech3	1m 48.810s	1.623s
12	Barbera	SPA	Ducati	Avintia Racing	1m 48.991s	Q1
13	Hernandez	COL	Ducati	Energy T.I. Pramac Racing	1m 49.051s	Q1
14	Aoyama	JPN	Honda	Drive M7 Aspar	1m 49.209s	Q1
15	Bautista	SPA	Honda	GO&FUN Honda Gresini	1m 49.274s	Q1
16	Redding	GBR	Honda	GO&FUN Honda Gresini	1m 49.703s	Q1
17	Abraham	CZE	Honda	Cardion AB Motoracing	1m 49.790s	Q1
18	Hayden	USA	Honda	Drive M7 Aspar	1m 49.835s	Q1
19	De Angelis	RSM	Yamaha	NGM Forward Racing	1m 50.263s	Q1
20	Petrucci	ITA	ART	Octo IodaRacing Team	1m 50.635s	Q1
21	Laverty	GBR	PBM	Paul Bird Motorsport	1m 51.280s	Q1
22	Parkes	AUS	PBM	Paul Bird Motorsport	1m 51.489s	Q1
23	Di Meglio	FRA	Avintia	Avintia Racing	1m 52.181s	Q1

1 JORGE LORENZO
Got a superb start and stayed with the Hondas, only dropping back as the rain got heavier. Pitted from third, was fourth on the next lap and in the lead next time round. Rode superbly, made no mistakes and won where neither he nor Yamaha had before.

2 ALEIX ESPARGARO
The first MotoGP podium finish for the rider and the team – and for an Open Class bike. Pitted from sixth place with seven laps left (Aleix was the first to come in), which turned out to be perfect timing.

3 CAL CRUTCHLOW
Made no mistakes, timed his bike change well, and almost got second after a barging match with Espargaro on the run to the flag. Unlike Dovizioso and Iannone, did not get an upgraded Ducati.

4 STEFAN BRADL
Had clutch problems off the start and then lacked confidence with the hard rear tyre. His pit stop went perfectly, putting Stefan within range of the podium – fourth was a good result after recent disappointments.

5 BRADLEY SMITH
An eventful race to say the least. Hit Rossi on the first lap then dropped to 20th avoiding a crash. Pitted at the right time but the choice of the harder wet tyre meant he could not keep pace with Crutchlow, with whom he exited pitlane.

6 POL ESPARGARO
His only mistake on an otherwise perfect weekend was staying out too long when it rained. But as he was a rookie following four much more experienced riders, it was an entirely understandable decision.

7 ALVARO BAUTISTA
Happier in the cool, dry conditions of race day than at any other time over the weekend. Unfortunately, a vibration on the brakes with his wet bike slowed him for a while, but he was closing fast on Smith and Espargaro at the flag.

8 HIROSHI AOYAMA
His best result of the year so far. Tentative at first on the harder tyre but quicker later on and also on wet tyres.

9 NICKY HAYDEN
Back at last from the operation to repair his wrist. Did not know whether he would be able to compete but did as many laps as anyone in practice. Under the circumstances, a top-ten finish has to be seen as a triumph.

10 SCOTT REDDING
His race was not as uncomfortable as the previous one. One of the first timers for a dry-to-wet bike change, so found the second part of the race tricky.

11 DANILO PETRUCCI
The first Italian home! Well up the Open Class bike fight in the dry, lost three places in the bike change, but recovered one of them before the flag.

LAP CHART

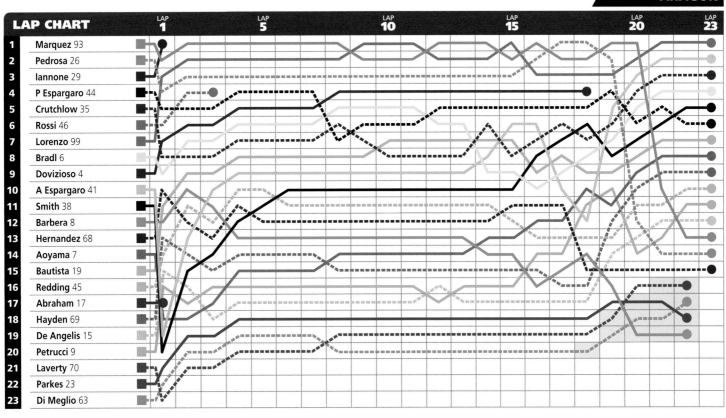

	Rider	LAP 1	LAP 5	LAP 10	LAP 15	LAP 20	LAP 23
1	Marquez 93						
2	Pedrosa 26						
3	Iannone 29						
4	P Espargaro 44						
5	Crutchlow 35						
6	Rossi 46						
7	Lorenzo 99						
8	Bradl 6						
9	Dovizioso 4						
10	A Espargaro 41						
11	Smith 38						
12	Barbera 8						
13	Hernandez 68						
14	Aoyama 7						
15	Bautista 19						
16	Redding 45						
17	Abraham 17						
18	Hayden 69						
19	De Angelis 15						
20	Petrucci 9						
21	Laverty 70						
22	Parkes 23						
23	Di Meglio 63						

RACE

	Rider	Motorcycle	Race time	Time +	Fastest lap	Avg. speed	
1	Lorenzo	Yamaha	44m 20.406s		1m 49.107s	98.2mph	S/M
2	Espargaro A	Yamaha	44m 30.701s	10.295s	1m 49.775s	97.8mph	M/M
3	Crutchlow	Ducati	44m 30.718s	10.312s	1m 49.994s	97.8mph	M/M
4	Bradl	Honda	44m 32.124s	11.718s	1m 49.826s	97.7mph	M/H
5	Smith	Yamaha	44m 49.889s	29.483s	1m 49.978s	97.1mph	M/M
6	Espargaro P	Yamaha	44m 50.092s	29.686s	1m 49.690s	97.1mph	M/M
7	Bautista	Honda	44m 50.169s	29.763s	1m 50.032s	97.1mph	S/M
8	Aoyama	Honda	44m 58.247s	37.841s	1m 50.832s	96.8mph	S/M
9	Hayden	Honda	45m 03.363s	42.957s	1m 51.199s	96.6mph	S/S
10	Redding	Honda	45m 14.343s	53.937s	1m 50.634s	96.3mph	M/S
11	Petrucci	ART	45m 20.230s	59.824s	1m 51.325s	96.0mph	M/M
12	De Angelis	Yamaha	45m 21.124s	1m 00.718s	1m 51.330s	96.0mph	S/M
13	Marquez	Honda	45m 35.633s	1m 15.227s	1m 49.133s	95.4mph	M/H
14	Pedrosa	Honda	45m 44.932s	1m 24.526s	1m 49.174s	95.1mph	M/H
15	Hernandez	Ducati	45m 58.661s	1m 38.255s	1m 50.850s	94.7mph	S/M
16	Laverty	PBM	44m 37.129s	1 lap	1m 52.144s	93.3mph	M/S
17	Di Meglio	Avintia	45m 02.913s	1 lap	1m 53.168s	92.4mph	M/S
18	Parkes	PBM	45m 02.992s	1 lap	1m 52.105s	92.4mph	M/S
19	Barbera	Ducati	45m 59.305s	1 lap	1m 51.040s	90.5mph	M/S
NF	Dovizioso	Ducati	33m 30.545s	5 laps	1m 49.553s	101.7mph	M/M
NF	Rossi	Yamaha	5m 34.194s	20 laps	1m 49.386s	102.0mph	S/M
NF	Iannone	Ducati	1m 53.663s	22 laps	–	99.9mph	M/M
NF	Abraham	Honda	1m 58.581s	22 laps	–	95.8mph	M/M

CHAMPIONSHIP

	Rider	Nation	Team	Points
1	Marquez	SPA	Repsol Honda Team	292
2	Pedrosa	SPA	Repsol Honda Team	217
3	Rossi	ITA	Movistar Yamaha MotoGP	214
4	Lorenzo	SPA	Movistar Yamaha MotoGP	202
5	Dovizioso	ITA	Ducati Team	142
6	Espargaro A	SPA	NGM Forward Racing	112
7	Espargaro P	SPA	Monster Yamaha Tech3	108
8	Iannone	ITA	Pramac Racing	92
9	Bradl	GER	LCR Honda MotoGP	87
10	Smith	GBR	Monster Yamaha Tech3	85
11	Bautista	SPA	GO&FUN Honda Gresini	73
12	Crutchlow	GBR	Ducati Team	63
13	Redding	GBR	GO&FUN Honda Gresini	60
14	Aoyama	JPN	Drive M7 Aspar	51
15	Hernandez	COL	Energy T.I. Pramac Racing	39
16	Hayden	USA	Drive M7 Aspar	36
17	Abraham	CZE	Cardion AB Motoracing	33
18	Edwards	USA	NGM Forward Racing	11
	Pirro	ITA	Ducati Team	11
20	Petrucci	ITA	Octo IodaRacing Team	9
21	Parkes	AUS	Paul Bird Motorsport	7
	De Angelis	RSM	NGM Forward Racing	7
23	Di Meglio	FRA	Avintia Racing	4
24	Laverty	GBR	Paul Bird Motorsport	2
	Barbera	SPA	Avintia Racing	2
26	Camier	GBR	Drive M7 Aspar	1

12 ALEX DE ANGELIS
Tried to make a mess of his first ever bike change by throwing his Yamaha at his crew – but happy with the result.

13 MARC MARQUEZ
Ripped the circuit record to shreds in qualifying and wanted to win at his favourite circuit, but a dry-to-wet race was new to Marc and trying to stay out on slicks was an error.

14 DANI PEDROSA
Followed Marquez, watching and waiting for him to pit, and they both stayed out too long. Dani crashed at Turn 1 but was able to remount and get back to the pits for the wet bike.

15 YONNY HERNANDEZ
Lost the chance of a top-ten finish when he crashed at the last corner as he was about to enter the pits; had to do another lap before changing bikes.

16 MICHAEL LAVERTY
This was the sixth time this year that Michael just missed out on a point, this time because he ran off-track on the first lap before clawing his way back to the group.

17 MIKE DI MEGLIO
Rode with recently plated bones in his left hand and had a rough weekend. Lots of modifications to chassis and electronics made things worse.

18 BROC PARKES
Stayed out too long on slicks, but happy with his pace.

19 HECTOR BARBERA
Got a GP14 Ducati with spec software that set the bike on fire in practice. Then a crash and technical problems kept him out of qualifying. Only had one bike, so changed wheels in the race.

DID NOT FINISH

ANDREA DOVIZIOSO
Looking good in fourth place right behind Lorenzo when he highsided at Turn 9 after putting his rear tyre on a damp patch. The mistake cost Dovi and the new GP14.2 a realistic chance of a rostrum at least.

VALENTINO ROSSI
Ran off-track on the fourth lap while up with the leaders, hit wet tarmac and fell. Momentarily lost consciousness and was taken to hospital for a precautionary scan.

ANDREA IANNONE
Fighting for the lead off the start but ran wide on the second lap and crashed at speed on wet grass.

KAREL ABRAHAM
The bike slowed on the first lap with an engine problem, so Karel pitted. The engine would not restart so his race was over.

MOTUL GRAND PRIX OF JAPAN
TWIN-RING MOTEGI

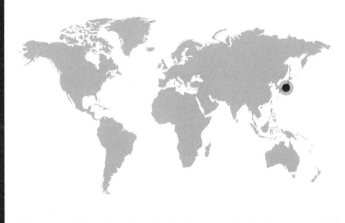

SECOND COMING

Marc Marquez retained his title at Honda's home track, but Jorge Lorenzo won again

There were no disasters. Super typhoon Vongfong arrived later than expected, and despite signs that things could have been a lot worse, Marc Marquez used his head and did not risk going for the win.

His job was to beat both his team-mate Dani Pedrosa and Valentino Rossi. If he did so he would retain his title and become the youngest man ever to win back-to-back championships in the top class of motorcycle racing. That record belonged, of course, to Mike Hailwood and dated from 1962–63, the great man's first two seasons with MV Agusta. The good thing, from Marc's point of view, was that he did not have to worry about Jorge Lorenzo.

While Marc managed, outwardly at least, to remain his normal smiling self, the team around him showed signs of the pressure. Honda had never before managed to clinch a title at its own circuit. No-one mentioned that beforehand, but a lot of people did afterwards. Last season the title should also have been won at Motegi but a foul-up in the previous race, at Phillip Island, prevented that and Honda hosted a Yamaha victory. This year's plan was very clear: do not mess up.

Circumstances tried to conspire against Marc right from the start. He fell on Friday morning when the bike shook its head coming out of Turn 3, knocking the brake pads back in the calipers, and he arrived at Turn 4 without much stopping power. Next morning he heard a nasty noise from the engine and rolled to a halt. A factory Honda breaking down? Almost unheard of. With Marc and his team looking and sounding as they did at Brno and Misano, it was almost unsurprising that he qualified off the front row for only the second time this year.

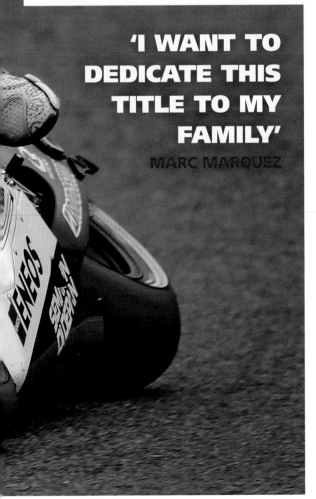

'I WANT TO DEDICATE THIS TITLE TO MY FAMILY'

MARC MARQUEZ

Seeing a Ducati on the front row was not a surprise either, but seeing one on pole was. Andrea Dovizioso used the super-soft rear tyre to good effect to beat Valentino Rossi and take pole for the first time in four years, while it was Ducati's first pole since Valencia 2010 – Casey Stoner's last race for the factory.

As usual, Dovi warned that the effort required to force the bike to go round corners properly would mean that both he and the tyres would be past their best after just a few laps. Which did not stop him getting ahead to the first corner and then hanging on to third place behind the fast-starting Yamahas for eight laps before Marquez came past and another five laps before Pedrosa also passed. Finishing 14 seconds behind the leader, in fifth place, was not quite the closest a Ducati had been all year, but it was not far off. Along with the pole, Dovi showed that stability on the brakes and good acceleration, both vital at Motegi, are not lacking on the Ducati.

Both of those features are usually thought to be Honda's strengths, so it was more than a little surprising to see Rossi get the holeshot closely followed by Lorenzo, who came through from the second row and followed for four laps before cutting past and then rapidly opening up a gap of nearly three seconds. It was imperious stuff from Jorge, whose form in free practice had been impressive, but Valentino was nearly as fast.

If we strike Dovi's super-soft tyre from the record, Rossi would have had his first pole for four years and, like Marquez, he knew that he could prolong the championship for another week. He tried – he

ABOVE Andrea Dovizioso and team celebrate Ducati's first pole position in four years.

LEFT The Yamahas set the pace but Rossi could not match Lorenzo and Marquez overhauled him.

By this stage of the season there was no doubt that the Yamaha was no longer losing out on the straight to the Honda, and the riders reported that this season's one-litre reduction in tank capacity had been addressed without making the motor difficult to use – quite the reverse, in fact, for throttle pick-up from low revs had become easier. All the same, fuel consumption was still marginal: both factory M1s had to be pushed down pitlane at the end of the race.

The Yamaha riders' form in the second half of the season guaranteed a fight to the finish, despite the fact that the title was decided with three races to go. Rossi's rostrum put him second in the championship table – and ahead of Pedrosa on 'countback' – for the first time since Assen, while Lorenzo's back-to-back wins put him in contention, only three points behind. Valentino was moved to observe that Jorge's form had him worried. Both Yamaha men were sporting enough to say that the right man had won the championship.

The double champion celebrated with a rather staged tribute to Japanese history featuring one of his retinue dressed as a 16th century samurai general, Honda Tadakatsu, who won 57 battles without suffering even a scratch despite the trademark horned helmet that advertised his presence. This character handed Marc a sword with which he cut free a celebratory balloon – you do not have to be Japanese to get the symbolism in that – before two accompanying geishas then handed him the slightly less traditional championship T-shirt and gold-plated Shoei helmet.

A general sense of relief descended on anyone and everyone wearing a Honda shirt.

ABOVE Yamaha's test rider Katsuyuki Nakasuga put in his annual appearance as a wild card.

BELOW Hayden's and Redding's customer Honda battle enters the tunnel.

really tried – to keep Marquez behind him but the second time the Spaniard came past he made it stick. Pedrosa's charge came too late to challenge Valentino's third place.

Watching Marquez celebrate, it was easy to overlook that this was the third Yamaha victory in a row and Jorge's second. Both of Jorge's wins came with the fastest lap of the race, and here he also set a new lap record. What would the season have looked like if he had not made those errors in the first two races?

RED DEVILS

Andrea Dovizioso's pole position was another indication of just how well the Ducati factory is working under its new race director Gigi Dall'Igna. The rider himself seemed reinvigorated and able to extract the maximum from the bike in a variety of circumstances.

At the start of the year, Andrea said that the objective was to halve the gap to the leader at most circuits, and at many places, notably Silverstone, he did even better than that. His podium finishes at Texas and Assen were little masterpieces of opportunism.

Andrea Iannone, promoted to factory rider status, also weighed in with some fine rides and the pair made Ducati a front-row fixture in the second part of the season, taking advantage of the dispensation that allows them to use a softer tyre than the other factory bikes; Ducati is a factory team but running with concessions because it has not won a dry race in two years.

It would be tempting to link this to the début at Aragón of the Desmosedici 'GP14.2', but that would be stretching a point. The revised bike was narrower, to allow the rider to move around more

easily, but addressed none of Ducati's fundamental understeering problems. Its arrival did coincide with a major revival in the fortunes of Cal Crutchlow, but those two facts were also unrelated.

Cal's bike received no updates all year. He certainly figured out a few things, and while the rostrum at Aragón could be considered fortuitous – Cal certainly thought so – he very much deserved second place in Australia.

History shows that Cal and Dovi are very closely matched, so it is difficult to judge exactly how much progress Dall'Igna and his engineers have been making. Dall'Igna declined to make too many changes to the bike as the rest of 2014 passed – 'I want to do this job only once' – so we await with much interest the 2015 redesign, the GP15, which will in all probability not appear until the Sepang test in February.

MOTUL GRAND PRIX OF JAPAN
TWIN-RING MOTEGI
ROUND 15
OCTOBER 12

RACE RESULTS

CIRCUIT LENGTH 2.983 miles
NO. OF LAPS 24
RACE DISTANCE 71.597 miles
WEATHER Dry, 19°C
TRACK TEMPERATURE 27°C
WINNER Jorge Lorenzo
FASTEST LAP 1m 45.350s,
101.905mph, Jorge Lorenzo (record)
PREVIOUS LAP RECORD 1m 45.589s,
101.656mph, Dani Pedrosa, 2012

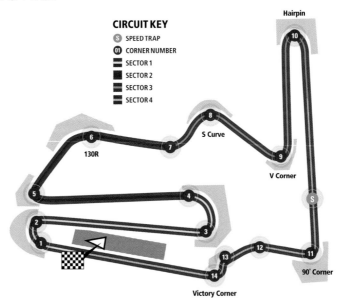

CIRCUIT KEY
- (S) SPEED TRAP
- (01) CORNER NUMBER
- SECTOR 1
- SECTOR 2
- SECTOR 3
- SECTOR 4

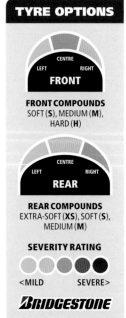

TYRE OPTIONS

FRONT

FRONT COMPOUNDS
SOFT (**S**), MEDIUM (**M**),
HARD (**H**)

REAR

REAR COMPOUNDS
EXTRA-SOFT (**XS**), SOFT (**S**),
MEDIUM (**M**)

SEVERITY RATING
<MILD   SEVERE>

BRIDGESTONE

QUALIFYING

	Rider	Nation	Motorcycle	Team	Time	Pole +
1	Dovizioso	ITA	Ducati	Ducati Team	1m 44.502s	
2	Rossi	ITA	Yamaha	Movistar Yamaha MotoGP	1m 44.557s	0.055s
3	Pedrosa	SPA	Honda	Repsol Honda Team	1m 44.755s	0.253s
4	Marquez	SPA	Honda	Repsol Honda Team	1m 44.775s	0.273s
5	Lorenzo	SPA	Yamaha	Movistar Yamaha MotoGP	1m 44.784s	0.282s
6	Iannone	ITA	Ducati	Pramac Racing	1m 44.854s	0.352s
7	Espargaro P	SPA	Yamaha	Monster Yamaha Tech3	1m 44.867s	0.365s
8	Crutchlow	GBR	Ducati	Ducati Team	1m 44.898s	0.396s
9	Bradl	GER	Honda	LCR Honda MotoGP	1m 45.005s	0.503s
10	Smith	GBR	Yamaha	Monster Yamaha Tech3	1m 45.044s	0.542s
11	Espargaro A	SPA	Yamaha	NGM Forward Racing	1m 45.315s	0.813s
12	Bautista	SPA	Honda	GO&FUN Honda Gresini	1m 45.677s	1.175s
13	Hernandez	COL	Ducati	Energy T.I. Pramac Racing	1m 45.971s	Q1
14	Hayden	USA	Honda	Drive M7 Aspar	1m 46.465s	Q1
15	Redding	GBR	Honda	GO&FUN Honda Gresini	1m 46.499s	Q1
16	Barbera	SPA	Ducati	Avintia Racing	1m 46.796s	Q1
17	Nakasuga	JPN	Yamaha	YAMALUBE Racing Team	1m 46.876s	Q1
18	Aoyama	JPN	Honda	Drive M7 Aspar	1m 46.915s	Q1
19	Abraham	CZE	Honda	Cardion AB Motoracing	1m 46.948s	Q1
20	De Angelis	RSM	Yamaha	NGM Forward Racing	1m 47.092s	Q1
21	Petrucci	ITA	ART	Octo IodaRacing Team	1m 47.757s	Q1
22	Laverty	GBR	PBM	Paul Bird Motorsport	1m 48.144s	Q1
23	Di Meglio	FRA	Avintia	Avintia Racing	1m 48.185s	Q1
24	Parkes	AUS	PBM	Paul Bird Motorsport	1m 48.261s	Q1

1 JORGE LORENZO
Took the lead on the fourth lap, set a new lap record four laps later, and opened up a lead of nearly three seconds. The win backed up Jorge's victory here last year and made it seven podium finishes in a row as well as two wins in a row.

2 MARC MARQUEZ
Knew that he had to finish ahead of Rossi and Pedrosa to retain his title – which is exactly what he did after a Friday and Saturday that saw him, respectively, crash and stop with an engine problem. Marc still smiled but later admitted he had felt the pressure.

3 VALENTINO ROSSI
Only beaten to pole by Dovizioso and the super-soft tyre, then got the holeshot and did his level best to keep the championship alive for another week. It took Marquez a few laps to get past but Valentino got back in front at the end of that lap. When Marc went by again, Rossi had to fend off Pedrosa for the final podium place.

4 DANI PEDROSA
As in several earlier races, Dani lost a chunk of time off the start but was lapping at the same speed as the leaders later in the race.

5 ANDREA DOVIZIOSO
Started from pole for only the second time in his career, and Ducati's first pole since Stoner at Valencia 2010. Was sure to tell everyone that this did not mean he could get on the rostrum. As predicted, he dropped back when the rear tyre dropped off but it took the Hondas and Yamahas 14 laps to get past him.

6 ANDREA IANNONE
Unhappy with both turning and acceleration at the start of the race. Both improved, so he was able to run a good pace, although the problems prevented him from running with the works bikes.

7 STEFAN BRADL
Qualifying on the back of the third row limited his possibilities, but Stefan got a good start, passed Pol Espargaro and closed up to Iannone – which is where he stayed for the rest of the race.

8 POL ESPARGARO
A solid ride to what Pol himself called an unimpressive finishing position. His main difficulty was with the full tank at the start but from the middle of the race he got faster, although he was not quite close enough to tackle Bradl on the last lap.

9 BRADLEY SMITH
Brad's race was a mirror of his team-mate's, complete with a mistake on the first corner of the last lap that prevented an attack on the two riders in front of him. Happy only with the gap to the leader, which would have been under 20 seconds without that mistake.

10 ALVARO BAUTISTA
The usual problems: rear tyre feel and stopping the bike. Got stuck behind Hernandez and by the time Alvaro made the pass it was too late to make further progress.

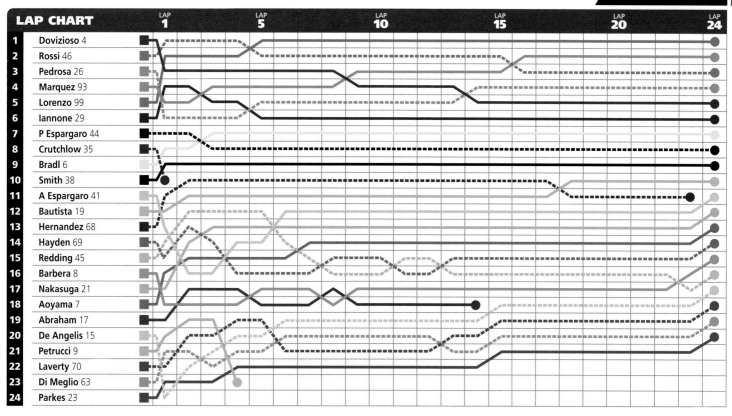

LAP CHART

	LAP 1	LAP 5	LAP 10	LAP 15	LAP 20	LAP 24
1 Dovizioso 4						
2 Rossi 46						
3 Pedrosa 26						
4 Marquez 93						
5 Lorenzo 99						
6 Iannone 29						
7 P Espargaro 44						
8 Crutchlow 35						
9 Bradl 6						
10 Smith 38						
11 A Espargaro 41						
12 Bautista 19						
13 Hernandez 68						
14 Hayden 69						
15 Redding 45						
16 Barbera 8						
17 Nakasuga 21						
18 Aoyama 7						
19 Abraham 17						
20 De Angelis 15						
21 Petrucci 9						
22 Laverty 70						
23 Di Meglio 63						
24 Parkes 23						

RACE

	Rider	Motorcycle	Race time	Time +	Fastest lap	Avg. speed	
1	Lorenzo	Yamaha	42m 21.259s		1m 45.350s	101.4mph	M/S
2	Marquez	Honda	42m 22.897s	1.638s	1m 45.389s	101.3mph	M/S
3	Rossi	Yamaha	42m 23.861s	2.602s	1m 45.545s	101.3mph	M/S
4	Pedrosa	Honda	42m 24.416s	3.157s	1m 45.381s	101.3mph	M/S
5	Dovizioso	Ducati	42m 35.612s	14.353s	1m 45.557s	100.8mph	M/S
6	Iannone	Ducati	42m 37.912s	16.653s	1m 45.880s	100.7mph	M/S
7	Bradl	Honda	42m 40.790s	19.531s	1m 45.772s	100.6mph	M/S
8	Espargaro P	Yamaha	42m 41.074s	19.815s	1m 46.183s	100.6mph	M/S
9	Smith	Yamaha	42m 44.834s	23.575s	1m 46.147s	100.5mph	M/S
10	Bautista	Honda	42m 56.946s	35.687s	1m 46.660s	100.0mph	M/S
11	Espargaro A	Yamaha	43m 01.927s	40.668s	1m 46.605s	99.8mph	M/S
12	Nakasuga	Yamaha	43m 12.286s	51.027s	1m 47.066s	99.4mph	M/S
13	Aoyama	Honda	43m 12.352s	51.093s	1m 47.104s	99.4mph	M/ES
14	Hayden	Honda	43m 17.051s	55.792s	1m 47.230s	99.2mph	M/ES
15	Barbera	Ducati	43m 20.348s	59.089s	1m 46.898s	99.1mph	M/S
16	Redding	Honda	43m 20.767s	59.508s	1m 47.289s	99.0mph	M/ES
17	De Angelis	Yamaha	43m 37.806s	1m 16.547s	1m 48.168s	98.4mph	M/ES
18	Laverty	PBM	43m 49.280s	1m 28.021s	1m 48.613s	98.0mph	M/ES
19	Di Meglio	Avintia	43m 50.729s	1m 29.470s	1m 48.934s	97.9mph	M/ES
20	Parkes	PBM	43m 54.512s	1m 33.253s	1m 49.004s	97.8mph	M/ES
NF	Hernandez	Ducati	41m 12.803s	1 lap	1m 46.735s	99.9mph	M/S
NF	Abraham	Honda	25m 22.849s	10 laps	1m 47.690s	98.7mph	M/ES
NF	Petrucci	ART	7m 26.499s	20 laps	1m 48.651s	96.2mph	M/ES
NF	Crutchlow	Ducati	1m 53.567s	23 laps	–	94.5mph	M/S

CHAMPIONSHIP

	Rider	Nation	Team	Points
1	Marquez	SPA	Repsol Honda Team	312
2	Rossi	ITA	Movistar Yamaha MotoGP	230
	Pedrosa	SPA	Repsol Honda Team	230
4	Lorenzo	SPA	Movistar Yamaha MotoGP	227
5	Dovizioso	ITA	Ducati Team	153
6	Espargaro A	SPA	NGM Forward Racing	117
7	Espargaro P	SPA	Monster Yamaha Tech3	116
8	Iannone	ITA	Pramac Racing	102
9	Bradl	GER	LCR Honda MotoGP	96
10	Smith	GBR	Monster Yamaha Tech3	92
11	Bautista	SPA	GO&FUN Honda Gresini	79
12	Crutchlow	GBR	Ducati Team	63
13	Redding	GBR	GO&FUN Honda Gresini	60
14	Aoyama	JPN	Drive M7 Aspar	54
15	Hernandez	COL	Energy T.I. Pramac Racing	39
16	Hayden	USA	Drive M7 Aspar	38
17	Abraham	CZE	Cardion AB Motoracing	33
18	Edwards	USA	NGM Forward Racing	11
	Pirro	ITA	Ducati Team	11
20	Petrucci	ITA	Octo IodaRacing Team	9
21	Parkes	AUS	Paul Bird Motorsport	7
	De Angelis	ITA	NGM Forward Racing	7
23	Di Meglio	FRA	Avintia Racing	4
	Nakasuga	JPN	YAMALUBE Racing Team	4
25	Barbera	SPA	Avintia Racing	3
26	Laverty	GBR	Paul Bird Motorsport	2
27	Camier	GBR	Drive M7 Aspar	1

11 ALEIX ESPARGARO
Top Open bike again, but given one penalty point by Race Direction for his last-corner move on Hernandez. Had trouble stopping the bike early on.

12 KATSUYUKI NAKASUGA
Yamaha's test rider did his usual job of collecting data for next year's M1.

13 HIROSHI AOYAMA
Two crashes in practice sapped his confidence, and a swing at a marshal after one of them cost him a penalty point, but after good work from his team finished as top customer Honda.

14 NICKY HAYDEN
Qualified as top customer Honda despite his still-painful wrist. Redding's first off-track excursion shot a couple of stones through Nicky's screen, which did not help his aerodynamics. Still happy with a couple of points at a place he knew would be hard work following his operation.

15 HECTOR BARBERA
Had to run his sole Ducati without the support of Ducati engineers. The Avintia team got most things right except the traction control, so Hector was sliding out of corners. Happy to score a point for the third time this season.

16 SCOTT REDDING
Big problems with holding a line under braking, so much so that he ran off the track twice. His efforts used up the front tyre, which then pushed nastily in the final five laps.

17 MIKE DI MEGLIO
Persevering with the old CRT Kawasaki, unlike his team-mate. Thought he might have a chance after warm-up but had trouble getting within half a second of those lap times in the race.

18 MICHAEL LAVERTY
Struggled for rear grip from the first session, improved slightly but at least had an entertaining race with his team-mate and di Meglio.

19 ALEX DE ANGELIS
Technical and electronics issues meant Alex could not get on terms with the other Open Class bikes.

20 BROC PARKES
Had problems with chatter, as usual, and with rear grip. Only dropped back from the other Open Class bikes in the final laps.

DID NOT FINISH

CAL CRUTCHLOW
Nearly jumped the start, which meant he lost ground to the front men. Trying to make up for the mistake, he crashed at Turn 3 second time round.

KAREL ABRAHAM
Ran out of brakes for the second time this season.

YONNY HERNANDEZ
Looking forward to a good finish when he was torpedoed by Aleix Espargaro on the last corner.

TISSOT AUSTRALIAN GRAND PRIX
PHILLIP ISLAND

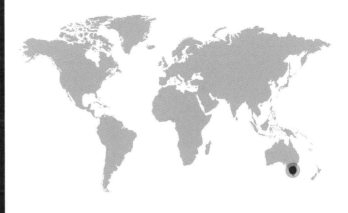

SOFTLY, SOFTLY

Valentino Rossi celebrated his 250th race in the top class with a win as Yamaha swept the podium

When Marc Marquez fell, Valentino Rossi was four seconds behind him. Rossi had been dicing with Jorge Lorenzo, who was just starting to lose ground with front tyre trouble. Valentino said one word to himself: 'Victory.'

Nine years since his last win at Phillip Island, a track he loves above all others with the possible exception of Mugello, the Doctor turned back time and won in the manner of old. He was in trouble in practice and qualifying did not go well, although not as badly as his grid position would imply. There followed a great start, then a short, sharp burst of aggression to get him to the front men, and finally the experience came into play.

It felt like an old, Jerry Burgess-inspired win, taken from what looked like an unpromising position thanks to the team working well right up to warm-up and the rider then using all his experience to deal with treacherous conditions so much better than the rest that he won by ten seconds. The only real difference was that Burgess is not in the garage any more – Silvano Galbusera is. Together, team and rider solved the problems of the trickiest track for tyres in the calendar.

The events of 12 months previously were fresh in everyone's mind – on that occasion Bridgestone's rear slicks could not cope with the new, abrasive surface. This year the debate was all about the front tyre and whether it could deal with the depressed temperatures of race day. Post-race, the two factory Yamahas stood side by side in parc fermé; one of them had a perfect-looking front tyre, the other a tyre so worn that it looked as if its left-hand side had been attacked with a file. Lorenzo muttered about getting a faulty tyre (again) but his times through 20 of the 27 laps were equal to

ABOVE Cal Crutchlow crashed out on the final lap, scant reward for a brave qualifying lap and a clever race.

RIGHT Three abreast in the battle for third; the Tech 3 Yamahas of Bradley Smith and Pol Espargaro sandwich Andrea Dovizioso's Ducati.

OPPOSITE Marc Marquez hits the deck at MG Corner.

those of Valentino. All three podium finishers used the softest rubber available – the supersoft front tyre – and Bridgestone politely pointed out that it was more likely that some set-up or riding-style variation had caused the problem than that Jorge had an inferior tyre.

The fact that the race started at 4pm local time to suit European TV audiences meant that track temperatures plummeted during proceedings. This definitely caught out a few men who had used the harder front-rubber option, the soft tyre, notably Marc Marquez and Cal Crutchlow, who both crashed straight after easing off for the first time. Marc was holding a comfortable lead when he lost the front on lap 18 as soon as he touched the brakes coming down off Lukey Heights. Cal had an identical crash at the Honda hairpin – on the final lap while in second place!

The Englishman had been the man to emerge from a mass brawl for fourth place behind Marquez and the duelling Yamahas. As Lorenzo's troubles magnified, Cal went past and looked set to back up his second place on the grid with the same position in the race – and best Ducati rider of the weekend. When the dust settled after his fall he could be seen standing by his bike, staring at it in utter disbelief.

There were a lot of retirements, not all of them due to the soft tyre. Both Dani Pedrosa and Aleix Espargaro were hit from behind at the hairpin, respectively by Andrea Iannone and Stefan Bradl. The rate of attrition let a few men who usually scrap for the last few points get a taste of the limelight. Hector Barbera made good use of his GP14 Ducati to finish as top Open Class rider for the first time this year. Mind you, he and Alvaro

'TO COME BACK AND TAKE THE FIRST POSITION AFTER TEN YEARS IS GREAT'

VALENTINO ROSSI

ABOVE Alvaro Bautista, Scott Redding and Hector Barbera fighting for fifth place.

BELOW Bautista was behind team-mate Redding for most of the race, but passed the Brit just before the flag.

Bautista only got past Scott Redding on the run to the flag; the Briton was far and away the fastest of the customer Honda riders and reminded everyone why HRC were so keen to sign him.

The early battle for fourth place was thinned down as the race went on. Three laps from the end, Pol Espargaro crashed at Honda. When Crutchlow followed suit, Bradley Smith found himself in third place. He had been at the heart of the action in the group dice, getting hung out to dry more than once and having to fight back to the front of the group. Bradley did not realise that he had made the podium until he saw a big screen halfway round the slow-down lap. His reaction when he got back to the Tech 3 team was emotional: Tech 3's first podium of the year and Bradley's first in MotoGP put the icing on Yamaha's cake. For the first time since France 2008 the marque had a clean sweep of the rostrum.

While Marquez's crash obviously had no adverse consequences given that he was unhurt, Pedrosa's most certainly did. Dani started the day level on points with Rossi and fighting for second in the championship, so giving up 25 points to Valentino with only 50 left on the table did not look good. Before the race Lorenzo had been three points behind the pair, so he overhauled Pedrosa and established a handy 17-point buffer, but now lay eight points adrift of his team-mate.

With Rossi back to his imperious best and Jorge on top form after a catastrophic start to the year, Yamaha had clocked up four race wins in a row – a feat that would have been unthinkable before the summer break. Never mind second in the championship – what mattered now was to be top man in that team.

A BRIDGESTONE BREAKTHROUGH

Bridgestone broke new ground by using a front tyre of asymmetric design for the first time in motorcycle racing.

The use of asymmetric construction for the rear tyre has been common practice for many years, the idea being to compensate for the differing number of right- and left-hand corners. Phillip Island is very much a left-handed track, so if the tyre is to work in the small number of right-handers it needs softer tread rubber on that side.

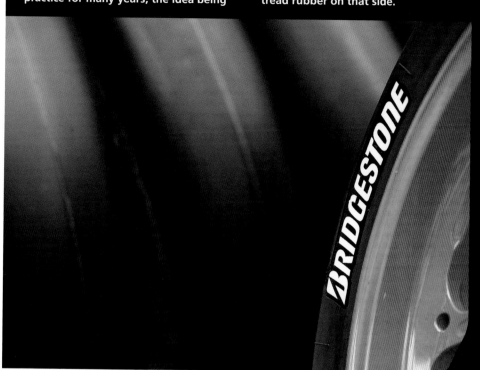

The new soft tyre had normal soft rubber over most of its surface but the right shoulder used the extra-soft compound. When the bike was banked over by about 30 degrees, the extra-soft compound came into play.

Because of the amount of time a bike spends on its side at high speed, Phillip Island provides tyre companies with their most difficult problem of the year. This is exacerbated by changeable weather and cooling breezes.

On the grid the worry was about rapidly cooling tarmac. The race was started at 4pm for the benefit of European TV audiences and in colder weather than at any other time during the weekend – and towards the end of the race it got colder very rapidly. That is what caused the crashes: it simply got too cold for the soft rubber and the men who had chosen the extra-soft tyre filled the podium.

Nine riders chose to run the new asymmetric soft tyre and it worked fine. There proved to be no problem with the transition between compounds.

The asymmetric design would also reappear at the final race of the year.

BELOW Bradley Smith did not know he had got his first podium in MotoGP until he saw a big screen halfway round the slow-down lap.

TISSOT AUSTRALIAN GRAND PRIX
PHILLIP ISLAND
ROUND 16
OCTOBER 19

RACE RESULTS

CIRCUIT LENGTH 2.764 miles

NO. OF LAPS 27

RACE DISTANCE 74.628 miles

WEATHER Dry, 16°C

TRACK TEMPERATURE 29°C

WINNER Valentino Rossi

FASTEST LAP 1m 29.605s, 111.039mph, Valentino Rossi

LAP RECORD 1m 28.108s, 112.903mph, Marc Marquez, 2013

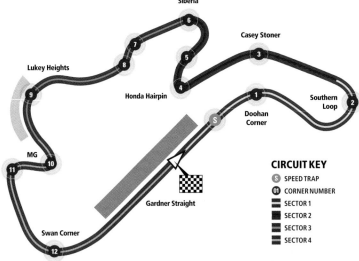

CIRCUIT KEY
- **S** SPEED TRAP
- **01** CORNER NUMBER
- SECTOR 1
- SECTOR 2
- SECTOR 3
- SECTOR 4

TYRE OPTIONS

FRONT

FRONT COMPOUNDS
EXTRA-SOFT (**ES**), SOFT (**S**)
SOFT (ASYMMETRIC) (**SA**)

REAR

REAR COMPOUNDS
SOFT (**S**), MEDIUM (**M**), HARD (**H**)

SEVERITY RATING

<MILD   SEVERE>

QUALIFYING

	Rider	Nation	Motorcycle	Team	Time	Pole +
1	Marquez	SPA	Honda	Repsol Honda Team	1m 28.408s	
2	Crutchlow	GBR	Ducati	Ducati Team	1m 28.642s	0.234s
3	Lorenzo	SPA	Yamaha	Movistar Yamaha MotoGP	1m 28.650s	0.242s
4	Smith	GBR	Yamaha	Monster Yamaha Tech3	1m 28.656s	0.248s
5	Pedrosa	SPA	Honda	Repsol Honda Team	1m 28.675s	0.267s
6	Espargaro A	SPA	Yamaha	NGM Forward Racing	1m 28.866s	0.458s
7	Iannone	ITA	Ducati	Pramac Racing	1m 28.887s	0.479s
8	Rossi	ITA	Yamaha	Movistar Yamaha MotoGP	1m 28.956s	0.548s
9	Espargaro P	SPA	Yamaha	Monster Yamaha Tech3	1m 28.968s	0.560s
10	Dovizioso	ITA	Ducati	Ducati Team	1m 29.088s	0.680s
11	Bradl	GER	Honda	LCR Honda MotoGP	1m 29.155s	0.747s
12	Aoyama	JPN	Honda	Drive M7 Aspar	1m 29.955s	1.547s
13	Redding	GBR	Honda	GO&FUN Honda Gresini	1m 30.280s	Q1
14	Barbera	SPA	Ducati	Avintia Racing	1m 30.348s	Q1
15	Hayden	USA	Honda	Drive M7 Aspar	1m 30.542s	Q1
16	Abraham	CZE	Honda	Cardion AB Motoracing	1m 30.569s	Q1
17	Bautista	SPA	Honda	GO&FUN Honda Gresini	1m 30.635s	Q1
18	Hernandez	COL	Ducati	Energy T.I. Pramac Racing	1m 30.729s	Q1
19	Petrucci	ITA	ART	Octo IodaRacing Team	1m 30.812s	Q1
20	Di Meglio	FRA	Avintia	Avintia Racing	1m 31.431s	Q1
21	Laverty	GBR	PBM	Paul Bird Motorsport	1m 31.492s	Q1
22	Parkes	AUS	PBM	Paul Bird Motorsport	1m 31.730s	Q1
23	De Angelis	RSM	Yamaha	NGM Forward Racing	1m 32.595s	Q1

1 VALENTINO ROSSI
In his 250th race in the top class Valentino made all that experience tell. Had to work hard from a third-row start to get to his team-mate, with whom he fought until the leader, Marquez, fell. Valentino then pulled away from Lorenzo to win by over ten seconds, nine years after his last win at Phillip Island.

2 JORGE LORENZO
Jorge called it the luckiest second place of his life. He finished with his supersoft front tyre showing the sort of damage Rossi experienced in Texas. After a great start to the race and a long battle with Valentino for second, it became obvious in the final ten laps that Jorge was having problems. The main damage may have been to his chances of finishing second in the championship.

3 BRADLEY SMITH
An emotional first rostrum in MotoGP to add to his 23 in smaller classes. Bradley raced the supersoft front tyre and despite a great start he found himself in a group dice for fifth, dodging tough moves and flying motorcycles. He hung on where others did not to make it an all-Yamaha rostrum.

4 ANDREA DOVIZIOSO
Surprised to be fourth after a weekend when he was never really in the hunt, as his tenth place on the grid demonstrates.

5 HECTOR BARBERA
The best result in MotoGP for both rider and team. Hector was able to achieve his ambition of beating the customer Hondas to finish top Open Class bike.

6 ALVARO BAUTISTA
Had his usual problems with the bike, plus some rear-tyre drop-off, but persevered and out-dragged his team-mate on the run to the flag.

7 SCOTT REDDING
Equalled his best finish of the season despite a run-on at Turn 4 that put him back to 20th place. Was fifth coming out of the last corner but Barbera and Bautista then passed him.

8 HIROSHI AOYAMA
Concentrated on the supersoft front after a practice crash, which was definitely a good thing for the race. The only problem was unexplained lack of grip early on.

9 ALEX DE ANGELIS
Got over two days of problems to have a great race on his favourite track.

10 NICKY HAYDEN
Was able to pass Hernandez in the corners but got repassed on the straight, which meant Nicky lost touch with the group in front.

11 YONNY HERNANDEZ
Thought he was on for a better finish and happy to be racing on a clear track, not fighting in a group, when his rear tyre went off steeply with five laps to go.

12 DANILO PETRUCCI
Raced with the customer Hondas in the early stages but could not stay with them, probably due to changes that were

LAP CHART

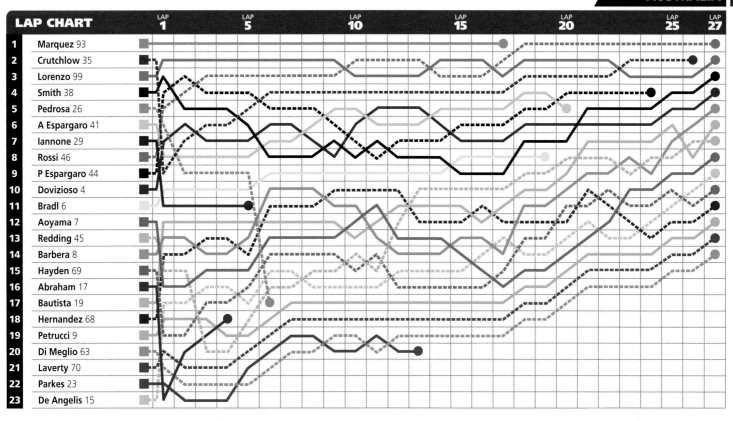

		LAP 1	LAP 5	LAP 10	LAP 15	LAP 20	LAP 25	LAP 27
1	Marquez 93							
2	Crutchlow 35							
3	Lorenzo 99							
4	Smith 38							
5	Pedrosa 26							
6	A Espargaro 41							
7	Iannone 29							
8	Rossi 46							
9	P Espargaro 44							
10	Dovizioso 4							
11	Bradl 6							
12	Aoyama 7							
13	Redding 45							
14	Barbera 8							
15	Hayden 69							
16	Abraham 17							
17	Bautista 19							
18	Hernandez 68							
19	Petrucci 9							
20	Di Meglio 63							
21	Laverty 70							
22	Parkes 23							
23	De Angelis 15							

RACE

	Rider	Motorcycle	Race time	Time +	Fastest lap	Avg. speed	
1	Rossi	Yamaha	40m 46.405s		1m 29.605s	109.8mph	ES/M
2	Lorenzo	Yamaha	40m 57.241s	10.836s	1m 29.771s	109.3mph	ES/M
3	Smith	Yamaha	40m 58.699s	12.294s	1m 30.437s	109.2mph	ES/M
4	Dovizioso	Ducati	41m 01.298s	14.893s	1m 30.363s	109.1mph	SA/M
5	Barbera	Ducati	41m 16.494s	30.089s	1m 30.888s	108.4mph	SA/M
6	Bautista	Honda	41m 16.559s	30.154s	1m 30.847s	108.4mph	SA/M
7	Redding	Honda	41m 16.563s	30.158s	1m 30.757s	108.4mph	ES/M
8	Aoyama	Honda	41m 19.571s	33.166s	1m 30.780s	108.3mph	ES/S
9	De Angelis	Yamaha	41m 19.982s	33.577s	1m 31.001s	108.3mph	ES/S
10	Hayden	Honda	41m 20.549s	34.144s	1m 30.821s	108.2mph	SA/M
11	Hernandez	Ducati	41m 25.873s	39.468s	1m 30.712s	108.1mph	ES/M
12	Petrucci	ART	41m 43.089s	56.684s	1m 31.594s	107.3mph	ES/S
13	Laverty	PBM	41m 59.218s	1m 12.813s	1m 32.409s	106.6mph	ES/S
14	Di Meglio	Avintia	42m 14.455s	1m 28.050s	1m 32.851s	105.9mph	S/S
NF	Crutchlow	Ducati	39m 19.584s	1 lap	1m 30.014s	109.6mph	SA/M
NF	Espargaro P	Yamaha	36m 24.206s	3 laps	1m 30.382s	109.3mph	SA/M
NF	Espargaro A	Yamaha	30m 22.059s	7 laps	1m 30.419s	109.2mph	ES/S
NF	Bradl	Honda	28m 50.687s	8 laps	1m 30.119s	109.2mph	SA/M
NF	Marquez	Honda	25m 34.041s	10 laps	1m 29.608s	110.2mph	SA/M
NF	Parkes	PBM	20m 22.443s	14 laps	1m 32.722s	105.8mph	ES/S
NF	Pedrosa	Honda	9m 19.978s	21 laps	1m 30.385s	106.6mph	SA/M
NF	Iannone	Ducati	7m 40.178s	22 laps	1m 30.265s	108.1mph	ES/M
NF	Abraham	Honda	6m 15.352s	23 laps	1m 31.130s	106.0mph	S/S

CHAMPIONSHIP

	Rider	Nation	Team	Points
1	Marquez	SPA	Repsol Honda Team	312
2	Rossi	ITA	Movistar Yamaha MotoGP	255
3	Lorenzo	SPA	Movistar Yamaha MotoGP	247
4	Pedrosa	SPA	Repsol Honda Team	230
5	Dovizioso	ITA	Ducati Team	166
6	Espargaro A	SPA	NGM Forward Racing	117
7	Espargaro P	SPA	Monster Yamaha Tech3	116
8	Smith	GBR	Monster Yamaha Tech3	108
9	Iannone	ITA	Pramac Racing	102
10	Bradl	GER	LCR Honda MotoGP	96
11	Bautista	SPA	GO&FUN Honda Gresini	89
12	Redding	GBR	GO&FUN Honda Gresini	69
13	Crutchlow	GBR	Ducati Team	63
14	Aoyama	JPN	Drive M7 Aspar	62
15	Hayden	USA	Drive M7 Aspar	44
	Hernandez	COL	Energy T.I. Pramac Racing	44
17	Abraham	CZE	Cardion AB Motoracing	33
18	Barbera	SPA	Avintia Racing	14
	De Angelis	RSM	NGM Forward Racing	14
20	Petrucci	ITA	Octo IodaRacing Team	13
21	Edwards	USA	NGM Forward Racing	11
	Pirro	ITA	Ducati Team	11
23	Parkes	AUS	Paul Bird Motorsport	7
24	Di Meglio	FRA	Avintia Racing	6
25	Laverty	GBR	Paul Bird Motorsport	5
26	Nakasuga	JPN	YAMALUBE Racing Team	4
27	Camier	GBR	Drive M7 Aspar	1

made to suit the lower temperatures but did not work as expected.

13 MICHAEL LAVERTY
The usual problems with rear grip lessened as the race went on so Michael gritted his teeth and scored points for the second time this year.

14 MIKE DI MEGLIO
Had major issues with the wind, which was much stronger on race day than the rest of the weekend. Swapped to the old fairing with holes in it and lost 20kph (12mph) on the straight! Grateful to finish in the points.

DID NOT FINISH

CAL CRUTCHLOW
Cal was in a safe second place when he lost the front, like several others, at Turn 4. Caught out on the last lap, the only time he backed off, by the cool track and the harder front tyre.

POL ESPARGARO
Used the harder front tyre and lost the front at Turn 4 three laps from the flag while pushing to catch Lorenzo, who was then in third. It looked like a first rostrum in MotoGP but the combination of the harder rubber and cooling track got him.

ALEIX ESPARGARO
Looking good in the fight for fourth and thinking about a rostrum finish when he was tailgated by Bradl.

STEFAN BRADL
Was trying to make up ground after being sent wide by the Pedrosa/Iannone incident – and did the same thing in the same place to Aleix Espargaro.

MARC MARQUEZ
Leading by two seconds and cruising when he lost the front at Turn 10.

BROC PARKES
A 130mph highside at Turn 1 in free practice meant Broc went to the line with damage to both his shoulder and his confidence, and had to pull out of the race.

DANI PEDROSA
Rammed by Iannone on lap 6 while mired in the pack after average qualifying and a bad start. Had to retire with a bent rear wheel rim – and not happy with the Italian.

ANDREA IANNONE
Rammed Pedrosa at Turn 4 while trying hard to make up time and places lost after a first-corner coming together with Crutchlow; not helped by being in neutral, not first.

KAREL ABRAHAM
Disappointed to crash out early on, with a highside that the electronics did not see coming; Karel's third non-finish in a row.

SHELL ADVANCE MALAYSIAN MOTORCYCLE GRAND PRIX
SEPANG INTERNATIONAL CIRCUIT

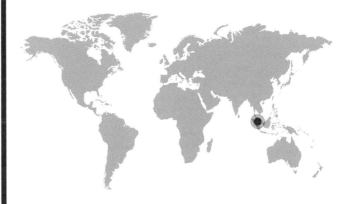

TWELVE AND COUNTING

Marc Marquez returned to winning ways and equalled Mick Doohan's record of wins in a season

Silverstone seemed a long time ago. The British round took place only eight weeks and four races before the Sepang race, but in that brief period the character of the season changed. Yamaha won those four races and Ducati became ever-present on the front row of the grid. Marc Marquez's aura of invincibility was dented.

With the world title safely retained in Japan, Marc had tried to win Australia 'in a new way' and paid the price. That new way was bolting from the start and seeing how much he could win by. This time he did not get to do that. Practice was difficult, although Marc disguised that fact with the grip of some new tyres and pole position. In the race he had to deal with both Yamahas: Jorge Lorenzo was strong at the start and Valentino Rossi harassed him to within sight of the flag.

Mind you, Valentino and Jorge had things on their minds other than the win. They and Dani Pedrosa were covered by just three points in the fight for second place in the championship. Normally these multiple World Champions would not give a thought to anything other than first place, and in truth the runner-up spot is still irrelevant to them. What does matter, however, is the status of being top man in the Yamaha team – that, as Rossi made clear, is well worth fighting for. Honda was also keen to occupy the top two places in the table, but Pedrosa contrived to crash – not just once but twice – and effectively consigned himself to fourth overall.

The other fight that would go to the final round was for sixth overall. Effectively that was the prize for first non-works bike and it was between the Espargaro brothers and Bradley Smith. The Englishman backed up his maiden rostrum in Australia with a good fifth place while Pol and Aleix both had bad weekends.

Aleix collided with Alvaro Bautista at the start of the second lap, an incident for which he accepted the blame, while Pol also made life difficult for himself. At the end of Free Practice 3 he was on the cusp of having to go through the first qualifying session when both Andrea Dovizioso and Scott Redding signalled that the Spaniard had a problem with his bike. Pol chose to ignore them and found himself fired down the road thanks to oil on his back tyre. He suffered a broken foot and the bike went up in flames, leaving the team distinctly unhappy. Having missed qualifying, on race day Pol rode to a heroic sixth. It could have been a lot worse: Pol narrowly avoided centre-punching a car on the service road when he used the short-cut back to the pits during warm-up.

It is usual for the Malaysian round to see higher track temperatures than anywhere else but even by the standards of Sepang this year's race was run in extreme conditions. An ambient temperature in the mid-30s does not sound too bad, but it is hell for riders when allied to extreme humidity as the weather builds up to the regular late-afternoon thunderstorm. And track temperatures

'THIS WAS ONE OF THE TOUGHEST RACES OF THE YEAR FOR ME PHYSICALLY'

MARC MARQUEZ

OPPOSITE The coming together between Aleix Espargaro and Alvaro Bautista at the start of the second lap; Aleix held his hands up.

ABOVE Marc Marquez had to work for his win; both Yamaha riders led before he got to the front.

RIGHT Pol Espargaro ignored warnings and this was the result: a broken metatarsal and a burning M1.

ABOVE Scott Redding pursues Alex de Angelis and Nicky Hayden, who both fell.

BELOW Yonny Hernandez finished top Ducati in seventh, a career-best result.

over 55 degrees make it hell for tyres too. Once the temperature is above 50, riders always describe the track as feeling 'greasy', which may help explain Pedrosa's brace of front-end crashes.

The weather at Sepang also makes massive demands on a rider's fitness and powers of concentration – the two, of course, are related. Jorge Lorenzo again made reference to his fitness, or lack of it, in explaining why he faded a little in third place. At the start of the season he had to recover from three operations over the close season and now he said he

had not trained enough during the three weeks outside Europe. He did have the excuse, though, of losing the rubber pad from the left side of the tank – he braces his knee against that under braking.

So what to make of Rossi in second place and pushing Marquez all the way at the age of 35? If you wanted to know just how much he has worked and how much he has desired to be back at the front, here was the evidence. After Rossi took the lead from his team-mate, Marquez took advantage of him running wide at the final corner to take the lead. Far from fading, the older man continued to press right to the end. When Marc told the post-race press conference that 'the strongest opponent today was the weather', Valentino felt moved to interrupt and pointedly remark, 'It was supposed to be me!' The contrast between the exhausted Stefan Bradl in fourth and the amazingly fresh Bradley Smith in fifth was also worth noting.

As usual, Marquez's pole and win broke and equalled some records. The pole was his 13th of the year, beating the 12 set by Mick Doohan and Casey Stoner. The win was his 12th of the year, equalling Doohan's dozen from 1997. In the interests of strict statistical accuracy, though, it should be pointed out that Mick's benchmarks were set in a 15-race season. It took Marc 17 races to beat the pole record and he left Sepang with one more chance to notch up the most victories in a single season. A little basic mathematics will demonstrate that Mighty Mick has the higher strike rate and therefore the boasting rights – not that he will care. Marc, on the other hand, has plenty of time ahead of him.

LOITERING WITH INTENT

Race Director Mike Webb, normally a man in control of his emotions, finally lost his rag with the Moto3 field.

The subject of Moto3 riders going slowly on the racing line, looking for a tow in qualifying, has been generating heat all year. There has been much arm-waving, notably by Jack Miller, and penalty points have been dished out, including one block-booking of seven Moto3 riders in Australia.

But what finally pushed Webb over the edge was the sight in qualifying at Sepang of half the field sitting up and cruising on the back straight, looking over their shoulders and waiting for a fast guy to come through and tow them to a better qualifying position.

The Race Director's problem was that, by the letter of the law, he could not punish the Sepang miscreants because they were not on the racing line. It seemed that a new rule was needed, but if the normal channels were gone through it would not come into force until 2015.

Race Direction took a different approach. It was decided that the rule covering dangerous riding would be invoked to cover what undoubtedly has been dangerous behaviour. You do not have to be very old to remember accidents caused by people going slowly on a live track, and the sort of collisions that happen under those circumstances rarely have trivial consequences.

The Moto3 riders were summoned to a special briefing at the next race, in Valencia, and told in no uncertain terms that anyone seen to be cruising, sitting up or looking over their shoulder would be penalised, no matter which bit of the track they were on. This would be applied to Moto2 and MotoGP as well, where there have also been several near misses in qualifying – although, it must be said, on nothing like the scale or regularity of the misbehaviour that has occurred in Moto3.

BELOW Marc Marquez photo-bombing the Rossi team's post-race celebrations.

OFFICIAL TIMEKEEPER

SHELL ADVANCE MALAYSIAN MOTORCYCLE GRAND PRIX
SEPANG INTERNATIONAL CIRCUIT

ROUND 17
OCTOBER 26

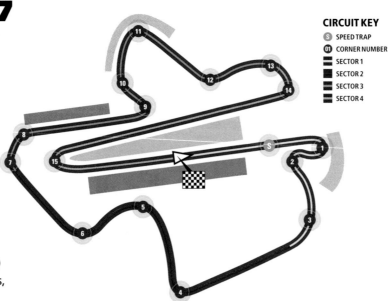

CIRCUIT KEY
- **S** SPEED TRAP
- **01** CORNER NUMBER
- SECTOR 1
- SECTOR 2
- SECTOR 3
- SECTOR 4

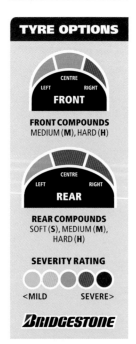

TYRE OPTIONS

FRONT

LEFT — CENTRE — RIGHT

FRONT COMPOUNDS
MEDIUM (**M**), HARD (**H**)

REAR

LEFT — CENTRE — RIGHT

REAR COMPOUNDS
SOFT (**S**), MEDIUM (**M**), HARD (**H**)

SEVERITY RATING

<MILD   SEVERE>

BRIDGESTONE

RACE RESULTS

CIRCUIT LENGTH 3.447 miles
NO. OF LAPS 20
RACE DISTANCE 68.94 miles
WEATHER Dry, 36°C
TRACK TEMPERATURE 54°C
WINNER Marc Marquez
FASTEST LAP 2m 01.150s, 102.340mph, Marc Marquez (record)
PREVIOUS LAP RECORD 2m 01.415s, 102.216mph, Marc Marquez, 2013

QUALIFYING

	Rider	Nation	Motorcycle	Team	Time	Pole +
1	Marquez	SPA	Honda	Repsol Honda Team	1m 59.791s	
2	Pedrosa	SPA	Honda	Repsol Honda Team	1m 59.973s	0.182s
3	Lorenzo	SPA	Yamaha	Movistar Yamaha MotoGP	2m 00.203s	0.412s
4	Bradl	GER	Honda	LCR Honda MotoGP	2m 00.472s	0.681s
5	Dovizioso	ITA	Ducati	Ducati Team	2m 00.703s	0.912s
6	Rossi	ITA	Yamaha	Movistar Yamaha MotoGP	2m 00.740s	0.949s
7	Espargaro A	SPA	Yamaha	NGM Forward Racing	2m 00.801s	1.010s
8	Crutchlow	GBR	Ducati	Ducati Team	2m 01.119s	1.328s
9	Smith	GBR	Yamaha	Monster Yamaha Tech3	2m 01.263s	1.472s
10	Bautista	SPA	Honda	GO&FUN Honda Gresini	2m 02.294s	2.503s
11	Aoyama	JPN	Honda	Drive M7 Aspar	2m 10.568s	10.777s
12	Espargaro P	SPA	Yamaha	Monster Yamaha Tech3	2m 01.885s	1.431s
13	Hernandez	COL	Ducati	Energy T.I. Pramac Racing	2m 02.184s	Q1
14	Hayden	USA	Honda	Drive M7 Aspar	2m 02.330s	Q1
15	Abraham	CZE	Honda	Cardion AB Motoracing	2m 02.548s	Q1
16	Barbera	SPA	Ducati	Avintia Racing	2m 02.682s	Q1
17	Redding	GBR	Honda	GO&FUN Honda Gresini	2m 02.874s	Q1
18	De Angelis	RSM	Yamaha	NGM Forward Racing	2m 03.165s	Q1
19	Petrucci	ITA	ART	Octo IodaRacing Team	2m 03.874s	Q1
20	Laverty	GBR	PBM	Paul Bird Motorsport	2m 04.539s	Q1
21	Di Meglio	FRA	Avintia	Avintia Racing	2m 04.784s	Q1
22	Parkes	AUS	PBM	Paul Bird Motorsport	2m 05.208s	Q1
23	Iannone	ITA	Ducati	Pramac Racing	2m 02.597s	Q1

1 MARC MARQUEZ
Pushed out of the way at Turn 1 but able to come back from eighth to fourth in one lap. Followed Rossi past Lorenzo at half distance, then took advantage of a mistake a lap later to take the lead and pull away to equal Mick Doohan's record of 12 wins in a season and to give Honda the constructors' title.

2 VALENTINO ROSSI
A brilliant comeback after disastrous qualifying and practice. Dealt with Lorenzo, which Vale said was the most important thing (because of the fight for second place in the championship).

3 JORGE LORENZO
Used the hard front tyre, unlike his team-mate, but Jorge's race was compromised by the loss of the rubber stop on the left side of his tank – he uses this to brace his knee when braking. Also blamed his 'soft' training during this period of three 'flyaway' races.

4 STEFAN BRADL
A quietly efficient weekend. Good qualifying and good pace in the race despite knowing after the first hard-braking effort that his Honda's front end was not up to any serious attacking manoeuvres.

5 BRADLEY SMITH
A great race after unpromising practice and qualifying. In the closing stages chased down a tiring Bradl but could not make a last-corner pass. Definitely helped by his fitness, Bradley looked better than most of them after the flag.

6 POL ESPARGARO
Rode with a broken metatarsal in his left foot after a big crash in qualifying. Tried to maintain a consistent pace but found the last ten laps very tough. Rewarded by moving up a place in the World Championship at the expense of his brother.

7 YONNY HERNANDEZ
What a way to celebrate your 50th GP – a career-best result. Got his best ever start and maintained good pace, despite serious sliding in the last five laps, to finish as top Ducati.

8 ANDREA DOVIZIOSO
Shadowed the three podium finishers for most of the race but suddenly started losing ground at around two-thirds distance. A fuel-pump problem meant the engine stuttered every time Andrea opened the throttle.

9 HECTOR BARBERA
Delighted to be top Open Class finisher for the second race running, but had a difficult race. Could not run the times he did on Saturday, probably due to the increased temperatures and consequent loss of grip.

10 SCOTT REDDING
Knew Aoyama was faster so went with the harder rear tyre in case it gave an advantage in the closing stages. It did not, but Scott still finished top customer Honda rider and extended his lead in the battle to be top customer Honda rider in the points standings.

LAP CHART

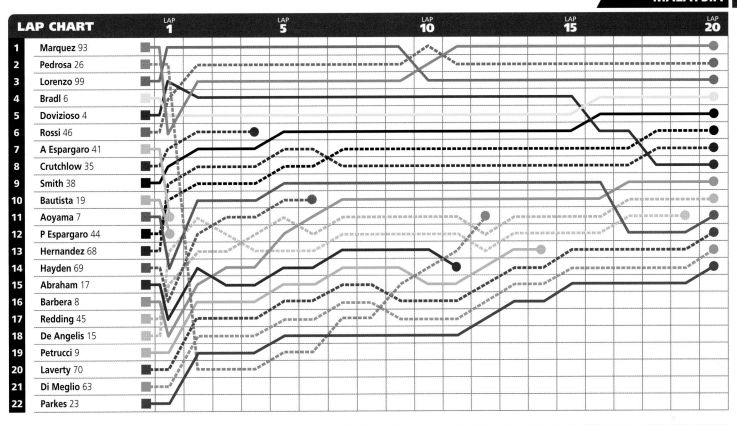

		LAP 1	LAP 5	LAP 10	LAP 15	LAP 20
1	Marquez 93					
2	Pedrosa 26					
3	Lorenzo 99					
4	Bradl 6					
5	Dovizioso 4					
6	Rossi 46					
7	A Espargaro 41					
8	Crutchlow 35					
9	Smith 38					
10	Bautista 19					
11	Aoyama 7					
12	P Espargaro 44					
13	Hernandez 68					
14	Hayden 69					
15	Abraham 17					
16	Barbera 8					
17	Redding 45					
18	De Angelis 15					
19	Petrucci 9					
20	Laverty 70					
21	Di Meglio 63					
22	Parkes 23					

RACE

	Rider	Motorcycle	Race time	Time +	Fastest lap	Avg. speed	
1	Marquez	Honda	40m 45.523s		2m 01.150s	101.3mph	M/M
2	Rossi	Yamaha	40m 47.968s	2.445s	2m 01.315s	101.3mph	M/M
3	Lorenzo	Yamaha	40m 49.031s	3.508s	2m 01.556s	101.2mph	H/M
4	Bradl	Honda	41m 06.757s	21.234s	2m 02.313s	100.5mph	M/M
5	Smith	Yamaha	41m 07.806s	22.283s	2m 02.519s	100.5mph	M/M
6	Espargaro P	Yamaha	41m 20.191s	34.668s	2m 02.854s	100.0mph	M/M
7	Hernandez	Ducati	41m 23.958s	38.435s	2m 02.739s	99.8mph	H/M
8	Dovizioso	Ducati	41m 34.362s	48.839s	2m 02.295s	99.4mph	H/M
9	Barbera	Ducati	41m 36.315s	50.792s	2m 03.694s	99.3mph	H/S
10	Redding	Honda	41m 44.611s	59.088s	2m 03.743s	99.0mph	M/M
11	Aoyama	Honda	42m 01.472s	1m 15.949s	2m 03.175s	98.3mph	M/S
12	Laverty	PBM	42m 03.489s	1m 17.966s	2m 05.305s	98.2mph	M/S
13	Di Meglio	Avintia	42m 13.296s	1m 27.773s	2m 05.392s	97.9mph	H/S
14	Parkes	PBM	42m 29.767s	1m 44.244s	2m 05.891s	97.2mph	H/S
NF	De Angelis	Yamaha	39m 39.875s	1 lap	2m 04.171s	99.0mph	M/S
NF	Petrucci	ART	29m 23.210s	6 laps	2m 04.790s	98.4mph	M/S
NF	Pedrosa	Honda	25m 00.691s	8 laps	2m 01.653s	99.1mph	M/M
NF	Abraham	Honda	22m 58.622s	9 laps	2m 04.151s	98.9mph	M/S
NF	Hayden	Honda	12m 29.154s	14 laps	2m 03.308s	99.3mph	M/S
NF	Crutchlow	Ducati	8m 15.778s	16 laps	2m 02.106s	100.0mph	H/M
NF	Espargaro A	Yamaha	2m 10.616s	19 laps	–	94.9mph	H/M
NF	Bautista	Honda	2m 10.687s	19 laps	–	94.9mph	M/M
NS	Iannone	Ducati	–	–	–	–	

CHAMPIONSHIP

	Rider	Nation	Team	Points
1	Marquez	SPA	Repsol Honda Team	337
2	Rossi	ITA	Movistar Yamaha MotoGP	275
3	Lorenzo	SPA	Movistar Yamaha MotoGP	263
4	Pedrosa	SPA	Repsol Honda Team	230
5	Dovizioso	ITA	Ducati Team	174
6	Espargaro P	SPA	Monster Yamaha Tech3	126
7	Smith	GBR	Monster Yamaha Tech3	119
8	Espargaro A	SPA	NGM Forward Racing	117
9	Bradl	GER	LCR Honda MotoGP	109
10	Iannone	ITA	Pramac Racing	102
11	Bautista	SPA	GO&FUN Honda Gresini	89
12	Redding	GBR	GO&FUN Honda Gresini	75
13	Aoyama	JPN	Drive M7 Aspar	67
14	Crutchlow	GBR	Ducati Team	63
15	Hernandez	COL	Energy T.I. Pramac Racing	53
16	Hayden	USA	Drive M7 Aspar	44
17	Abraham	CZE	Cardion AB Motoracing	33
18	Barbera	SPA	Avintia Racing	21
19	De Angelis	RSM	NGM Forward Racing	14
20	Petrucci	ITA	Octo IodaRacing Team	13
21	Edwards	USA	NGM Forward Racing	11
	Pirro	ITA	Ducati Team	11
23	Parkes	AUS	Paul Bird Motorsport	9
	Laverty	GBR	Paul Bird Motorsport	9
	Di Meglio	FRA	Avintia Racing	9
26	Nakasuga	JPN	YAMALUBE Racing Team	4
27	Camier	GBR	Drive M7 Aspar	1

11 HIROSHI AOYAMA
Best qualifying of the year and a good warm-up followed by a good start. Had a problem with his drinks system and the conditions took their toll. Ran off track four laps from home and lost the chance to be top Open Class finisher.

12 MICHAEL LAVERTY
Delighted to score points for the second race in a row. Did not have the grip early on to go with the group but maintained a consistent pace to overtake Petrucci and open a gap to di Meglio.

13 MIKE DI MEGLIO
Happy with finishing in the points but not with the performance of his bike. Not enough power to stay with Laverty on the straights and after seven laps a lot of chatter.

14 BROC PARKES
Still seriously affected by the shoulder injury he picked up in his home race the previous weekend, but toughed it out to collect two points.

DID NOT FINISH

ALEX DE ANGELIS
Retirement on the last lap but Alex was happy with the race as he got a good start and was able to stay with Redding.

DANILO PETRUCCI
His ART bike stopped four laps from the flag while he was 13th – which would have been a great result.

DANI PEDROSA
Slid off when he lost the front at the final corner; got back on but had the same crash again.

KAREL ABRAHAM
His lack of confidence in the brakes continued. Running last of the customer Hondas when he crashed.

NICKY HAYDEN
Was chasing his team-mate when he made a mistake at Turn 9 and lost the front – apologised to the team.

CAL CRUTCHLOW
Looked to be on for a good race but coasted to a halt with terminal electrical problems on lap five.

ALVARO BAUTISTA
Collided with Aleix Espargaro while braking for the first corner of lap two. Rider perplexed; team blamed Espargaro.

ALEIX ESPARGARO
Went wide on the brakes, touched Bautista and crashed, taking the Honda down as well. Apologised for causing the incident, but got some consolation by being confirmed as Open Class Champion.

VALENCIA
ROUND 18

GRAN PREMIO GENERALI DE LA COMUNITAT VALENCIANA
CIRCUITO RICARDO TORMO

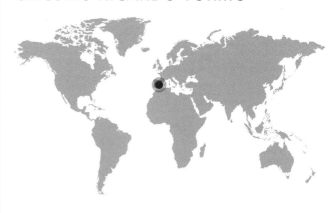

THE FINAL COUNTDOWN

Marc Marquez won for the 13th time and broke the record for the number of victories in a season

For quite a lot of the weekend it looked as if Marc Marquez was going to finish another astonishing season on an uncharacteristically flat note. He was, in his terms, slightly off the pace, and he crashed in qualifying, consigning himself to a second-row start from fifth, his worst of the year. He had never won from anywhere other than the front row – so were we in for a finale that would underline the superb Yamaha renaissance of the second half of the season? When Valentino Rossi took his first pole position for over four years, his 50th in the top class, it looked like the Doctor's scriptwriter was at work again.

There was also the matter of second place overall to sort out. Valentino made it very clear that it was being top Yamaha rider that concerned him, not the second place as such. There was also the matter of the dispute for top satellite bike – sixth place – between the Espargaro brothers and Bradley Smith. It does not sound important but it triggers all sorts of bonuses and contractual obligations.

Just to make things even more complicated on the convoluted stadium circuit, there was a new version of the customer Honda as well as two extra motorcycles on track. The Honda was ridden by Hiro Aoyama and was considerably faster down the straight than the 2014 model. Michele Pirro made his usual appearance as a wild card but on a slightly more finished-looking Ducati than normal; the factory obviously wanted to stop him defecting to Aprilia. But most attention focused on the singleton Suzuki, which was entered as a wild card in preparation for the post-season tests.

In truth, Suzuki's entry was as much a 'thank you' to test rider Randy de Puniet as anything. The team

'I AM SO PLEASED, ESPECIALLY FOR MY BROTHER! IT IS A VERY HAPPY DAY, EVEN MORE THAN IN MOTEGI WHEN I WAS CROWNED CHAMPION'

MARC MARQUEZ

just hoped to get through the race without a disaster and then concentrate on the real business of testing with their young Spanish signings, Aleix Espargaro and Maverick Viñales. Suzuki was allocated three engines for the weekend and two were out of commission by race day, while in the race the gearbox cried enough. The bike looked competitive, only 1.3 seconds off the best time on Friday and a second off pole in qualifying. In the race, though, de Puniet's best lap was 1.9 seconds slower than Marquez's new lap record. Frankly, anything much better would have been a bit of a surprise; most commentators decided to do what the team suggested and concentrate on how the Suzuki would fare in testing.

The performance of the Ducatis was again slightly puzzling. Andrea Iannone qualified fastest of them and led the opening laps as the works riders indulged in their own private dice. Cal Crutchlow and Andrea Dovizioso spent most of the race swapping places in a hard but fair fight that was eventually won by Dovi. However, it was hard not to wonder at Cal's late-season form and Andrea was moved to offer a slightly backhanded compliment by saying he was 'a bit sorry' that the Brit was leaving the Ducati team.

Iannone's initial pace was wasted when he followed Jorge Lorenzo's example and swapped bikes early in the race when part of the circuit was affected by a light shower. At Aragón, where Jorge won, he had been complimented on his brave race but had replied that he had been lucky – and that Aleix Espargaro, the first to pit, was the one who had been brave. At Valencia it looked as if Jorge remembered that and gambled on the weather getting worse. Instead, he found himself lapping over

OPPOSITE Jorge Lorenzo enters pitlane as he gambles on changing bikes – it did not pay off.

LEFT Andrea Iannone led the first ten laps, underlining what a good season he has had.

ABOVE Valentino Rossi started from pole position for the first time since Le Mans 2010.

ABOVE The Paul Bird Motorsport team said goodbye to MotoGP with a double finish.

BELOW Suzuki entered Randy de Puniet as a wild card prior to the factory's return to MotoGP in 2015.

ten seconds slower than the leaders and retired, handing second in the championship to Rossi.

The arrival of the rain slowed down the whole field for a few laps. Marquez said he was thinking of his mistake at Aragón; quite a few others, it seemed, were thinking about the tests starting on Monday. Earlier in the day they would have seen Suzuki recruit Maverick Viñales crash out of the Moto2 race and walk away holding his previously injured shoulder – just what you want the day before your first ride on a MotoGP machine.

Marc Marquez had also been watching the smaller classes. Specifically, he had been watching his younger brother Alex emerge from a fraught Moto3 finale as World Champion. All of a sudden, though, Marc had his mind back on his own game. Although it took a few laps to catch and pass Rossi and Iannone, Marc's performance was reminiscent of the start of the season. The outcome was only in doubt for a moment when the rain came and Rossi closed, but once the Spaniard had assessed the situation he was able to open up the gap again.

The race was a metaphor for the whole season. Marc looked vulnerable for a while but it was an illusion. His fellow Spaniards, Pedrosa and Lorenzo, had seriously flawed seasons – Dani with lack of pace early in races, Jorge with a mad start to the year. The threat to Marquez's domination came from Valentino Rossi, revitalised this year at the age of 35. He has remodelled his riding style, and, in contrast to his early years, works ferociously hard on his fitness. Rossi understood that if he wanted to compete with a man 14 years younger than him, that was what it would take. Where does he get his motivation from?

Wherever and however he gets his motivation, Valentino is going to need all he can get over his next two seasons with Yamaha. Marc Marquez did not just retain his title in 2014, but managed to win races in ways he has not shown before.In Valencia he did it without the benefit of a front-row start; all 17 other MotoGP wins came from the front row. Marquez has won wet races, dry races and bike-change races (from wet to dry and dry to wet) – and he has won from pitlane.

Perhaps there are ways Marquez has not won. No doubt we will find out in 2015.

TEAM RUFEA

The traditional photocall after the last race for the three World Champions – Marc Marquez, Tito Rabat and Alex Marquez – featured not just two brothers but three close friends.

They call themselves Team Rufea and all three of them use that name on various forms of social media, such as Instagram, if you want to follow. Rufea is a small dirt-track oval outside the Marquez brothers' home town of Lleida where the three practice hard when Rabat is not wearing a groove in the Almeria circuit. At the end of the Valencia weekend, it emerged that the brothers had had a coming-together the week before and, according to Marc, it could have been rather a big deal – he thought for a moment that he had put Alex out of the last race.

The trio's history goes back to Spanish championship days when Tito and the slightly younger Marc Marquez became friends. Both were supported by the Royal Automobile Club of Catalunya, so were effectively team-mates. At races Tito became a regular visitor to the Marquez family caravan

2014 FIM MotoGP World Champions

for breakfast. It was notable at the photo shoot how Alex's and Marc's mother, Rosal, made a point of being attentive to Tito, who lost his own mother two years ago.

Before the traditional photocall, which the trio delayed as they insisted

on taking group selfies, Team Rufea's best day had occurred earlier in the year at Catalunya, which was the first time all three of them had won on the same day. It is difficult to imagine them having a better day than the last Sunday of the 2014 season.

RIGHT Oh My God, there are two of them! HRC rewarded Moto3 Champion Alex Marquez with a ride on its MotoGP bike in post-race testing on the Monday after Valencia; big brother kept an eye on him.

GRAN PREMIO GENERALI DE LA COMUNITAT VALENCIANA
CIRCUITO RICARDO TORMO

ROUND **18**
NOVEMBER 9

RACE RESULTS

CIRCUIT LENGTH 2.489 miles

NO. OF LAPS 30

RACE DISTANCE 74.658 miles

WEATHER Dry, 18°C

TRACK TEMPERATURE 22°C

WINNER Marc Marquez

FASTEST LAP 1m 31.515s, 97.866mph, Marc Marquez (record)

PREVIOUS LAP RECORD 1m 31.628s, 97.742mph, Dani Pedrosa (2013)

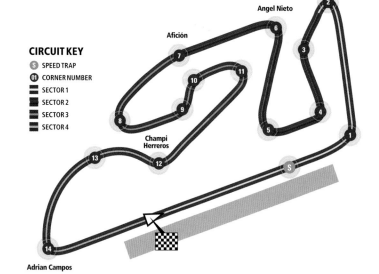

CIRCUIT KEY
- **S** SPEED TRAP
- **01** CORNER NUMBER
- ▬ SECTOR 1
- ▬ SECTOR 2
- ▬ SECTOR 3
- ▬ SECTOR 4

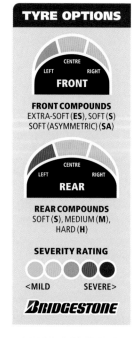

TYRE OPTIONS

FRONT

FRONT COMPOUNDS
EXTRA-SOFT (**ES**), SOFT (**S**)
SOFT (ASYMMETRIC) (**SA**)

REAR

REAR COMPOUNDS
SOFT (**S**), MEDIUM (**M**),
HARD (**H**)

SEVERITY RATING

<MILD   SEVERE>

BRIDGESTONE

QUALIFYING

	Rider	Nation	Motorcycle	Team	Time	Pole +
1	Rossi	ITA	Yamaha	Movistar Yamaha MotoGP	1m 30.843s	
2	Iannone	ITA	Ducati	Pramac Racing	1m 30.975s	0.132s
3	Pedrosa	SPA	Honda	Repsol Honda Team	1m 30.999s	0.156s
4	Lorenzo	SPA	Yamaha	Movistar Yamaha MotoGP	1m 31.049s	0.206s
5	Marquez	SPA	Honda	Repsol Honda Team	1m 31.144s	0.301s
6	Espargaro P	SPA	Yamaha	Monster Yamaha Tech3	1m 31.307s	0.464s
7	Smith	GBR	Yamaha	Monster Yamaha Tech3	1m 31.324s	0.481s
8	Crutchlow	GBR	Ducati	Ducati Team	1m 31.359s	0.516s
9	Dovizioso	ITA	Ducati	Ducati Team	1m 31.426s	0.583s
10	Bradl	GER	Honda	LCR Honda MotoGP	1m 31.443s	0.600s
11	Espargaro A	SPA	Yamaha	NGM Forward Racing	1m 31.486s	0.643s
12	Pirro	ITA	Ducati	Ducati Team	1m 32.617s	1.774s
13	Bautista	SPA	Honda	GO&FUN Honda Gresini	1m 32.160s	Q1
14	Redding	GBR	Honda	GO&FUN Honda Gresini	1m 32.315s	Q1
15	Hernandez	COL	Ducati	Energy T.I. Pramac Racing	1m 32.321s	Q1
16	Hayden	USA	Honda	Drive M7 Aspar	1m 32.395s	Q1
17	Barbera	SPA	Ducati	Avintia Racing	1m 32.443s	Q1
18	Aoyama	JPN	Honda	Drive M7 Aspar	1m 32.449s	Q1
19	De Angelis	RSM	Yamaha	NGM Forward Racing	1m 32.453s	Q1
20	De Puniet	FRA	Suzuki	Team Suzuki MotoGP	1m 32.509s	Q1
21	Petrucci	ITA	ART	Octo IodaRacing Team	1m 32.683s	Q1
22	Laverty	GBR	PBM	Paul Bird Motorsport	1m 32.808s	Q1
23	Abraham	CZE	Honda	Cardion AB Motoracing	1m 33.019s	Q1
24	Parkes	AUS	PBM	Paul Bird Motorsport	1m 33.972s	Q1
25	Di Meglio	FRA	Avintia	Avintia Racing	1m 34.510s	Q1

1 MARC MARQUEZ
Rounded off the year with a record-breaking 13th win to beat Mick Doohan's achievement. Appeared distracted during practice, but once his brother had secured the Moto3 title Marc got his mind back on the job.

2 VALENTINO ROSSI
Pushed Marquez all the way from his 50th pole position in the top class, which seemed to please more than some of his victories as his last pole was four years ago. Doubly satisfied with the result as he has never had much luck at Valencia.

3 DANI PEDROSA
Continued his pattern of average starts, thus wasting his front-row start. Happy to finish on the podium after two no-scores, but made the point that he has not had a good year.

4 ANDREA DOVIZIOSO
A suitable end to his ultra-professional season. Major improvements in qualifying and a race-long fight with his team-mate at a track that he and the bike do not really like.

5 CAL CRUTCHLOW
Bowed out of the factory Ducati team with another good ride. Like his team-mate, with whom he diced for most of the race, thought he could have pushed harder when conditions got tricky.

6 POL ESPARGARO
Won the battle with his brother and Smith for sixth in the championship but was displeased with his race. Dropped as low as 13th as he worried about his lack of experience in the mixed conditions but fought back, as befits the best non-factory rider of the year.

7 ALEIX ESPARGARO
Arrived with the Open Class title already in his pocket and secured seventh overall with another impressive ride. Finished top Open Class bike again and overtook Smith in the points table.

8 STEFAN BRADL
Another man who is not a fan of this track and erred on the side of caution when the rain came: Stefan's last race for the LCR team was not the event he hoped for after a three-year association.

9 MICHELE PIRRO
Ducati's test rider rode as a wild card. Delighted with the best finish of his six races this year on the test team's machine – which looked a little more finished than in previous races.

10 SCOTT REDDING
Superb in the mixed conditions, and another top-ten finish cemented his place as top customer Honda rider.

11 HECTOR BARBERA
Not sure whether to be pleased about scoring points again or disappointed about not being top Open Class rider,

LAP CHART

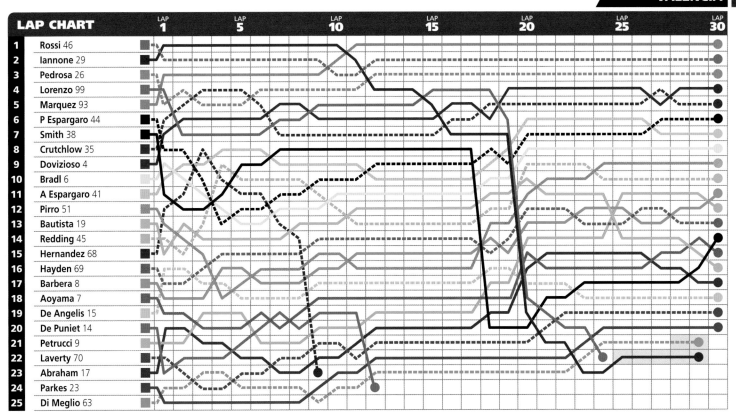

		LAP 1	LAP 5	LAP 10	LAP 15	LAP 20	LAP 25	LAP 30
1	Rossi 46							
2	Iannone 29							
3	Pedrosa 26							
4	Lorenzo 99							
5	Marquez 93							
6	P Espargaro 44							
7	Smith 38							
8	Crutchlow 35							
9	Dovizioso 4							
10	Bradl 6							
11	A Espargaro 41							
12	Pirro 51							
13	Bautista 19							
14	Redding 45							
15	Hernandez 68							
16	Hayden 69							
17	Barbera 8							
18	Aoyama 7							
19	De Angelis 15							
20	De Puniet 14							
21	Petrucci 9							
22	Laverty 70							
23	Abraham 17							
24	Parkes 23							
25	Di Meglio 63							

RACE

	Rider	Motorcycle	Race time	Time +	Fastest lap	Avg. speed	
1	Marquez	Honda	46m 39.627s		1m 31.515s	95.9mph	S/M
2	Rossi	Yamaha	46m 43.143s	3.516s	1m 31.688s	95.9mph	S/M
3	Pedrosa	Honda	46m 53.667s	14.040s	1m 31.715s	95.5mph	S/M
4	Dovizioso	Ducati	46m 56.332s	16.705s	1m 31.966s	95.4mph	S/M
5	Crutchlow	Ducati	46m 56.400s	16.773s	1m 32.019s	95.4mph	S/M
6	Espargaro P	Yamaha	47m 17.511s	37.844s	1m 32.104s	94.7mph	SA/M
7	Espargaro A	Yamaha	47m 17.795s	38.168s	1m 32.446s	94.7mph	SA/S
8	Bradl	Honda	47m 21.430s	41.803s	1m 32.500s	94.6mph	S/M
9	Pirro	Ducati	47m 25.337s	45.710s	1m 33.094s	94.5mph	S/M
10	Redding	Honda	47m 30.818s	51.191s	1m 33.127s	94.3mph	SA/S
11	Barbera	Ducati	47m 36.139s	56.512s	1m 32.918s	94.1mph	SA/S
12	Petrucci	ART	47m 36.627s	57.000s	1m 33.552s	94.1mph	SA/M
13	Hayden	Honda	47m 36.889s	57.262s	1m 32.989s	94.1mph	SA/S
14	Smith	Yamaha	47m 37.144s	57.517s	1m 31.989s	94.0mph	SA/M
15	Aoyama	Honda	47m 38.402s	58.775s	1m 33.399s	94.0mph	SA/M
16	Bautista	Honda	47m 38.491s	58.864s	1m 32.538s	94.0mph	SA/M
17	Abraham	Honda	47m 42.016s	1m 02.389s	1m 33.627s	93.9mph	ES/S
18	De Angelis	Yamaha	47m 55.422s	1m 15.795s	1m 33.013s	93.5mph	SA/S
19	Laverty	PBM	48m 05.936s	1m 26.309s	1m 33.636s	93.1mph	SA/S
20	Parkes	PBM	48m 16.839s	1m 37.212s	1m 34.071s	92.8mph	SA/S
21	Di Meglio	Avintia	46m 40.210s	1 lap	1m 34.640s	92.8mph	S/S
22	Iannone	Ducati	47m 55.140s	1 lap	1m 32.054s	90.4mph	SA/M
NF	Lorenzo	Yamaha	38m 47.139s	6 laps	1m 31.817s	92.3mph	S/M
NF	De Puniet	Suzuki	19m 31.033s	18 laps	1m 33.445s	91.8mph	SA/S
NF	Hernandez	Ducati	14m 24.721s	21 laps	1m 33.511s	93.2mph	S/M

CHAMPIONSHIP

	Rider	Nation	Team	Points
1	Marquez	SPA	Repsol Honda Team	362
2	Rossi	ITA	Movistar Yamaha MotoGP	295
3	Lorenzo	SPA	Movistar Yamaha MotoGP	263
4	Pedrosa	SPA	Repsol Honda Team	246
5	Dovizioso	ITA	Ducati Team	187
6	Espargaro P	SPA	Monster Yamaha Tech3	136
7	Espargaro A	SPA	NGM Forward Racing	126
8	Smith	GBR	Monster Yamaha Tech3	121
9	Bradl	GER	LCR Honda MotoGP	117
10	Iannone	ITA	Pramac Racing	102
11	Bautista	SPA	GO&FUN Honda Gresini	89
12	Redding	GBR	GO&FUN Honda Gresini	81
13	Crutchlow	GBR	Ducati Team	74
14	Aoyama	JPN	Drive M7 Aspar	68
15	Hernandez	COL	Energy T.I. Pramac Racing	53
16	Hayden	USA	Drive M7 Aspar	47
17	Abraham	CZE	Cardion AB Motoracing	33
18	Barbera	SPA	Avintia Racing	26
19	Pirro	ITA	Ducati Team	18
20	Petrucci	ITA	Octo IodaRacing Team	17
21	De Angelis	RSM	NGM Forward Racing	14
22	Edwards	USA	NGM Forward Racing	11
23	Parkes	AUS	Paul Bird Motorsport	9
	Laverty	GBR	Paul Bird Motorsport	9
	Di Meglio	FRA	Avintia Racing	9
26	Nakasuga	JPN	YAMALUBE Racing Team	4
27	Camier	GBR	Drive M7 Aspar	1

as he had been in the previous two races. Thought that this was probably the true level of the bike at the moment.

12 DANILO PETRUCCI
Marked his 50th GP with a fine race. When conditions got tricky he went past Aoyama, Hayden and Bautista. He also got Barbera's Ducati but it went by him on the straight, then Danilo repassed but ran wide making the effort.

13 NICKY HAYDEN
Rode hard on a track he loves but destroyed his rear tyre in the process. Still handicapped by his healing right wrist.

14 BRADLEY SMITH
Lost two places in the championship to the Espargaro brothers. Ran on when the rain started and was prevented by a marshal from getting back on track.

15 HIROSHI AOYAMA
Raced the totally unsorted prototype of the 2015 customer Honda with pneumatic rather than steel valve springs. Hiro reported that it needs a lot of work!

16 ALVARO BAUTISTA
Another horrible race in a season he described as 'a disaster'. No feeling in the dry and worse in the wet.

17 KAREL ABRAHAM
Happier in the wet and was looking set for some points to end a bad end-of-season run, but when the track dried he was outgunned by Aoyama and Bautista.

18 ALEX DE ANGELIS
Started well but lost confidence, especially in the rear tyre, when the rain came down. Last race for the Forward Yamaha team; will be with Ioda in 2015.

19 MICHAEL LAVERTY
Bowed out of MotoGP with a cracking qualifying lap and good pace but got some cold-tearing to his rear tyre.

20 BROC PARKES
Similar problems to his team-mate but gave the PBM team a double finish at its last MotoGP race.

21 MIKE DI MEGLIO
A difficult final race, especially when it rained.

22 ANDREA INANNONE
Took the same gamble on the rain continuing as Lorenzo did – in fact he followed him up pitlane – and with the same result. Ran on at Turn 8 but was considerably slower than the field at that point.

DID NOT FINISH

JORGE LORENZO
Took a punt on swapping to his wet bike when light rain fell. The rain did not persist and he retired.

RANDY DE PUNIET
Said farewell to MotoGP with a wild-card ride on the Suzuki. Put out of the race by downshifting problems.

YONNY HERNANDEZ
Up to eighth on the third lap when he suddenly lost all feeling with the front tyre and retired.

SPORTSMART²

THE ONLY SPORT TYRE YOU'LL EVER WANT

/ MULTI-TREAD TECHNOLOGY FOR WET AND DRY GRIP
/ JLB TECHNOLOGY FOR HANDLING AT ALL SPEEDS
/ JLT TECHNOLOGY FOR COMFORT

DUNLOP

www.dunlopmotorcycle.eu

RIDE WITH CONFIDENCE

Follow us... **f** */DunlopMoto* 🐦 *@DunlopMoto*

WORLD CHAMPIONSHIP CLASSIFICATION

MotoGP

	Rider	Nation	Motorcycle	QAT	AME	ARG	SPA	FRA	ITA	CAT	NED	GER	INP	CZE	GBR	RSM	ARA	JPN	AUS	MAL	VAL	Points
1	Marquez	SPA	Honda	25	25	25	25	25	25	25	25	25	25	13	25	1	3	20	–	25	25	362
2	Rossi	ITA	Yamaha	20	8	13	20	20	16	20	11	13	16	16	16	25	–	16	25	20	20	295
3	Lorenzo	SPA	Yamaha	–	6	16	13	10	20	13	3	16	20	20	20	20	25	25	20	16	–	263
4	Pedrosa	SPA	Honda	16	20	20	16	11	13	16	16	20	13	25	13	16	2	13	–	–	16	246
5	Dovizioso	ITA	Ducati	11	16	7	11	8	10	8	20	8	9	10	11	13	–	11	13	8	13	187
6	Espargaro P	SPA	Yamaha	–	10	8	7	13	11	9	–	9	11	–	10	10	10	8	–	10	10	136
7	Espargaro A	SPA	Yamaha	13	7	1	9	7	7	10	13	10	–	8	7	–	20	5	–	–	9	126
8	Smith	GBR	Yamaha	–	11	9	8	6	–	6	8	–	10	7	–	9	11	7	16	11	2	121
9	Bradl	GER	Honda	–	13	11	6	9	–	11	6	–	–	9	9	–	13	9	–	13	8	117
10	Iannone	ITA	Ducati	6	9	10	–	–	9	7	10	11	–	11	8	11	–	10	–	–	–	102
11	Bautista	SPA	Honda	–	–	–	10	16	8	–	9	7	–	6	–	8	9	6	10	–	–	89
12	Redding	GBR	Honda	9	–	2	3	4	3	3	4	5	7	5	6	3	6	–	9	6	6	81
13	Crutchlow	GBR	Ducati	10	–	–	–	5	–	–	7	6	8	–	4	7	16	–	–	–	11	74
14	Aoyama	JPN	Honda	5	4	6	4	2	2	1	–	4	6	3	2	4	8	3	8	5	1	68
15	Hernandez	COL	Ducati	4	3	4	2	3	6	5	–	–	–	–	5	6	1	–	5	9	–	53
16	Hayden	USA	Honda	8	5	5	5	–	–	4	–	2	–	–	–	–	7	2	6	–	3	47
17	Abraham	CZE	Honda	3	2	3	–	1	4	–	2	3	5	2	3	5	–	–	–	–	–	33
18	Barbera	SPA	Ducati	–	1	–	1	–	–	–	–	–	–	–	–	–	–	1	11	7	5	26
19	Pirro	ITA	Ducati	–	–	–	–	–	5	2	–	–	–	4	–	–	–	–	–	–	7	18
20	Petrucci	ITA	ART	2	–	–	–	–	–	–	1	1	–	–	–	–	5	–	4	–	4	17
21	De Angelis	RSM	Yamaha	–	–	–	–	–	–	–	–	–	–	1	2	4	–	7	–	–	14
22	Edwards	USA	Yamaha	7	–	–	–	1	–	–	–	–	3	–	–	–	–	–	–	–	–	11
23	Parkes	AUS	PBM	1	–	–	–	–	–	5	–	1	–	–	–	–	–	–	2	–	9
	Laverty	GBR	PBM	–	–	–	–	–	–	–	–	2	–	–	–	–	–	–	3	4	–	9
	Di Meglio	FRA	Avintia	–	–	–	–	–	–	–	–	4	–	–	–	–	–	–	2	3	–	9
26	Nakasuga	JPN	Yamaha	–	–	–	–	–	–	–	–	–	–	–	–	–	–	4	–	–	–	4
27	Camier	GBR	Honda	–	–	–	–	–	–	–	–	–	1	–	–	–	–	–	–	–	1

CONSTRUCTOR

	Motorcycle	QAT	AME	ARG	SPA	FRA	ITA	CAT	NED	GER	INP	CZE	GBR	RSM	ARA	JPN	AUS	MAL	VAL	Points
1	Honda	25	25	25	25	25	25	25	25	25	25	25	25	16	13	20	10	25	25	409
2	Yamaha	20	11	20	20	20	20	20	11	16	20	20	20	25	25	25	25	20	20	354
3	Ducati	11	16	10	11	8	10	8	20	11	9	11	11	13	16	11	13	9	13	211
4	Forward Yamaha	13	7	1	9	7	7	10	13	10	3	8	7	2	20	5	7	–	9	138
5	ART	2	–	–	–	–	–	–	1	1	–	–	–	–	5	–	4	–	4	17
6	PBM	1	–	–	–	–	–	–	5	–	2	–	–	–	–	–	3	4	–	15
7	Avintia	–	1	–	1	–	–	–	–	4	–	–	–	–	–	–	2	3	–	11

TEAM

	Motorcycle	QAT	AME	ARG	SPA	FRA	ITA	CAT	NED	GER	INP	CZE	GBR	RSM	ARA	JPN	AUS	MAL	VAL	Points
1	Repsol Honda Team	41	45	45	41	36	38	41	41	45	38	38	38	17	5	33	–	25	41	608
2	Movistar Yamaha MotoGP	20	14	29	33	30	36	33	14	29	36	36	36	45	25	41	45	36	20	558
3	Ducati Team	21	16	7	11	13	10	8	27	14	17	10	15	20	16	11	13	8	24	261
4	Monster Yamaha Tech 3	–	21	17	15	19	11	15	8	9	21	7	10	19	21	15	16	21	12	257
5	GO&FUN Honda Gresini	9	–	2	13	20	11	3	13	12	7	11	6	11	15	6	19	6	6	170
6	Pramac Racing	10	12	14	2	3	15	12	10	11	–	11	13	17	1	10	5	9	–	155
7	NGM Forward Racing	20	7	1	9	7	8	10	13	10	3	8	8	2	24	5	7	–	9	151
8	LCR Honda MotoGP	–	13	11	6	9	–	11	6	–	–	9	9	–	13	9	–	13	8	117
9	Drive M7 Aspar	13	9	11	9	2	2	5	–	6	–	6	4	2	4	15	–	14	5	4	116
10	Avintia Racing	–	1	–	1	–	–	–	–	4	–	–	–	–	–	1	13	10	5	35
11	Cardion AB Motoracing	3	2	3	–	1	4	–	2	3	5	2	3	5	–	–	–	–	–	33
12	Paul Bird Motorsport	1	–	–	–	–	–	–	5	–	3	–	–	–	–	–	3	6	–	18
13	Octo IodaRacing Team	2	–	–	–	–	–	–	1	1	–	–	–	–	5	–	4	–	4	17

THE
PLACE
TO BE

- **COMFORTABLE SURROUNDINGS**
- **FINEST CATERING**
- **THE MOST EXCLUSIVE LOCATION**

MotoGP VIP Village™, the official and exclusive Corporate Hospitality programme of the MotoGP™ World Championship, offering the highest level of services at every Grand Prix.

motogpvipvillage@dorna.com
www.motogpvipvillage.com

Moto2™
CHAMPIONSHIP

RUN
RABAT RUN

**It was the year of Tito Rabat
and the Marc VDS team, and
it was the year of the rookie**

Between them, Marc VDS team-mates Tito Rabat and Mika Kallio won over half of the season's 18 races. Given the quality of personnel and the ambition of the team owner, perhaps that is no surprise.

Tito – he prefers the diminutive to the full Esteve – started the year with a reputation for putting in enormous distances in practice and winning races by escaping off the start. As he is also gentle on the tyres, he does not fade late in a race. So, went the theory, if you disrupt his rhythm, push him about a bit, he will crack. That perceived weakness was shown to be fiction at Silverstone when Rabat caught his fast-starting team-mate and did a bit of pushing and shoving of his own to take the win. It also ended an impressive run by Kallio that had put him in range of a title challenge.

Rabat's late-season rivals came from some surprising quarters. Once the Suter factory started delivering its evolution chassis, which gave more front-end feel, Dominique Aegerter, Tom Lüthi and Johann Zarco all became regular front-runners and, in the case of Aegerter and Lüthi, race winners. However, the German Kalex chassis were so superior at the start of the season that there were fears that the ten Suters on the grid in 2014 might become none by 2015 as teams seek any advantage in a tightly regulated class. The smaller chassis manufacturers, such as Speed Up, are thinly represented and suffer from lack of data, hampered by the Catch 22 situation that they cannot gather the data needed for development without more bikes on the grid.

News came at Misano that the two Swiss teams that led the Suter challenge would be amalgamating for 2015 and would run Kalex bikes. In a class with controlled engine, electronics and tyres it may be inevitable that

RIGHT Ten years after his other win, also in the wet at Assen, Ant West won on the Qatari Federation team's Speed Up.

BELOW One of Tito Rabat's 11 wins was in Argentina. He shared the rostrum with Xavier Simeon and rookie Luis Salom, neither of whom managed another top-three finish.

one maker finds the right answer to an equation that is simpler than normal, but it most certainly would not be good for a Grand Prix class to effectively become a one-make series. The pace of the Suters at the end of the year and the wet-weather win at Assen by Ant West on a Speed Up helped maintain the variety the class needs, as did the appearance of the All-Japan GP2 Championship-winning NTS chassis with the JiR team from Motegi onwards.

At the last count the grid featured 16 Grand Prix winners, so this is not an easy class in which to make an instant impact. This year's crop of novices, however, was an exception to that rule. They were led by Maverick Viñales, who set the fastest lap in his first race, won his second race, took pole in his 14th, and finished lower than fourth only four times as he

1 – QATARI GP

Title favourite Tito Rabat (Marc VDS Kalex) won a tense duel with Takaaki Nakagami (Idemitsu Kalex) by half a bike's length, with Rabat's team-mate Mika Kallio a close third. Nakagami was later disqualified for an illegal air filter, promoting Kallio to second and Thomas Lüthi (Interwetten Suter) to third.

'I made a very good start but then I made a mistake and lost several places,' said Rabat. 'After that I needed to find my rhythm and catch the fast guys.'

Lüthi beat reigning Moto3 champ Maverick Viñales (Pons Kalex) by just three tenths of a second.

Josh Herrin's GP début on the Caterham Suter lasted just a few corners. After a spirited start from 27th on the grid he went down in a pile-up caused by Xavier Simeon.

'It's disappointing but at least I have a lot of confidence going into the next races because the bike felt really good and I was able to pass a lot of the riders I hadn't been able to pass in practice,' said Herrin.

2 – AMERICAS GP

Moto3 world champ Maverick Viñales (HP 40 Kalex) destroyed his rivals to win his first Moto2 race at Austin. The 19-year-old charged through from eighth place to overpower race leader Dominique Aegerter (Technomag Suter) and Qatar winner Tito Rabat (Marc VDS Kalex). Rabat followed Viñales through into second but had no answer to the leader's stunning end-of-race pace. Viñales finally crossed the line four seconds in front, with Aegerter a further 1.3 seconds down.

'It's an incredible feeling to win my second Moto2 race,' said Viñales. 'We spent most of our time during practice working with used tyres.'

Mika Kallio (Marc VDS Racing) finished fourth, just ahead of Simone Corsi (NGM Forward Kalex). A multiple pile-up at the first corner triggered by Josh Herrin (AirAsia Caterham Suter) claimed six riders.

3 – ARGENTINIAN GP

Tito Rabat (Marc VDS Kalex) continued his Moto2 domination with an impressive start-to-finish win while Austin winner and his most feared title rival Maverick Viñales (Pons HP40 Kalex) crashed out. With three rounds gone, Rabat has scored two wins and a second to enjoy a 28-point lead, the largest across all three classes.

'I got a good start and rode a good first few laps, which isn't usually my strong point,' said Rabat, who increases his confidence at every race. 'It was very difficult to keep concentration, but you must, because if you relax just a little bit the others catch you!'

While Rabat made good his escape, Xavier Simeon (Federal Oil Suter) established himself alone in second place and Luis Salom (Pons HP40 Kalex), Dominique Aegerter (Technomag Suter) and Simone Corsi (Forward Kalex) disputed third. That battle eventually went the way of former Moto3 title-hope Salom. Aegerter got the better of Corsi despite an oil leak that caused rear tyre and brake problems.

4 – SPANISH GP

The Marc VDS team celebrated its second consecutive start-to-finish win, this time with Mika Kallio taking victory. The Finn led from pole to chequered flag on his Kalex, untroubled by closest rivals Dominique Aegerter (Technomag Suter) and Jonas Folger (AGR Kalex). Certainly no-one, least of all the 119,000 fans present on race day, had expected a Finnish/Swiss/German podium at Jerez.

Aegerter tried everything he knew to get close enough to attack but Kallio rode like a robot, grinding out the laps. 'It was hard but the plan was to do what I did, push all the race and make no mistakes,' said Kallio who was 2.4 seconds ahead at the finish.

Former Moto3 race-winner Folger – who rides for a small team, owned by a Spanish celebrity chef – was delighted with his first Moto2 podium. He kept the pressure on Aegerter and held off points leader Tito Rabat (Marc VDS), who started badly following problems with his water bottle on the grid.

5 – FRENCH GP

Finn Mika Kallio (Marc VDS Kalex) won his second Moto2 race in a row, but this time he did not lead from start to finish. Instead he lost the lead to Simone Corsi (NGM Kalex) in the early stages and was happy to stay there for a while.

'I told myself, okay, cool down, save the tyres,' said Kallio. 'Then when he slowed a bit, I decided to go.'

Kallio pounced with six laps to go and then got his head down so no-one could mount a last-gasp attack. The plan worked perfectly, Kallio crossing the line a second ahead of Corsi to close the points gap on slow-starting series leader and team-mate Tito Rabat.

Austin winner Maverick Viñales (HP40 Kalex) established a new lap record on his way to fourth, just ahead of team-mate Luis Salom and pole-starter Jonas Folger (AGR Kalex).

took a solid third overall. His stats are comparable to those of Marc Marquez at the same stage of his career – no wonder Suzuki snapped him up for MotoGP in 2015.

Fellow class rookies Luis Salom and Jonas Folger scored podium finishes and fastest laps early on but failed to keep their momentum going. Franco Morbidelli and Sam Lowes were a little more erratic but impressed mightily. In the Briton's case, the fact that he was on the Speed Up chassis – with its carbon-fibre swinging arm and other left-field chassis ideas – was certainly a mitigating factor in his patchy form, but by the end of the year he was looking at home on a Grand Prix grid. Kudos, too, to Tech 3 team-mates Ricard Cardus and Marcel Schrötter, who regularly put the unfavoured Mistral in the top ten.

ABOVE LEFT Dominique Aegerter celebrates his first Grand Prix win.

ABOVE RIGHT British rookie Sam Lowes and his Speed Up turned out in a variety of colours, including a slightly shocking pink.

LEFT Mika Kallio on his way to victory at Indianapolis – part of the mid-season charge that took him to within seven points of his team-mate.

6 – ITALIAN GP

Tito Rabat (Marc VDS Kalex) won his third race of the year after making a dogged and successful pursuit of early leaders Jonas Folger (AGR Kalex) and Luis Salom (Pons Kalex).

On the first lap Rabat collided with Salom and nearly ran off the track and at half-distance it seemed like he would have to settle for third. But the Spaniard steadily closed the gap, finally getting ahead for the first time with four laps remaining.

'I made a very good race because on the first lap I nearly went outside the track, so I had a lot of distance to make up,' he said.

If Rabat was happy with his latest success – which extended his points lead over team-mate and sixth-place finisher Mika Kallio – Moto2 rookies Salom and Folger had just as much reason to smile.

Five seconds behind them Simone Corsi (NGM Kalex) won a tight tussle for fourth, a fraction ahead of Dominique Aegerter (Technomag Kalex), Kallio and Johann Zarco (Caterham Suter)

7 – CATALAN GP

Tito Rabat (Marc VDS) won his fourth race of 2014, comfortably dismissing early challenges from team-mate Mika Kallio and Austin winner Maverick Viñales (Paginas Amarillas Kalex).

Once clear, he left Viñales in second and Kallio fighting for the final podium slot with Johann Zarco (AirAsiaSuter) and Thomas Lüthi (Interwetten Suter). Zarco won that battle when Lüthi attacked Kallio, both men ran wide, opening the door for the Frenchman to score Caterham's first GP podium.

'This is an unbelievable moment: the best thing that can happen to a rider is to win at home,' said Rabat.

Mattia Pasini (NGM Kalex) and Ricard Cardus (Tech 3) were sixth and seventh, while Axel Pons (AGR Kalex), son of former 250 World Champion Sito Pons, won a busy skirmish for eighth, his best-ever GP finish.

Zarco's team-mate Josh Herrin was 16th, two tenths away from his first world title point.

8 – DUTCH TT

Following a delay caused by a hailstorm, the Moto2 race got underway on a soaking track, perfect conditions for Aussie rain-master Ant West (QMMF Speed Up). After qualifying 27th fastest in the dry, West assumed control of the race and fought off a determined challenge from Austin winner Maverick Viñales (Paginas Amarillas Kalex) and Mika Kallio (Marc VDS Kalex).

West was delighted with his first win in over a decade. 'I just tried to ride it wide and keep it smooth. Once I was ahead I knew it would be difficult to overtake because there was only one dry line.'

Viñales did get ahead for one brief moment but in the final laps he was unable to retake the lead. Nine riders crashed during the race, including Simone Corsi (NGM Kalex) and Sam Lowes (Speed Up) who had been battling for the lead. Corsi remounted to finish 13th, Lowes got back on and immediately crashed once again.

Championship leader Tito Rabat (Marc VDS Kalex) crashed on the sighting lap and finished the race

9 – GERMAN GP

Dominique Aegerter (Technomag Suter) won a brilliant début GP victory. The Swiss was in the battle for the win from the start, spending most of the race shadowing leader Mika Kallio (Marc VDS Racing). In the final few laps Aegerter grabbed the lead, Kallio grabbed it back, before finally Aegerter prevailed, by 0.091 seconds.

'After I passed him on the last lap I closed my line at the last corner and it worked,' said 23-year-old Aegerter, whose win gave Suter its first success of 2014.

Third place went to Simone Corsi (NGM Kalex) whose duel with series leader Tito Rabat (Marc VDS Kalex) lasted to the final corner. Maverick Viñales (Pons Kalex) had a great race, coming through from 15th to finish right behind Rabat and less than a second off the podium.

10 – INDIANAPOLIS GP

Mika Kallio (Marc VDS Kalex) ramped up the pressure on his team-mate Tito Rabat with a dominating win from pole position. Rabat could only finish fourth, which cut his championship lead to a mere seven points. In fact Kallio had to do it twice because the first start was red-flagged after four laps following a pile-up that left Mattia Pasini unconscious at the trackside. Thankfully he walked to the ambulance after a few minutes of careful observation.

Kallio did not scorch away from the field at the second time of asking quite as he had done first time but he built up a comfortable lead over Rabat. The surprise came four laps from the flag when both Maverick Viñales (Paginas Amarillo Kalex) and Dominique Aegerter (CIP Suter) passed him in the same corner. AMA Champion Josh Herrin (Caterham Suter) had a nightmare: he was involved in the group crash that stopped the race and crashed out of the restart.

Disappointments? The terrible form of one of last year's stars, Takaaki Nakagami, in a team built around him, and Nico Terol's problems. The sacking of the reigning American champion, Josh Herrin, after failing to score a point in 12 races was also painful to watch.

Moto2 continued to field a grid full of professional teams and quality riders, and in 2014 Marc VDS were just that bit more professional than the rest. For 2015 Marc VDS will abandon its Moto3 effort in order to run Scott Redding on a factory MotoGP Honda as well as continuing with a two-man Moto2 team. One of the team's Moto2 riders will be Rabat, who will therefore become the first Moto2 champion to defend his number-one plate in the five-year history of the class. If all goes according to plan, Rabat will then move to MotoGP with the team in 2016.

ABOVE Maverick Viñales was an outstanding rookie with four race wins and third in the championship.

RIGHT The Marc VDS riders finished third in the championship and – naturally – won the teams' title as well.

OPPOSITE TOP Johann Zarco scored three third places in the final six races as the Suters struck back.

OPPOSITE BOTTOM Tom Lüthi won two of the last four races on the evo Suter chassis.

11 – CZECH REPUBLIC GP

Remember the days when every Moto2 race was a Rollerball event? Those days are long gone as the top teams and top riders stretch out the pack. This time Tito Rabat led from the start to regain the title initiative from Marc VDS Kalex team-mate Mika Kallio, who had beaten him at the previous three races to reduce the championship gap to just seven points. Rabat gradually increased his lead over Kallio and looked to be home and dry. Then it started to rain. Kallio closed in, but Rabat girded his loins to win by 3.3 seconds.

'It's difficult to race alone – I was pushing so hard to make the gap and then the rain came and it became slightly dangerous,' said the Spaniard after extending his title lead to 12 points.

Kallio was well clear of former Moto3 champ and Moto2 podium first-timer Sandro Cortese (Dynavolt Kalex). Tom Lüthi (Interwetten) just beat fellow Suter rider Dominique Aegerter (Technomag) for fourth, with Maverick Viñales (Paginas Amarillas Kalex) fifth.

12 – BRITISH GP

Marc VDS team-mates and title contestants Tito Rabat and Mika Kallio had a battle that made the Marquez/Lorenzo duel look tame. Rabat eventually came out on top, by just six hundredths of a second, after a heroic ride that saw him come back from almost two seconds down on his team-mate.

The pair rubbed tyres and leathers as they fought for supremacy in the final two laps, Rabat triumphing thanks to his better pace on used tyres.

'I think this was the best race of my life,' he grinned. 'The beginning was difficult. I was angry and asking myself why don't I brake later?'

And brake later he did, catching the lead group of Kallio, Maverick Viñales (Paginas Amarillas Kalex) and Johann Zarco (Air Asia Suter) in the closing stages. Viñales crossed the line third, 0.15 seconds behind a disappointed Kallio.

'As usual, I was fast in the beginning but Tito was faster at the end,' said the Finn.

13 – SAN MARINO GP

Once again Marc VDS team-mates Mika Kallio and Tito Rabat dominated and once again Kallio had the pace in the early stages while Rabat was faster as fuel loads and traction decreased.

Rabat slowly closed for the kill and planned to make his move at the end, but with ten laps to go Kallio had a big moment, when he suddenly lost grip, and Rabat was through. Kallio was powerless to counter-attack and took his third consecutive finish behind Rabat, who seemed to have blunted the Finn's earlier championship surge.

'Mika is impossible to follow at the start but step by step I can catch him,' said Rabat. 'I wanted to follow him for longer because it is easier with the slipstream but then he made a mistake. Now we have to work to improve our speed at the start of races.'

Johann Zarco (AirAsia Suter) came in third with Maverick Viñales (Paginas Amarillas Kalex) closing in the final stages after getting the better of Dominique Aegerter (Technomag Suter) and Tom Lüthi (Interwetten Suter).

14 – ARAGÓN GP

Maverick Viñales (Paginas Amarillas Kalex) underlined his MotoGP value with a runaway victory of the sort that is difficult to achieve in Moto2. The Spaniard took control from Mika Kallio (Marc VDS Kalex) at one-quarter distance and left the rest of the pack to fight among themselves.

He controlled the race from the front to cross the line 1.3 seconds ahead of series leader Tito Rabat (Marc VDS Kalex).

Riders had to contend with a dry line that gave them zero room to make any errors. 'The track conditions were so difficult but I felt really good on the bike from the start, so I was able to ride very hard and make a gap,' said Viñales.

Rabat finished well clear of a five-man battle for the last podium finish that was won by Johann Zarco (AirAsia Suter) ahead of Tom Lüthi (Interwetten Suter), Franco Morbidelli (Italtrans Racing Team Kalex) and Dominique Aegerter (Technomag Suter). Kallio finished seventh, putting him 33 points behind team-mate Rabat.

15 – JAPANESE GP

Swiss rider Thomas Lüthi produced the biggest surprise of the weekend with a start-to-finish win – his first visit to the podium since the season-opener in Qatar.

Lüthi's riding was an exercise in Swiss precision as he rocketed away from the start to establish a good gap, which in the closing stages came under determined attack from Maverick Viñales (Paginas Amarillas Kalex).

'I had a great rhythm from the start and was surprised to make a gap but then I was under a lot of pressure and the last laps felt very long!' smiled Lüthi (Interwetten Suter), whose victory gave Suter its second Moto2 win of the year.

Viñales finished 1.2 seconds down and two seconds up on series leader Tito Rabat (Marc VDS Kalex), who suffered the same start-line nerves that Marquez displayed in the MotoGP race.

'Everyone passed me at the start,' said Rabat. 'I need to change this for Australia.'

Nonetheless Rabat increased his points lead over team-mate Mika Kallio, who slipped to fifth behind Johann Zarco (AirAsia Suter).

CHAMPIONSHIP STANDINGS

	Rider	Nat	Team	Motorcycle	Points
1	Esteve Rabat	SPA	Marc VDS Racing Team	Kalex	346
2	Mika Kallio	FIN	Marc VDS Racing Team	Kalex	289
3	Maverick Viñales	SPA	Paginas Amarillas HP 40	Kalex	274
4	Thomas Lüthi	SWI	Interwetten Sitag	Suter	194
5	Dominique Aegerter	SWI	Technomag carXpert	Suter	172
6	Johann Zarco	FRA	AirAsia Caterham	Caterham Suter	146
7	Simone Corsi	ITA	NGM Forward Racing	Kalex	100
8	Luis Salom	SPA	Paginas Amarillas HP 40	Kalex	85
9	Sandro Cortese	GER	Dynavolt Intact GP	Kalex	85
10	Marcel Schrötter	GER	Tech 3	Tech 3	80
11	Franco Morbidelli	ITA	Italtrans Racing Team	Kalex	75
12	Anthony West	AUS	QMMF Racing Team	Speed Up	72
13	Sam Lowes	GBR	Speed Up	Speed Up	69
14	Xavier Simeon	BEL	Federal Oil Gresini Moto2	Suter	63
15	Jonas Folger	GER	AGR Team	Kalex	63
16	Jordi Torres	SPA	Mapfre Aspar Team Moto2	Suter	57
17	Julian Simon	SPA	Italtrans Racing Team	Kalex	56
18	Ricard Cardus	SPA	Tech 3	Tech 3	45
19	Hafizh Syahrin	MAL	Petronas Raceline Malaysia	Kalex	42
20	Alex de Angelis	RSM	Tasca Racing Moto2	Suter	37
21	Mattia Pasini	ITA	NGM Forward Racing	Kalex	35
22	Takaaki Nakagami	JPN	IDEMITSU Honda Team Asia	Kalex	34
23	Axel Pons	SPA	AGR Team	Kalex	28
24	Randy Krummenacher	SWI	Octo IodaRacing Team	Suter	24
25	Lorenzo Baldassarri	ITA	Gresini Moto2	Suter	20
26	Louis Rossi	FRA	SAG Team	Kalex	18
27	Gino Rea	GBR	AGT REA Racing	Suter	7
28	Nicolas Terol	SPA	Mapfre Aspar Team Moto2	Suter	2
29	Roberto Rolfo	ITA	Tasca Racing Moto2	Suter	2

16 – AUSTRALIAN GP

This was Mika Kallio's last real opportunity to stage a comeback in his title fight with Marc VDS Kalex team-mate Tito Rabat. And if ever he had the chance this was it because Rabat made several mistakes during the race. However, the Spaniard always came back, finally taking third, three tenths ahead of Kallio.

Victory went to hard-charging Maverick Viñales (Paginas Amarillas Kalex) who got stronger as the race progressed. After battling for the lead in the mid-stages he escaped to win by 1.3 seconds.

'The first part of the race was a problem, I didn't have a good feeling,' he said. 'But at the end we were so fast.'

Rabat had started the final lap in second place but succumbed to Motegi winner Tom Lüthi (Interwetten Suter), making the most of Suter's recent chassis update.

2013 World Supersport champ Sam Lowes (Speed Up) ran with the lead group before slipping back to a lonely fifth, his best Moto2 result so far.

17 – MALAYSIAN GP

Maverick Viñales (Paginas Amarillas Kalex) scorched to his third Moto2 win in four races, beating Mika Kallio (Marc VDS Kalex) with a typically strong pace in the final laps.

Kallio's team-mate Tito Rabat led from pole position and built a gap but Viñales and Rabat sensibly decided not to get involved; he knew that a third-place finish would give him the title.

Kallio did everything he could to win the race but in the end he had no reply to Viñales.

'That was the hardest race ever!' said the Spanish rookie. 'But I had a good plan – to be really smooth with the gas during the first part, otherwise the tyre temperature gets too high. So I saved my tyres and in the end that helped me to pull away.'

A few seconds behind the delighted Rabat a three-way battle raged for fourth place, with Dominique Aegerter (carXpert Suter) caught and passed on the last lap by Johann Zarco (AirAsia Suter), with Julian Simon (Italtrans Kalex) just metres behind.

18 – VALENCIAN GP

Tito Rabat rode one hell of a Moto2 race, refusing to give into relentless pressure from Tom Lüthi and determined to win in front of his home fans. Lüthi (Interwetten Suter) had made several lunges at Rabat (Marc VDS Kalex), getting ahead for an instant, only to immediately relinquish the lead.

As the pair exited the final corner Rabat was several yards ahead and appeared to have the race won. But suddenly his bike slowed and Lüthi sped past to take the win by 0.133 seconds.

'What a surprise, but it was a nice present and I'd like to thank Tito for it,' joked the Swiss after his second win in four races. Lüthi's season was transformed at Aragón where he received a longer-wheelbase chassis.

Rabat was crestfallen but magnanimous. 'I wanted to stay in front of Tom because his bike was faster,' he said. 'But the cooler temperature made the bike slide more, which used more fuel, so after the last corner I had fuel starvation.'

The pace of Rabat and Lüthi left the rest of the pack trailing.

MotoGP™2014

WORLD CHAMPION

Congratulations!

The Only One

Bridgestone for MotoGP™ 2014

Moto3™
CHAMPIONSHIP

THE GLOVES COME OFF

Honda versus KTM, Alex Marquez versus Jack Miller. Moto3 got ugly at times but provided stunning racing every time

Some time last year somebody said something that annoyed HRC. Resources were suddenly diverted to the Moto3 project and at the very end of pre-season testing Honda's new bike made its appearance. The Estrella Galicia team swapped from KTM to the very rapid new machines, as did the Ongetta-Rivacold and SaxoPrint teams.

KTM continued to supply Aki Ajo's teams (although some of the bikes were badged as Husqvarnas) and Valentino Rossi's new Sky Racing Team VR46 as well as Gresini and last year's winners Team Calvo. The Indian Mahindra factory again fielded a works team but also sold bikes to three privateer squads. In contrast to Moto2, the Kalex-chassis KTMs were not competitive with the exception of the one ridden by Juanfran Guevara, who, along with Isaac Viñales (cousin of Maverick) and John McPhee, was one of the breakthrough men of the year.

It took a while for the Hondas to find a base setting and the Mahindas had transmission problems, allowing KTM riders Jack Miller and Romano Fenati to share the first six wins. It looked as if it was all over and done with – but then things started to get weird. Fenati's form dropped off the edge of a cliff, shortly followed by the VR46 team manager being fired. By now Estrella Galicia was getting its Hondas competitive, allowing Alex Marquez (younger brother of Marc) to win two in a row.

Then two class veterans, Efren Vazquez and Alexis Masbou, took début wins on Hondas as Miller's form faltered. Miller lost the championship lead at Aragón when he touched Marquez and fell, consequently losing the points lead. It was a racing incident, but it set the tone for a sour end-of-season confrontation – one that

RIGHT Jack Miller after winning the GP of the Americas; he started the year in dominant form, winning three of the first five races.

FAR RIGHT Romano Fenati won in Argentina to give Team Sky VR46 its first victory. Team manager Vitto Guareschi did not last the season.

BELOW Miguel Oliveira gave Mahindra its first podium of the season with third at Assen.

boiled down to a confrontation between Miller, combative and brilliant on the brakes, and the speed of the Hondas.

The last four races of the season turned into a soap-opera script of rider errors, fairing banging, ill-advised protests, arm twisting, arguments about team orders, arguments about lack of team orders, a sulking Aussie and the Spanish media ganging up on him. Amid the off-track dramas, both championship contenders put in superb rides at their home events. Miller's win in Australia was probably the best single ride of the championship, while Marquez's ride to third place in Valencia was the next best.

Early in the season Marquez had managed to squander several winning positions on the last lap, and in the Malaysian fight he put himself in the wrong position repeatedly. If he had employed a fraction of the guile of

1 – QATARI GP

New Red Bull KTM signing Jack Miller won the Moto3 race after a great duel with Alex Marquez (Estrella Galicia Honda). Marquez – riding a factory-backed Honda designed to end KTM's domination of the class – made a mistake on the last lap that dropped him into the second group. He beat Efren Vazquez (RTG Honda) for third by just five hundredths of a second.

'We've been fast all weekend but we couldn't put it all together until the race,' said Miller after his first win. 'The feeling is indescribable – I can't thank my parents enough for all the sacrifices they've made for my career.'

Marquez's team-mate Alex Rins would surely have been in the fight but for an early mistake that dropped him down to 21st. He crossed the line a close fifth, just behind Miguel Oliveira (Mahindra).

2 – AMERICAS GP

Jack Miller (Red Bull KTM) won the best race of the day, topping the podium by seven hundredths ahead of Romano Fenati (Sky VR46 KTM) and a further 0.17 seconds ahead of Efren Vazquez (RTG Honda).

Miller, who also won the Qatar opener, led pretty much all the way, instantly regaining the lead whenever Vazquez drafted past him on Austin's back straight. Vazquez's speed proved that Honda have found a heap of horsepower over the winter. Fenati never quite made it to the front but was only a whisper behind at the flag. Alex Marquez (Estrella Galicia Honda) was right with the leading group when he crashed with a few corners to go.

'I had a lot of pressure,' said Miller. 'The good thing is that we've improved the set-up since Qatar, so I had a lot more tyre left at the end.'

3 – ARGENTINA GP

Romano Fenati won the first victory for Valentino Rossi's new Sky VR46 KTM team after a heated, race-long fight with Jack Miller (Red Bull KTM), winner of the first two races.

Fenati came out on top after a wild encounter at the penultimate turn which had Alex Marquez (Estrella Galicia Honda) ahead, then Miller and finally Fenati, who barged into both the Spaniard and the Australian. He crossed the line 0.099 seconds ahead of Marquez, with a very unhappy Miller a further four tenths back.

'It's two years since my first win, so I'm very happy,' grinned Fenati. 'The fight with Jack was great. I'd like to say sorry because I lost the front at the end, which is why I hit him and Alex.'

Livio Loi (Marc VDS KTM) celebrated his 17th birthday with a stirring ride to fourth, right behind Miller. Marquez's team-mate Alex Rins led the next group, just ahead of Efren Vazquez (RTG Honda) who had earlier run with the leaders.

4 – SPANISH GP

Romano Fenati (Sky VR46 KTM) won his second consecutive victory with another last-corner move, though unlike Argentina there was no bumping and barging. By halfway through the final lap there were just three riders in it: Fenati, Efren Vazquez (RTG Honda) and Alex Rins (Estrella Galicia Honda). Rins dived into the lead at the final turn, only to run wide, allowing the other two to come back past him on the run to the line.

'The race was difficult from tenth on the grid,' said Fenati, who had had a problematic qualifying. 'I don't know what happened at the last corner – Rins was strong on the brakes but I won the race!'

Championship leader Jack Miller (Red Bull KTM) was fourth after being pushed wide by Isaac Viñales (Calvo KTM) at the start of the last lap.

5 – FRENCH GP

It felt like it would not be long before punches were thrown in the 2014 Moto3 championship. This race was marked by innumerable changes of position in the lead group and several collisions, most notably four corners from the flag when Efren Vazquez dived inside leader Jack Miller and had the door slammed in his face. The pair collided, Vazquez thrown off line, while Miller won the race.

It was a remarkable victory by the Australian teenager whose KTM was down on the speed against the Hondas, especially that of diminutive Vazquez. On the last lap he twice grabbed the lead from the Spaniard, braking later than late.

'It was a great fight and that's why I'm extremely happy,' said Miller, who was joined on the podium by Alex Rins (Estrella Galicia Honda) and Isaac Viñales (Calvo KTM).

Vazquez, not unknown for his robust riding tactics, was mad at finishing sixth. 'Jack was crazy. He kept closing the line. If I hadn't braked I would've crashed.'

LEFT Efren Vazquez leads the pack at Indianapolis on his way to the first win of his career.

BELOW Jack Miller's crash at the Dutch TT gifted Alex Marquez his second win in a row and put him in the title fight.

his big brother, the championship would have been over a long time before the final race of the year. Similarly, Miller was guilty of errors when he crashed at Mugello and Assen, and of questionable judgement in Aragón. We are, after all, talking about teenagers.

Both Marquez and Miller move out of Moto3 next year, with the Aussie making the leap to MotoGP. Alex Rins, the other Estrella Galicia rider and the man who finished third overall, also moves up. Their departures will make room at the top of the junior class for the Ajo team's new recruits Brad Binder and Miguel Oliveira to spearhead the KTM challenge. Estrella Galicia will field the young Frenchman Fabio Quartararo and Jorge Navarro, while Mahindra will again supply customer teams rather than run a works team. Binder provided

6 – ITALIAN GP	7 – CATALAN GP	8 – DUTCH TT	9 – GERMAN GP	10 – INDIANAPOLIS GP

This was a typically epic Mugello slipstreaming race, with a dozen or so riders in the lead group for most of the 20 laps.

Inevitably, the man who led out of the final corner didn't win the race, and the top seven crossed the line separated by less than six tenths of a second.

Once again it was Romano Fenati (Sky VR46 KTM) who crossed the line first, slipstreaming past Isaac Viñales (Calvo KTM) and Alex Rins (Estrella Galicia Honda) to win by just 0.010 seconds. Viñales and Rins dead-heated for second but Viñales got the nod following a video replay. Fourth went to Mahindra's Miguel Oliveira, a further 0.121 seconds down

It probably would have been 10 or 11 crossing the line within a second if it had not been for a last-lap pile-up – no one was surprised when it happened – which claimed title leader Jack Miller (Red Bull KTM) and three others. Miller was controversially awarded two penalty points for the incident.

Alex Marquez (Estrella Galicia Honda) destroyed the pack, grabbing the holeshot from pole and leaving the rest to do their worst to each other. While the 18-year-old made good his escape, a gang of seven riders fought for the final two podium places.

Marquez crossed the line 3.2 seconds ahead to score Honda's first Moto3 win since 2012. Fellow teenager Enea Bastianini (Go&Fun KTM) beat Efren Vazquez (RTG Honda) for second by two tenths, with series leader Jack Miller (Red Bull KTM) fighting his way from eighth to fourth on the last lap to preserve his points lead over Romano Fenati (Sky VR46 KTM), who finished a tenth behind the Aussie.

'I knew it would be difficult, so I wanted to gain an advantage from the start and I succeeded,' said Marquez, whose team-mate Alex Rins went out of the race with a broken gear linkage.

Alex Marquez (Estrella Galicia Honda) won his second consecutive race to repeat Catalunya's brotherly double and put himself in the fight for the Moto3 title.

Marquez dominated the only dry race of the day, easing away from his pursuers while the top two men in the championship had a disastrous day. Points leader Jack Miller (Red Bull KTM) crashed out of the lead when he lost the front on the bumps into Turn One, while Romano Fenati (Sky VR46 KTM) crashed out of the group contesting third place having fought his way back after running off the track on the first lap.

'It was easy to crash because the wind was strong and the track had very bad grip,' said Marquez the younger. 'After I saw Miller crash I understood that I must ride a very good race to make the finish.'

Estrella team-mate Alex Rins won his second-place duel with Miguel Oliveira (Mahindra) at the final chicane.

Jack Miller (Red Bull KTM) put his championship campaign back on course with his first win since May's French GP. The Aussie had to fight all the way, bettering podium first-timer Brad Binder (Ambrogio Mahindra) by less than two tenths of a second. Even more significantly, two of his main title rivals Romano Fenati and Alex Rins crashed out and on-form Alex Marquez only finished fourth.

'We gave away a lot of points at the last few races, so this is an important win for us,' said Miller, who had crashed out of the lead at Assen two weeks earlier. 'We were also lucky… er, sorry, it was unfortunate that Fenati and Rins crashed out.'

Binder was delighted with his podium but even happier he had been with the leaders for so long. 'I learned so much… irreplaceable!' he said.

Efren Vazquez (SaxoPrint Honda) took the first win of his long career when he out-dragged Romano Fenati (Sky VR46 KTM) on the dash from the final corner to the line. The pair were part of a ten-bike pack that had swapped positions on nearly every corner. Vazquez used the speed of his Honda, reliably the fastest bike all year, to pull out and pass the Italian to win by 0.006sec, with the whole group covered by just over two and a half seconds.

Championship leader Jack Miller (Red Bull Ajo KTM) was third, putting more distance into the Estrella Galicia Honda duo of Rins and Marquez. They were fifth and six behind Alexis Masbou (Ongetta-Rivacold Honda), who had been last at the end of the first lap. He had also had a big crash in qualifying yet managed to lead the race for several laps in the closing stages. The win was Vazquez's first after 116 attempts. Just another day in Moto3.

ABOVE LEFT By mid-season both Estrella Galicia team riders were championship contenders.

ABOVE RIGHT The top three at Brno were covered by less than two-tenths of a second at the flag. Alexis Masbou won, Enea 'The Beast' Bastianini was second and Danny Kent third.

RIGHT Jack Miller carries the flag after winning his home race at Phillip Island – probably the best race of the year.

Mahindra with its best result so far, second place at the Sachsenring, and Aspar Martinez's squad will be the Indian factory's lead team next year.

It has not taken long for the class that was supposed to be an affordable entry to Grand Prix racing to become a fight between the factories. Changes to the regulations for 2014 prevented any rider getting special engines and for 2015 the rev limit will be reduced in another attempt to keep costs down and make the playing field more level.

For such a young formula, Moto3 has done what it set out to do, with the possible exception of being inexpensive. What it did this season was reliably provide superb racing, often the best race of the day, thanks to a brilliant cast of characters from the Aussie 'larrikin' Jack Miller to the cool, professional Alex Rins, with some crash-happy kids such as Nico Antonelli in between. The good news is that there is absolutely no reason for that to change. Especially as Honda won the riders' title but finished equal on points with KTM in the constructors' competition only to see the Austrians take the prize by virtue of more race wins. That one will hurt.

11 – CZECH REPUBLIC GP	12 – BRITISH GP	13 – SAN MARINO GP	14 – ARAGÓN GP	15 – JAPANESE GP
This race produced the second-closest top nine since the Yugoslavian 1990 125 GP. Seventh place finisher Miguel Oliveira (Mahindra) crossed the finish line just 0.91 seconds behind first-time winner Alexis Masbou (Ongetta-Rivacold Honda). The Frenchman was joined on the podium by Enea Bastianini (Go&Fun KTM) and Danny Kent (Red Bull Husqvarna), the three of them separated by 0.187 seconds. 'My bike was very fast and I was very strong on the brakes – this is the best way to be in this kind of fight,' grinned Masbou. Of course, anyone of the top group could have won the race and indeed it should have been Alex Rins (Estrella Galicia Honda) who led the pack over the line at the end of the penultimate lap, then sat up to celebrate. He finished ninth. His team-mate Alex Marquez was fourth, just ahead of title leader Jack Miller (Red Bull KTM).	Until the last few laps there were more than a dozen riders in the lead group, proving that old racing maxim: fast, open tracks make brilliant racing. Only in the final three laps did the leading quartet manage to escape, with the Hondas of Estrella Galicia team-mates Alex Rins and Alex Marquez doing battle with the Go&Fun bike of teenage rookie Enea Bastianini and Miguel Oliveira's Mahindra. All four led at one stage or another, but in the final few hundred yards it was Rins who jumped past Marquez and Bastianini into the penultimate turn. Marquez counter-attacked out of the fast final corner, the difference at the line just 11 hundredths of a second! Bastianini took third, a further six hundredths down with Oliveira another five hundredths behind. Title-leader Jack Miller (Red Bull KTM) could only manage sixth, his bike outgunned by the Hondas.	Miller took pole and was confident he could fight for the win, having reverted to an older chassis spec. But a huge moment in the early stages put him out of the lead group of Rins, Marquez and Miguel Oliveira (Mahindra). Rins dragged Marquez and Oliveira with him until Oliveira crashed out. In the final stages Marquez girded his loins and attacked, bravely jumping out of the slipstream to dive past at the flat-out right at the end of the back straight, only for his team-mate to repay the complement at the same place on the final lap. On the run to the flag they were side by side, Rins getting the win by four hundredths. 'It was a race of strategy, because the slipstream is very important here, and my strategy worked perfectly,' said Rins after closing the championship gap on both Marquez and Miller. Isaac Viñales (Calvo KTM) won a thrilling three-man scrap for third ahead of Enea Bastianini (Go&Fun KTM) and Brad Binder (Ambrogio Mahindra). Just two tenths covered the trio at the flag	Rossi's Moto3 rider Romano Fenati (Sky VR46 KTM) scored his first victory in four months after a titanic scrap with Alex Marquez (Estrella Galicia Honda). His advantage at the flag was just five hundredths of a second, with Danny Kent (Husqvarna) right behind. Fenati rode an amazing race, charging through from 19th on the first lap despite a narrow racing line. In the closing stages he battled back and forth with Marquez and his team-mate Alex Rins, who ran wide, then fought back to fourth. 'My tyre was finished by the end but I really enjoyed the last-lap fight!' grinned Fenati. But the most crucial moment of the race happened at the end of lap four when series leader Jack Miller (Red Bull KTM) rode round the outside of Marquez. With only a slender dry line available, the two collided and Miller went cart-wheeling off the track. The incident lost him the title lead he had held since the start of the season.	Alex Marquez led a World Championship for the first time after a last lap that was crazy even by Moto3 standards. The teenager – who won his first GP victory at Motegi 2013 – spent the entire race battling with title rival Jack Miller (Red Bull KTM), Danny Kent (Red Bull Husqvarna), Brad Binder (Mahindra) and fellow Honda riders Efren Vazquez and John McPhee. Marquez made his move as the group raced down the back straight for the final time, using his Honda's superior speed to pass Miller and Kent, who refused to give in on the brakes. They both passed Marquez but then ran wide, leaving Marquez to win ahead of Vazquez and Binder. 'I saw Jack and Danny come past, completely sliding, so I knew they would go wide,' grinned Marquez. Miller crossed the line fifth but left Japan trailing Marquez by 25 points. The title hopes of Marquez's team-mate Alex Rins suffered a blow when he was pushed off the track at the very first turn. He recovered to finish tenth.

TOP Scottish rider John McPhee was one of the breakthrough riders of the year.

ABOVE Danny Kent got back into his Moto3 stride in the second half of the year, giving the Husqvarna marque its first ever Grand Prix pole position and podium finish.

CHAMPIONSHIP STANDINGS

	Rider	Nat	Team	Motorcycle	Points
1	Alex Marquez	SPA	Estrella Galicia 0,0	Honda	278
2	Jack Miller	AUS	Red Bull KTM Ajo	KTM	276
3	Alex Rins	SPA	Estrella Galicia 0,0	Honda	237
4	Efren Vazquez	SPA	SaxoPrint-RTG	Honda	222
5	Romano Fenati	ITA	SKY Racing Team VR46	KTM	176
6	Alexis Masbou	FRA	Ongetta-Rivacold	Honda	164
7	Isaac Viñales	SPA	Calvo Team	KTM	141
8	Danny Kent	GBR	Red Bull Husqvarna Ajo	Husqvarna	129
9	Enea Bastianini	ITA	Junior Team GO&FUN Moto3	KTM	127
10	Miguel Oliveira	POR	Mahindra Racing	Mahindra	110
11	Brad Binder	RSA	Ambrogio Racing	Mahindra	109
12	Jakub Kornfeil	CZE	Calvo Team	KTM	97
13	John McPhee	GBR	SaxoPrint-RTG	Honda	77
14	Niccolò Antonelli	ITA	Junior Team GO&FUN Moto3	KTM	68
15	Niklas Ajo	FIN	Avant Tecno Husqvarna Ajo	Husqvarna	52
16	Francesco Bagnaia	ITA	SKY Racing Team VR46	KTM	50
17	Juanfran Guevara	SPA	Mapfre Aspar Team Moto3	Kalex KTM	46
18	Karel Hanika	CZE	Red Bull KTM Ajo	KTM	44
19	Alessandro Tonucci	ITA	CIP	Mahindra	20
20	Zulfahmi Khairuddin	MAL	Ongetta-AirAsia	Honda	19
21	Livio Loi	BEL	Marc VDS Racing Team	KTM	17
22	Matteo Ferrari	ITA	San Carlo Team Italia	Mahindra	12
23	Jorge Navarro	SPA	Marc VDS Racing Team	Kalex KTM	11
24	Philipp Oettl	GER	Interwetten Paddock Moto3	Kalex KTM	10
25	Andrea Migno	ITA	Mahindra Racing	Mahindra	8
26	Hiroki Ono	JPN	Honda Team Asia	Honda	5
27	Jasper Iwema	NED	CIP	Mahindra	4
28	Hafiq Azmi	MAL	SIC-AJO	KTM	3
29	Arthur Sissis	AUS	Mahindra Racing	Mahindra	3
30	Jules Danilo	FRA	Ambrogio Racing	Mahindra	2
31	Eric Granado	BRA	Calvo Team	KTM	2
32	Remy Gardner	AUS	Calvo Team	KTM	1

16 – AUSTRALIAN GP

Seven days earlier Jack Miller (Red Bull KTM) had lost the world title lead he had held since the first race, so he knew that he had to stop the rot at his home race.

The race was a typically hectic Phillip Island skirmish, with 11 men in the lead group. But one by one they fell by the wayside, or rather two by two, as several pairs hit the deck after collisions.

By the end the group was down to six men and they crossed the line almost side by side, covered by a mere 0.24 seconds. Miller beat title rivals and Estrella Galicia Honda team-mates Alex Marquez and Alex Rins by 0.029 and 0.032 seconds respectively after grabbing the lead as the group attacked the 120mph Turn One for the final time.

'I got the last corner nailed and hoped and prayed the finish line would come up quick,' said Miller. 'It's great to be back in the title hunt after a couple of difficult weekends.'

RTG Honda team-mates Efren Vazquez and John McPhee were fourth and fifth and Alexis Masbou (Ongetta Honda) sixth.

17 – MALAYSIAN GP

This was a battle royal with the world title fully at stake. It was also Jack Miller (Red Bull KTM) against the full might of Honda, in this case Estrella team-mates Alex Marquez and Alex Rins and RTG team-mates Efren Vazquez and John McPhee.

The Hondas clearly had more speed than Miller's KTM but the Aussie was prepared to do anything to keep his rivals behind him and there was plenty of bumping and barging, especially with series leader Marquez, who several times found himself pushed back a few places by Miller, who was quite rightly unwilling to give a single inch.

'I did what I could to survive and take the title fight to Valencia,' said Miller, who finally finished second behind the super-quick Honda of the diminutive Vazquez, who tips the scales at just 56 kilos.

Vazquez beat Miller by two tenths, with Rins completing the podium. A last-lap mistake dropped Marquez to fifth, but that was better than McPhee who slid off on the final lap.

18 – VALENCIAN GP

Alex Marquez (Estrella Galicia Honda) made history by taking the Moto3 title at the end of a nerve-wracking race. The maths were simple: if Jack Miller (Red Bull KTM) won the race, Marquez had to finish third to take the title.

The race was less simple. The lead group sometimes numbered ten riders, with positions changing dramatically every few corners.

In the final laps Miller assumed control ahead of Isaac Viñales (Calvo KTM), with Marquez in third and chased hard by Danny Kent (Red Bull Husqvarna). On the last lap Kent closed remorselessly and looked ready to make a move and push the title in Miller's direction, until he ran wide with three corners to go.

Thus Marquez crossed the line in third, to become, with his older brother, GP racing's first sibling World Champions.

'The dream has come true – this is such a special day for our family!' he smiled, dazed with his success. 'It was such a tricky race but it's been a perfect weekend and I knew we could do it.'

For Miller, however, the result was a stunning blow. 'I'm completely disappointed after all our hard work this year,' he said. 'I got pushed wide by a couple of people a few times but there's no need to cry about it.'

Alex Rins (Estrella Galicia Honda) and Efren Vazquez (SaxoPrint Honda) were the last men in the lead group in fifth and sixth.

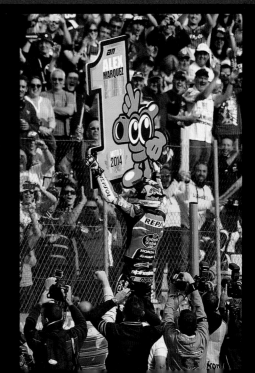

The eighth year of the Red Bull MotoGP Rookies Cup saw another great season of close racing and new emerging talents. Spanish 16-year-old Jorge Martín put in a virtually faultless performance to claim the title so impressively that the day after he won the final race in Aragón the Aspar Martinez team announced that it had signed him for its Moto3 World Championship team for 2015.

Martín had ended the 2013 season second to Karel Hanika with two race wins and was an obvious favourite starting this year. He did not disappoint, becoming a master on the KTM RC 250 R, but he certainly did not cruise to victory and did not win at the opening weekend in Jerez.

Race 1 of the year went to Japanese 15-year-old Soushi Mihara, who was unstoppable, but Martín picked up second, already prepared to accept good points when victory is not possible. Strangely Mihara was completely off form the following day and only finished ninth, a fluctuation in performance that he could not explain and that came to infect his year.

Sunday in Jerez saw Joan Mir, the 16-year-old Spaniard, get the best of a superb five-rider scrap to win over Manuel Pagliani with a great last-lap move on the 17-year-old Italian. Coupled with fourth from the day before, this gave Mir the Cup lead over Martín, whose second and third matched Pagliani's third and second.

On to Mugello for the single race there and after a wet day of practice and qualifying on Friday the weekend started dry and Martín kicked his Cup bid into top gear with a lights-to-flag win that left the others trailing. That was enough to snatch the points lead but Mir added misery to his own dreams by pulling off the track and out of the podium fight when he mistook a botched gearchange for a gearbox problem.

Mir would rue the points loss for the rest of the season, especially as the following weekend in Assen did not go his way. Martín put in two more great rides, second behind Mihara in a treacherously slippery Race 1 and runner-up in Race 2 to local hero Bo Bendsneyder, who would not be denied this dry race from pole. The 15-year-old Dutchman was already acquitting himself well in his first season, the quickest of the new boys, but he would unfortunately miss the Sachsenring races thanks to an arm injury suffered in a Spanish Championship round.

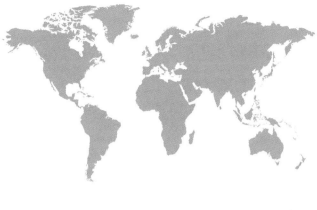

SPANISH HUSTLE

Jorge Martín is the new champion, and he was impressive enough to be offered a ride with the Aspar team in Moto3

LEFT Eventual winner Jorge Martín (88) chases Joan Mir (36) and Stefano Manzi (29), who finished second and third.

INSET Still only 16 years old, Jorge Martín was impressive enough to earn a place in Aspar Martinez's Moto3 team for 2015.

Germany proved a tough weekend for many with Race 1 being one of Martín's two off races of the year. He made a mess of the start, collided with another rider and later crashed trying to make up places. He remounted to finish 12th but points rival Mir had taken second and closed the gap. The winner was Toprak Razgatlıoglu and for the popular Turkish 17-year-old it was the only time he could completely overcome his height disadvantage to win a race.

Sunday's winner in Germany was Martín ahead of 17-year-old Bradley Ray, who had a hand in triggering a late-race collision that took out Stefano Manzi, Oscar Gutierrez and Pagliani. It was a lousy weekend for Pagliani as he had been the runaway leader in Race 1 only to fall while lapping a slower rider with victory in sight. Razgatlıoglu's third place made it a rostrum double for him in Germany and he always displayed great skill, sportsmanship and determination.

Although it was only halfway through the season, the first seven races had set up the defining pattern. Martín was the man to beat and while he would not win every race he kept stacking up the points. Italians Pagliani and Manzi were both super-fast and would lead at any time other than crossing the line on the last lap. Their season played out that way with Manzi stacking up a run of six third-place finishes before a second and finally victory in great style at Misano. A total of nine rostrum finishes for the year gave him third in the points table and a Moto3 Grand Prix ride in 2015 with Mahindra.

Pagliani missed out on a win, was second four times and fifth in the points table behind Ray. He did win the Italian Moto3 title. Ray also missed out on a win in 2014 and so, like Pagliani, he has a single 2013 victory as his best Cup result, but he ran at the front most of the time in

2014, scoring three rostrum finishes and an equal number of fourths. With the others struggling to claim victories it was left to Mir to challenge Martín and his effort was revived in Race 2 at Brno when Martín collided with Bendsneyder going into the last lap and they both crashed out of the lead group. Mir took the win on that final lap from an impressive Fabio di Giannantonio with the Italian 15-year-old chasing him across the line.

Martín bounced back with double victory at Silverstone and put the Cup beyond too much doubt. Mir kept things alive with a third to Martín's fifth in Misano but the final weekend in Aragón produced no shock reversals. Mir did his part with a great win in Race 1 but Martín was able to take the title comfortably as he eased off from the lead battle on the final lap to finish fourth.

Not only did Martín have the Cup but he was able to cap his wonderful season in perfect style with victory in Race 2, taking risks in the slipperiest of wet conditions to pass the very impressive Marc Garcia, who took second ahead of Ray.

Garcia, the 14-year-old Spaniard, had made excellent progress all the way through his début season to take tenth in the standings behind di Giannantonio and Bendsneyder, two riders who had also put in perfect first years. With the seven Rookies ahead of them all moving on from the Cup, these three become the favourites for 2015 and they have already demonstrated that the pace will not slacken.

Martín and Manzi are GP-bound, and Mir probably to the Spanish Championship. The other graduates will continue to develop their careers around the globe as a fresh intake joins the Cup in the pursuit of racing dreams.

RIDERS FOR HEALTH
BARRY COLEMAN

BATTLING TO HALT EBOLA

Health workers on Riders for Health motorcycles are playing a vital role in getting blood samples to labs quickly

Let's measure history in MotoGP dates. When we all met for Day of Champions and the British Grand Prix at Silverstone, no-one had heard much of Ebola. There were early signs of an outbreak in a very remote part of Guinea Conakry, but then not everybody had heard of Guinea Conakry.

We had all heard of Sierra Leone because of the British military intervention there to put an end to the Charles Taylor war. Some people had heard of Liberia, because it gave rise to the same war and was itself seriously devastated by conflict.

By the time we got to Aragón, the very nasty cat was out of the bag. Guinea, Sierra Leone and Liberia were all suffering from Ebola. By the time of Phillip Island, the whole world was suffering, or thought it was. Fear stalked the whole globe.

In some ways it was a reasonable fear. Ebola really is nasty. It destroys the nervous system and the vital organs from within. It was generally thought to have a mortality rate of something close to 98 per cent. In other words, assume that everyone who gets it dies.

The United States in particular shivered in its hand-tooled boots. The end of the world was nigh. Politicians lined up to call for total isolation of the countries concerned and brutal quarantine for all US-bound visitors who had been to West Africa.

But statistics matter. They shed light on these things. It turned out that more people had married Kim Kardashian than had died of Ebola in the US. But panic seized the nation. Fear of marrying Kim Kardashian is also perfectly reasonable.

Enough levity: Ebola is ghastly. But among its most ghastly characteristics is that it need never happen at all.

ABOVE Sulayman Senghore, a Riders mechanic, checks health worker Bubacarr Jallow's motorcycle in The Gambia.

BELOW RIGHT Joel Otieno, a Clinical Health Assistant in Kenya, distributing polio vaccinations.

Not that there is a vaccine, because there isn't, but for two other reasons. Firstly, it is actually hard to catch and, secondly, it can – in spite of the supposed mortality rate – be treated if it is detected in time.

And there is the problem. These outbreaks first occurred in the most remote parts of all three countries. Just before Valencia, the UN's head of Ebola action told us that what we have to remember is that the remote parts really are remote – there are no roads out there.

The name of this man, as I remember it, is Dr Sherlock Something. I remember admiring his perspicacity. I remember it because both Liberia and Sierra Leone had got in touch with MotoGP's very own humanitarian organisation, the one we all started, Riders for Health, and asked us to go and help them with their problems of isolation before Ebola had ever crossed their minds.

We went to have a look – we representatives of the motorcycle community – and said 'yes', of course we could help. Gratified, the ministries of health in both countries said that they would now talk to their various funders and supporters, among them the governments of both the UK and the US.

Sometime before Assen they told us that they were about ready for the next round of discussions as to how we could put the Riders system in place throughout their countries. And nothing happened. We were all waiting, as ever, for the funders to make up their minds.

And then, around and about the time of Malaysia, the British government called.

We are having trouble in Sierra Leone. We can't get Ebola blood samples to the labs quickly enough and

OUR IMPACT IN 2014

- Riders for Health's reliable vehicles are improving access to regular health care for millions of people across Africa. This year, thanks to your support, we have managed to achieve an incredible amount.

- We've improved access to health care for 14 million people across Africa.

- Our sample couriers transported over 470,000 medical samples and test results between health centres and laboratories and turnaround time has been cut in half. This means diseases like TB and HIV can be diagnosed quicker and patients can be treated faster.

- In Kenya, health workers have cut the time they spend travelling from four hours to one hour thanks to their motorcycles. Now they can spend these extra hours with their patients.

- Health workers can now run 3,500 extra health-education meetings every month, sharing information on how to control and prevent diseases.

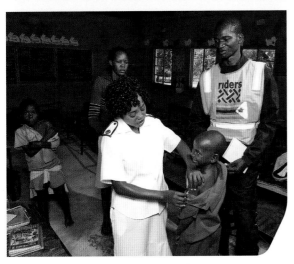

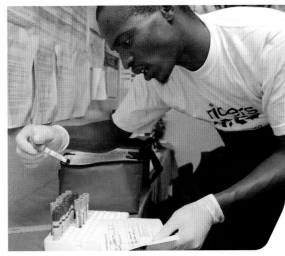

ABOVE Mr Palikobila Solomon Mwembe, an Environmental Health Officer in Binga, Zimbabwe, tells families about immunisations.

FAR LEFT A nurse assisting with a National Immunisation Campaign in Binga, Zimbabwe.

LEFT Phuthi Chabeli, a Riders for Health sample courier, in Mafeteng, Lesotho.

so we are putting people in holding centres without knowing whether they are infected or not. You are good at collecting and carrying samples (that's true: we do it – very quickly and very safely – for HIV samples in Lesotho, Zimbabwe and Malawi) so we would like you to come yesterday and help us.

Of course we are willing to help, and then some. It is what we do. We began working with the government in Sierra Leone to help them build a system for getting their samples to labs. Just in time for Valencia. And it started to make a difference.

When Qatar comes around, check our website to see how we are doing.

And try to be nice to your friends who are golf, tennis and F1 fans. Try to be polite and not to boast too shamelessly that ours is the only sport ever to have given rise to a humanitarian movement. I know I say that every year, but I can't help it.

Malaria, measles, threatening pregnancy, cuts, bruises, snakebites, cholera, HIV/AIDS, Ebola – glad to be of help.

RIDERS AND MotoGP IN 2014

In 2014, the stars and fans of MotoGP have raised hundreds of thousands of pounds to get more health workers on the road in Africa. Riders for Health holds events at MotoGP races around the globe, bringing motorcycling together to make a difference.

Day of Champions at Silverstone is a chance for fans to meet their heroes, ride the Silverstone track and own a piece of MotoGP history at the annual auction. This year it raised an incredible £193,802 for our work.

We held our Day of Stars event at the Circuit of the Americas in Texas and, in Spain, more than 300 people attended our Paddock Experience Days in Jerez, Catalunya and Valencia. These events allowed fans to go behind-the-scenes and experience the buzz of the MotoGP paddock.

We also gave fans the opportunity to win incredible MotoGP experiences. This year we held a competition to meet World Champion Marc Marquez and Dani Pedrosa. We auctioned grid passes for Silverstone and Valencia, and we even gave two fans the chance to attend the end-of-season awards ceremony.

This year MotoGP – its riders, its teams and, of course, its fans – has helped to raise an incredible £335,000 for Riders for Health.

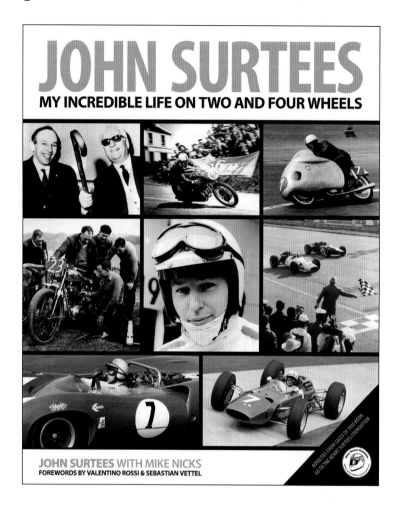
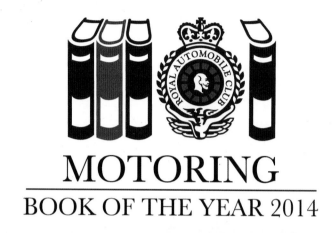
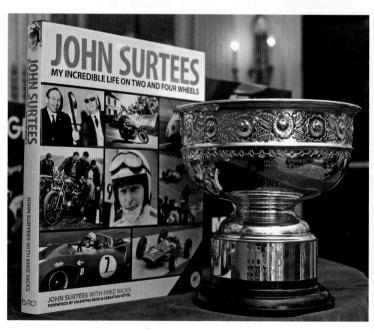